DICKENS STUDIES ANNUAL

Robert B. Partlow, Jr., *Editor*

Sub-editors:

William Axton   Robert Patten

Jerome Meckier   Richard Stang

Advisory Board:

Trevor Blount   Madeline House

Philip Collins   J. Hillis Miller

Ross Dabney   Steven Marcus

Earle Davis   Sylvère Monod

George Ford   Harry Stone

K. J. Fielding   Graham Storey

DICKENS
STUDIES
ANNUAL

VOLUME
4

Edited by

ROBERT B. PARTLOW, JR.

SOUTHERN ILLINOIS UNIVERSITY PRESS

Carbondale and Edwardsville

FEFFER & SIMONS, INC.

London and Amsterdam

Contents

Preface

OVER THE last year, while reading the sixty or so manuscripts submitted for publication in this volume of the *Dickens Studies Annual,* I noticed that not one author mentioned that Charles Dickens was a genius, the greatest of Victorians, a writer of Shakespearian importance, or a centrally significant figure in the development of prose fiction. After thirty years of major critical and scholarly effort, all this now seems to be taken for granted, worth mentioning only in sophomore classes. It struck me also that Dickens has been thoroughly accepted as a superb craftsman: a prose poet, a notable creator of memorable characters, a master of fictional structures and techniques. In a negative sense, then, these submissions are a tribute to the voluminous, rigorous, persuasive criticism of the last three decades.

Citing all those who have contributed to the establishment of Dickens in his proper place would require a lengthy bibliography, but certainly all students of Dickens owe an especial debt to John Butt, Kathleen Tillotson, Barbara Hardy, George Ford, Edgar Johnson, Sylvère Monod, Philip Collins, Kenneth Fielding, Madeline House, Humphry House, Graham Storey, and Hillis Miller (a listing manifestly incomplete), all of whom have contributed importantly to our understanding of Dickens, his relationships to his own age, and the nuances of his fictions. These and others have prepared for us reasoned editions of his works, his letters, his speeches, his dramatic performances; they have studied his poetics of the novel; they have provided detailed, subtle analyses of his fictional structures; and they have considered his transmutation of memory and perception into fictional characters, settings, plots, and patterns of meaning. Many of their projects are still continuing, the Pilgrim edition of the letters and the Clarendon edition of the works for example, as well as the bibliographical studies of Joseph Gold and the continuing productivity of The Dickens Fellowship and its *Dickensian,* now ably edited by Michael Slater.

In the last ten or fifteen years a host of younger scholar-critics has joined the earlier leaders—a measure of the attractiveness of those leaders, even more a measure of the power that Dickens has come to exert over careful readers—carried on their work, and, in many instances, broadened and deepened our understanding of the Inimitable. Humanistic studies are not usually cumulative, in the sense that studies in the sciences are; they are not sequential except in the broadest terms and over a span of time. Hence the rapid development of a massive body of Dickens scholarship and criticism is a notable phenomenon. As George Ford pointed out in his "Dickens in the 1960s" (in the 1970 Centenary number of the *Dickensian*), the 1940s were distinguished chiefly by fresh critical appraisals, the 1950s by biographical explorations, and the 1960s by textual studies. Since about 1970, however, although the earlier approaches have been in continuous use, major attention seems to have shifted back again to fresh critical evaluations and analyses. The quarterly Checklist of publications published in the *Dickens Studies Newsletter*, which grows longer annually, reveals that more and more interest is devoted to Dickens as a serious artist and thinker, not to be sure in the mold of Carlyle or Mill or any other formal philosopher, but as a sensitive man deeply concerned with contemporary and local issues and with the universal cruxes as well.

Many of the younger scholar-critics are still exploring areas opened up earlier, in biography, cultural pressures, and craftsmanship, but the shift to newer approaches is evident. The task assumed by these critics, including Robert Patten, Michael Goldberg, N. M. Lary, Joseph Gold, and James Kincaid, has been twofold: to investigate with increasing rigor certain previously opened-out aspects of Dickens' work, and to open out previously ignored aspects for initial investigation. Once acceptance had been gained that Dickens was a genius, that he was a prose poet whose writing demands detailed study, and that his values and beliefs call for close attention (as with George Eliot and Henry James, for example, in whom this matter is more obvious), then the problem lies in such questions as: what are the dimensions of his achievement? what *precisely* did he say and mean? what are the arcs of his meanings? what conflicts and anomalies exist in a given text and in the whole corpus? how are they resolved? in what exact ways does his technique, his imagery and symbolism for instance, embody his meanings? what is his relationship to contemporary and subsequent intellectual, cultural, and emotive *Gestalten*? despite what appears to be only a presentation of surfaces, how do his characters embody sophisticated psychological and mythic insights?

This volume of the *Dickens Studies Annual* was designed to exhibit recent thought in some of these newer areas of research, for the most part in the work of younger critics; the editors think the volume has not only considerable interest for this reason, but intrinsic merit and utility as well. This is not to imply that the other essays submitted have no interest or merit; many of them are in process of reconsideration, expansion, and rewriting for Volumes 5 and 6. The studies here included, primarily for the benefit of other scholars and students, were those most clearly ready for publication and most representative of strictly contemporary approaches.

Stephen Franklin's long article entitled "Dickens and Time: The Clock without Hands" is an example of the way in which the work of preceding writers such as John Henry Raleigh and Hans Meyerhoff is being expanded. Especially since the beginning of the nineteenth century, and (for us) especially in time-structures like the novel and in poetry like that of Yeats and T. S. Eliot concerned with man's place in history, Western man has become deeply curious about the concept of time: real time, virtual time, subjective time, historical time, space-time, relative time, duration, remembered time, simultaneous times, divergent times, time as fantasy—a whole range of considerations and problems which have revolutionized basic frames of reference. The work of such writers as Proust and Joyce, Yeats and Eliot, has been extensively investigated but, until recently, few critics have studied the less obvious handling of time in Dickens. Franklin's analysis is not trailblazing: Hillis Miller, Alexander Welsh, Robert Patten, and others have already published brilliant explorations, and of course all depend heavily on the formally philosophic studies of Bergson, Meyerhoff, Poulet, and Berdyaev, so that Franklin's article may be considered an extension or an application. Franklin's essay, like that of Patten, demonstrates that Dickens' attitude toward time was firmly embedded in his essential Christianity. Ranging over much of the corpus of Dickens' fiction rapidly yet with enough attention to detail and close reading of characters and situations so that theory is grounded in the facts of the texts, this essay seems admirably clear and persuasive.

The placing of the Ganz' study next in sequence suggests that, fortunately, all scholar-critics do not share the same interests, utilize the same techniques of analysis, or come to the same conclusions. In small compass, this pair of essays demonstrates that our humanistic discipline thrives on multiversity, lack of agreement, confrontations of insights and values, out of which come, we hope, renewed understandings. Seen thus, Margaret Ganz' article on "Humor and the Refashioning of Reality" is a counterargument: it takes issue with the interpretations of *Pickwick Papers* presented by Hillis Miller, Steven Marcus, and others. She insists that recent oversolemn preoccupation with Existentialist, Kierkegaardian, Jungian, Freudian, Marxian, Etceteran overtones in Dickens' novels has tended to the misestimation of Dickens' humor and so to misreading, at least partially, what these novels are about. In thus returning to earlier "appreciations" of *Pickwick,* Ganz insists that its richness may be located most satisfyingly in the imaginative devices with which it "challenges and affirmatively resolves the contradictions of experience." She reasserts the sheer funniness of *Pickwick,* which everyone acknowledges but which is sometimes overlooked or ignored in favor of the darker, more sinister elements. We might note, however, that in so returning to earlier views, she does not at the same time return to earlier modes of analysis and discussion; instead, her techniques of deployment and discussion are as incisive and meticulous as those of the critics she opposes, for example Steven Daniels, whose treatment of *Pickwick* is quite different.

Although not denying the humor in the novel, he considers it secondary to other more significant aspects. Following Steven Marcus' suggestion that *Pickwick* is "an activity of self-creation," Daniels argues that what emerges is not only the Mr. Pickwick of immortal memory, but Charles Dickens, the novelist who, in the process of creating his first novel, discovered his own identity and the path he was to follow in his ensuing fictions. Daniels sees in that process a complex interaction of creative imagination, personal values, and formal requirements; his close reading of the novel emphasizes the philosophic dimension, the structure of values, that grew as Dickens learned while in the creative activity of writing his book. Mr. Pickwick triumphs not only over such enemies as Dodson and Fogg—they remain undefeated, even triumphant, socially admired and approved—but over common and persistent temptations. The central issue, as Daniels sees it, is here dramatized: the individual *can* preserve his humanity in an indifferent or hostile world, and this is the real triumph, not success, not money, not respectability, not power. Such an interpretation, though apparently at odds with the analysis of Ganz, is not in actuality: we do not have to opt for one or the other; both are plausible and enriching.

The relationship between Dickens and Henry Mayhew, already explored in part by John Butt, Philip Collins, and Harland Nelson among others, is the subject of Anne Humpherys' essay. Instead of replowing old grounds, however, she emphasizes the fundamental differences between the two reporters of the world of the London poor. She points out that, in his journalism, Dickens tends to distance himself from those he is observing, while Mayhew tends to make himself part of the total situation. The differences between their major works are, Humpherys shows, not attributable merely to the fact that they used different genres, but rather to their handling of literary techniques. Dickens, for example, tends to be more general, Mayhew more particularizing; Dickens uses more imagery and personification, often symbolically. Humpherys proceeds to ground such differences in biography, in personal pressures, life-experiences and psychological structures, which influenced the ways in which they responded to the lower classes and to changing public sentiments. In general, by contrasting two powerful writers whose subject matter is apparently similar, Humpherys expertly analyzes some of the devices by which Dickens projected a unified and moving vision of the realities of life in Victorian London.

In comparable manner Lawrence Frank vivifies what seems like a hackneyed topic. How can anyone write vividly and freshly about Esther Summerson after the persuasive analyses of Axton, Miller, and Zwerdling? While not ignoring her role as a narrator and the problems caused by the split narration, Frank utilizes a psychological theory, in this case his own variety of existential psychology, to discuss her as a person and a character in this complex novel. He points out that the psychological is perhaps the least readily accepted part of Dickens' achievement and hence calls for the utmost care in treatment. While it is impossible adequately to summarize Frank's subtle analysis of Esther's essential being and her motivations or the changes they undergo while living out her life-situation, one intriguing insight is worth singling out: that Esther, warped by the knowledge of her illegitmate birth and by the religious-cultural bigotry of her aunt, more or less consciously ignores signs that might become clues to her real identity, her real being, and thus becomes a mystery to herself, a person of masks and surfaces who is afraid to expose her own reality, at least until the traumatic events near the end of the novel. In his analysis Frank considers the psychological, moral, religious, and cultural aspects of Esther, and demonstrates how these sometimes merge, sometimes confront each other in the minds and actions of those who make up the world of *Bleak House.* The essay is a sensitive reading of a novel whose complex interplay of forces so captures and baffles the imagination of modern readers.

Gordon Hirsch's "The Mysteries of *Bleak House:* A Psychoanalytic Study" is a companion piece to Frank's essay: both seek to disclose the basic meanings of the novel by sophisticated application of psychological theory, but Hirsch selects classic Freudian categories. A point by point comparison of the two essays would be rewarding, but this is the place only to suggest that, although both authors touch on many of the same elements of Esther's character and her reactions to events, they come to divergent conclusions about her motives. Hirsch, for example, agrees with Frank in seeing *Bleak House* as a mystery novel in which both characters and readers must make connections and find links in a fragmented and frightening world, but Hirsch indicates that the key to understanding is Freudian psychoanalytical theory: "the prototype for all curiosity and investigation of mysteries is the infantile sexual research that occurs at the Oedipal phase of development." Much that seems mysterious in the novel becomes clearer, he insists, when we see that many of the mysteries are connected with the desire to come to terms with one's parents and their sexuality. After infancy the drive to know about the parents' sexuality may be inhibited, may be converted and expressed neurotically, or may emerge in a sublimated, approvable way. Using this classic paradigm, Hirsch locates the characters' responses along this spectrum, and so provides what he labels "the underlying psychological coherence" of *Bleak House*. Given his assumptions and his frame of reference, he offers a rich, provocative reading of the novel.

An entirely different, more traditional, approach to *Bleak House* is that of Harvey Peter Sucksmith, who opts in his "The Role of the Ironmaster" for a cultural, historical analysis. One significant thread in the tapestry is Wat Tyler, intricately interconnected with Sir Leicester and Mr. Rouncewell, with Dickens' attitudes toward history and politics, with his involvement in such contemporary events as Chartism, and with his value-system. Sucksmith traces Dickens' evaluation of the rebel, Wat Tyler, from the first mention in 1840 through the Chartist troubles of the middle and late forties to *A Child's History of England* published in *Household Words* in 1852, and shows that Dickens, in this matter at least, shared popular Victorian radical sentiments. Rouncewell can therefore be considered not another Bounderby, as some critics insist, but rather a predecessor of Daniel Doyce and hence a sympathetic character. (This is, of course, merely the conclusion of an essay thick with facts and references and acutely argued analyses of Dickens' political and moral beliefs.) The rehabilitation of Mr. Rouncewell, after the adverse conclusions of Trevor Blount, is justifiable and certainly necessary to be considered. But this conclusion is perhaps less significant than the supporting study of Dickens' political, social, economic, and moral position in the fifties—or, to put the matter in other terms, the framework that Sucksmith posits in order to "place" Mr. Rouncewell seems at least as significant as the specific application. I think most Dickens scholars would welcome the expansion of this essay into a full-length study with some such title as *Dickens and the Condition-of-England Question;* we could all benefit from a cool, detailed account of Dickens' "radicalism" in the full meaning of that term.

Somewhat the same comment could be made about Edward Heatley's "The Redeemed Feminine of *Little Dorrit*," a title which suggests the conjoined religious and psychological thrust of his analysis of the novel. Heatley investigates the religious ethos which informs the novel and gives it so much of its meaning. As he points out, "The vindictive God of the dark law has a larger presence in *Little Dorrit* than in any other of Dickens' novels" except possibly *Bleak House*. Such arguments are valuable and enlightening when presented by a writer with a fine syncretic mind and a fundamental sympathy with religious concepts. Changing from religious ethos to psychology, or rather yoking the two together, may initially seem less than satisfactory, but Heatley demonstrates that it is necessary in order to accommodate "the full dynamic of the religious life" in the novel—it is in keeping with some provocative thinking stemming from Freud and Jung. Thus the novel may be read as a conflict between Masculine and Feminine, between masculine power and feminine love, paralleled with the Old and New Testaments. This essay is perhaps the most tantalizing in this volume, primarily because so much is crammed into such brief compass. The author could easily have expanded his material, digging more deeply into both the theories that shape his analysis and into the specific analyses of characters and events, perhaps completing a monograph or book. As an investigatory effort, somewhat like that of Joseph Gold, there is much to admire.

The editors wish to thank the administration of Southern Illinois University for its decision to continue the financial support without which the *Dickens Studies Annual* cannot exist. For over a year there was serious doubt that the University could continue its subsidy in these times of financial exigency so the final decision to support scholarly effort, perhaps even at the expense of other worthwhile activities, was laudable and generous. We can therefore look forward to at least two more volumes in this series and quite possibly to an indefinite extension beyond 1977. The Senior Editor also wishes to express his gratitude to the subeditors and readers who have labored with little public recognition, unselfishly, as a service to the profession. Professors Axton, Meckier, Patten, and Stang have been unstinting of their time and skills, most particularly in the writing of detailed criticism of manuscripts submitted by younger, less experienced authors. Without these practical helps and advice, the *Annual* would have little chance of success.

With their help this volume was assembled out of the dozens of manuscripts submitted; the intent was to present a cross-section of approaches and possibilities. We are modestly convinced of our success: these explorations of various psychological, philosophical, cultural, and literary elements of Dickens and his fictions are stimulating and instructive, and may lead to further study in the same areas. The editors look forward to reading such articles.

Carbondale, Illinois   *Robert B. Partlow, Jr.*
15 November 1974

Notes on Contributors

STEVEN V. DANIELS, Assistant Professor at Southern Methodist University, is working on a long study of structural patterns in Dickens' fiction.

LAWRENCE FRANK, Assistant Professor at the University of Washington, is in process of expanding his earlier work on Dickens and the double into book length.

STEPHEN L. FRANKLIN, Assistant Professor at Miami University, is preparing a book on *In Memoriam*.

MARGARET GANZ, Associate Professor at Brooklyn College, has published widely in journals devoted to Victorian literature, has published the fine book on Elizabeth Gaskell, *The Artist in Conflict*, and is now finishing an essay on Ibsen and Shaw.

EDWARD HEATLEY is a postgraduate research student at the University of Adelaide. The essay in this volume derives from his doctoral dissertation, concerned with religious humanism in Dickens' novels.

GORDON D. HIRSCH, an Assistant Professor at the University of Minnesota, has articles on Tennyson and on Dickens published, and is presently working up essays on John Stuart Mill, Mary Shelley, and Dickens.

ANNE HUMPHERYS, Associate Professor at Herbert H. Lehman College, is General Editor of the Cass Liberty of Victorian Times and has published *Voices of the Poor*, selections from Henry Mayhew. Her book on Mayhew is scheduled to appear shortly.

HARVEY PETER SUCKSMITH, formerly at Monash University and now at Dalhousie University, has many articles on Dickens to his credit, but he is best known for his fine study *The Narrative Art of Charles Dickens*.

Dickens Studies Annual

Stephen L. Franklin

DICKENS AND TIME

The Clock without Hands

In the works of neither Dickens nor Trollope . . . is there any of what we might call "metaphysical" concern with time.—John Henry Raleigh, "The English Novel and the Three Kinds of Time"

Literary works show directly how the qualities of time function . . . in the lives and experiences of the characters. The "truth" of these qualities, therefore, is first exhibited and realized within the specific aesthetic context.—Hans Meyerhoff, *Time in Literature*

THE WORKS of Charles Dickens are notable, among many other things, for his lifelong interest in, even his obsession with, certain abiding topics such as imprisonment, the law, and the divided personality. Time is another such topic in his fiction, one which engages his attention in novel after novel, for Dickens, like most of his contemporaries, felt the threat of change and the appeal of the past,[1] and yet he consciously embraced time and rejected escape from it, an attitude that underlies all the novels from *The Old Curiosity Shop* onward and that assumes major thematic and artistic relevance in several of them.

This acceptance of time by Dickens has caused a certain amount of discomfort on the part of those critics who would like to see him above such apparently strident Victorianism. The major among them, George H. Ford, connects this attitude with Dickens' rejection of the past and generally dislikes the fact that Dickens could be so apparently superficial.[2] John Henry Raleigh, feeling much the same way, calls Dickens' "philosophical attitude toward temporality" "sententious and more or less conventional,"[3] but both critics find also that, in Ford's words, Dickens developed "the secret prose, the music of memory, as a counterbalance to the vigorous Whig tone, with its castigations of the outmoded."[4] In short, he wrote like Proust, chiefly in *David Copperfield* and *Great Expectations,* but elsewhere, too, a fact noted first by Graham Greene and elaborated in some detail by J. Hillis Miller.[5]

One might question this interpretation of Dickens' temporal attitude on at least two scores. First, on the score of ideological motivation, one might ask whether Dickens' acceptance of time, or even his supposed rejection of the past, are really so much a part of the "vigorous Whig tone, with its castigations of the outmoded," as Ford and others [6] seem to think. Two recent critics of time in Dickens' work, Alexander Welsh and Robert L. Patten, connect Dickens' temporal attitude, not to a politically active stance or to Macaulayesque cheerleading, but to religious belief.[7] Since I intend to make the same connection shortly, but on different grounds, I shall only point out here that Dickens never regarded himself as a political person, but he always, however individualistically, considered himself a Christian.

Second, on the score of profundity, one might question the central point at issue: that Dickens' attitude toward time is superficial or "sententious and more or less conventional." Begging altogether the problem of how really profound the Proustian attitude toward time is, I would still suggest that Dickens criticism across the years has consistently followed the pattern of 1) assertion that in one way or another Dickens was shallow, contrived, or inept; 2) discovery that, on the contrary, Dickens was highly original, skillful, and complex, but in ways that do not fit the usual categories and criteria.[8]

In the long run, Dickens, like Shakespeare, was almost never superficial, regardless of his relative lack of formal learning. His attitudes toward time and his incorporation of them into his novels, however idiosyncratic, are no exceptions to this rule, either in what I would prefer to call his Wordsworthian, not Proustian, retrospections, or in his other treatments of temporality. I am especially interested in those other treatments, not only because several critics have examined Dickens' retrospections in some detail, but also because, in forging an acceptance of temporality into his fiction, Dickens performs the signal creative act of transforming one of the key elements of his world view into literary art of high skill and complexity.

At the heart of Dickens' creative treatment of time is his use of clocks and other timepieces to symbolize or heighten various facets of time and change. As my title, "The Clock without Hands," is meant to suggest, Dickens' undoubted fascination with clocks rests on what they record, the flow of time and the action of time on existence, rather than on any particular form of time, such as history or the past. One of the great stumbling blocks to an understanding of Dickens' temporal view is the conceptualization of time in such forms, for, to Dickens, that the clock ticks on is of the utmost relevance; where its hands point means little.

Dickens' view of time, in this respect, bears a surprisingly strong resemblance to that of Henri Bergson: both relate time to free will;

both reject what Bergson describes as the spatialization of time,[9] the envisioning of time as discrete blocks lying side by side [10]—seconds, minutes, and years or past, present, and future; and both consider time the mode of experience that endures—Bergson's *durée*—in a flow of continuity, the temporal continuum that Dickens signifies so often by the ticking of a clock or the chiming of a bell.[11] Where Dickens differs philosophically from Bergson is in his locating of duration in the exterior universe rather than solely in the consciousness.[12] As a Christian,[13] Dickens believes in the reality of the external world, believes that it takes precedence as the locus of man's activities over internal reality, which has its own mode of duration. Thus, when David Copperfield sits waiting for news of Ham in the storm, his mind a confusion of images from various times in his life, what most "torments" him is "the steady ticking of the undisturbed clock" that calls his attention to the reality outside him, the world as a temporal continuum in which man must act.

Although this view of time underlies all of Dickens' works to a greater or lesser degree, the earliest to express it as a central part of a larger construct is, fittingly enough, *Master Humphrey's Clock* [14] and, by extension, the novel which it frames, *The Old Curiosity Shop.* In the works that follow in the next decade, notably *Barnaby Rudge, A Christmas Carol, Dombey and Son,* and *David Copperfield,* Dickens, through the form of each, examines various problems regarding temporal flow that issue out in his most ideologically comprehensive and artistically intricate statement on time in *Bleak House.* Further, *Great Expectations* and *Edwin Drood,* following *Bleak House* at ten-year intervals, show Dickens approaching new temporal considerations through the complex integration of symbol, theme, plot, and characterization that is the outstanding feature of his artistic expression. All of these works, nevertheless, tend toward the one central ideal, that Christian man has no choice but to accept time and to confront its reality. Any other course, no matter how tempting, leads only to self-delusion and social evil.

The singularity of Dickens' creative genius expresses itself in no better way than in the fact that he is the only novelist about whose works a mere listing of clocks would be revealingly worthwhile. Although important clocks do appear in *Tristram Shandy, Mrs. Dalloway,* and a few other novels, Dickens' use of them amounts to a virtual monopoly in English fiction. Master Humphrey's clock, the first that I shall examine, sets the tone for those that follow, insofar as it stands juxtaposed to an attitude about time that Dickens sees as inadequate. Various theories have been proposed as to why *Master Humphrey's Clock* became "one of the lost books of the earth," [15] but the one that the work itself suggests is that either consciously or unconsciously Dickens came to realize that Master Humphrey and his companions, with their fondness, not for the past,[16] but for stasis in a world of change, simply could not function as a vehicle for the stories they frame.

In a letter to John Forster, Dickens describes his idea for the work, which presents a group of characters, Master Humphrey and his friends, who meet periodically to listen to stories written by members of the group: "I have a notion of this old file in the queer house, opening the book by an account of himself, and among other peculiarities, of his affection for an old quaint queer-cased clock. . . . Then I mean to tell how that he has kept odd manuscripts in the old, deep, dark, silent closet where the weights are . . . and how when the club came to be formed, they, by reason of their punctuality and his regard for his dumb servant, took their name from it." [17]

What Dickens fails to mention in this letter, perhaps because he did not realize it himself until later, is that Master Humphrey and his friends are philosophically at odds with the clock and the stories that are kept in it, for they, meeting periodically, living the existence of recluses, and preferring memories of the past to action in the present, are enamored of a stasis which is denied by the clock's perpetual advance. As Master Humphrey notes: "We are men of secluded habits . . . who are content to ramble through the world in a pleasant dream, rather than ever waken again to its harsh realities." The stories read at their once-weekly meetings are attempts "to beguile our days" and are kept in the clock case symbolically by Master Humphrey to derive stasis rather than temporality from that inexorable instrument—to "draw means to beguile time from the heart of time itself."

The first story Humphrey extracts from the clock, however, while it may "beguile" the members of his group, in truth presents a parody on the whole of their proceedings from the point of view of temporal change, a fact that suggests much about Dickens' difficulty in carrying on with the work. In the second, interior frame of the story, "The First Night of the Giant Chronicles," the statues of the giants Gog and Magog in the gallery of the London Guildhall come alive to talk and drink wine in the small hours of the morning. Magog says to Gog: "Our compact . . . is, if I understand it, that, instead of watching here in silence through the dreary nights, we entertain each other with tales of the past, the present and the future; with legends of London and her sturdy citizens from the old simple times. That every night at midnight, when Saint Paul's bell tolls out one, and we may move and speak, we thus discourse, nor leave such themes till the first gray gleam of day shall strike us dumb." This compact between Gog and Magog bears a strong resemblance to the mutual agreement of Master Humphrey's club, but it differs in several respects which make clear that it is meant to parody and to comment upon the other.[18] The first significant difference between the two arises from the nature of the members of the compact. Gog and Magog, the symbolic guardians of London, are in one sense immortal and in another representative of all mankind up to the Apocalypse (Rev. 20: 7–9). As such, they are associated with the time continuum of the cosmos, a fact that comes out [19] in Gog's first remark to his boisterous fellow: "Is this becoming demeanour for a watchful spirit over whose bodiless head so many years have rolled, so many changes swept like empty air—in whose impalpable nostrils the scent of blood and crime, pestilence, cruelty, and horror, has been familiar as breath to mortals—in whose sight Time has gathered in the harvest of centuries, and garnered so many crops of human pride, affectations, hope and sorrows?"

In contrast to these immortals and their grimly realistic view of time and change, a view that Dickens associates with Christian man in a fallen world, Master Humphrey and his friends are aging fast—the old, decaying house in which they meet signalizing their own mortality—and their view of time and change is, as I have already indicated, hopelessly unrealistic: "We are alchemists who would extract the essence of perpetual youth from dust and ashes." Dickens, perhaps coming to realize more clearly the disparity between his own aims and those of his characters, exposes the foolishness of their desire to see the world as a "pleasant dream" and their disregard of time in the face of the evidences of their own mortality through the realism of Gog and Magog in a parallel circumstance.

The second difference between the two compacts relates to the aim and presentation of storytelling. Rather than desiring to dwell on "spirits of past times [and] creatures of imagination" as does Master Humphrey's group, Gog and Magog want to tell tales "of the past, the present, and the future," regarding themselves as "Chroniclers" of life, not as "alchemists" of "fancies." This realistic approach toward storytelling is matched, notwithstanding the overall fantasy of giants and animated statues, by a comic realism of attitude and action on the part of the giants, who, with their relaxed drinking, occasional disagreement, and casual attitude toward observance of the moment, are at once more real and more truly immortal than their human counterparts, who behave with sobriety, formality, and punctuality, according to the fraudulent law of stasis, which masks a will to corporeal immortality that is altogether inconsistent with the ticking of the clock that marks their perpetual decay.

A final point of difference between the two compacts arises from the subject matter of the stories themselves. The story told within the Gog and Magog frame, like the others that follow, including *The Old Curiosity Shop,* does indeed display an element of pathos no doubt pleasing to such a "romantic spirit" as Master Humphrey, but the inner core of all the tales is more consistent with the somber world view of the giants, a view that is not belied for all their slapstick. Seduction and mob violence, child-murder and greed, political execution and cruelty,[20] these are the real subjects of the three tales taken along with those of Little Nell and, later, Barnaby Rudge from the case of Master Humphrey's clock, a clock which, notwithstanding Master Humphrey's pretense, is in its marking of temporal flow, the fitting receptacle of the stories it contains, something which cannot be said for the *Master Humphrey's Clock* frame as a whole.

That Dickens grew more and more concerned with the disparity between Master Humphrey's point of view on time and that of the stories shows up in Master Humphrey's gradual awakening to the implications of temporality at the close of *The Old Curiosity Shop* and again at the close of *Barnaby Rudge*. After the first of these is completed Master Humphrey relates an anecdote about a visit he made to St. Paul's to look at its clock (which, by no accident, is the clock Gog and Magog use in their compact). He finds that "it did not mark the flight of every moment with a gentle second stroke, as though it would check old Time"—the attitude he wrongly attributes to his own clock—"but measured it with one sledge-hammer beat, as if its business were to crush the seconds as they came trooping on, and remorselessly to clear a path before the Day of Judgment" (vi). This phenomenon, in its indifference to life, bids him to "have some thought for the meanest wretch that passes." In awakening him to the reality of time, St. Paul's clock awakens him to the reality of the fallen state of the human condition as well.

After the conclusion of *Barnaby Rudge* he comes to the further realization that his own clock, like the one at St. Paul's, beats out time inexorably. Although he once felt differently, he now finds that inexorability the "greatest kindness" of time and "the only balm for grief and wounded peace of mind" (vi). His growth of awareness in these last two appearances, I would suggest, marks, long after the fact, Dickens' discovery that *Master Humphrey's Clock* runs too much counter in tone to his own philosophical attitude to serve as a fitting frame for stories based on a Christian acceptance of time. Thus, its gradual disappearance from the weekly numbers.

— 2 —

The Present is the point at which time touches eternity. Of the present moment, and of it only, humans have an experience analogous to the experience which our Enemy has of reality as a whole; in it alone freedom and actuality are offered them. He would therefore have them . . . obeying the present voice of conscience, bearing the present

cross, receiving the present grace, giving thanks for the present pleasure.
   Our business is to get them away from the eternal and from the
Present. With this in view, we sometimes tempt a human . . . to live in
the Past.—C.S. Lewis, *The Screwtape Letters*

"Can time be adequately represented by space?" To which we answer:
Yes, if you are dealing with time flown; No, if you speak of time flowing. Now, the free act takes place in time which is flowing and not in
time which has already flown.—Henri Bergson, *Time and Free Will*

The Old Curiosity Shop, for all its flaws, is a much more consistently
unified exploration of time than *Master Humphrey's Clock.* Its success can
be measured, in part, by the surety with which it carries over from its
frame the symbolical use of clocks and other timepieces and the time-
based theme of withdrawal from reality into the past and the manner
in which it adds to them a second theme, the opposition between rural
past and urban present. Critical investigation of the novel has always
paid a great deal of attention to Nell's retreat into the countryside and
the scenes of squalor in the nameless industrial town through which
she and her grandfather pass.[21] Moreover, Miller and Malcolm Andrews have gone on to draw what seems the almost inevitable conclusion, that Nell's retreat into the country is actually an attempt to retreat
into the past and that the industrial town symbolizes the harsh present
she is trying to escape.[22]
   There is more to her withdrawal into the past than the rural setting, however, and more to the urban present than the blackened city
she encounters along the way. Dickens' treatment of time, far from
including these things only, underlies nearly all the significant actions
and the behavior of most of the important characters in the novel. Both
in the main plot, which treats of Nell and her grandfather, and in the
subplot, which centers on Dick Swiveller, attitudes toward past and
present, and temporality and evanescence, determine in great measure
the course of the action.
   With reference to time, Little Nell and her grandfather are on a
fool's errand. As has already been noted, they attempt to withdraw
from reality (urban life, the present) into a fantasy world (rural life, the
past) that never advances. The crux of Little Nell's development in the
novel rests on her growing awareness that such withdrawal cannot succeed. Her attempt to retreat into the static past comes instead to be an
education in the inexorable pervasiveness of time.
   At the root of Nell's desire to flee London for the country is her
grandfather's helplessness. Just as the Old Curiosity Shop itself is an
anachronism in London's contemporary bustle, so is its proprietor,

Nell's grandfather, a man of the past, totally incapable of coping with the present. In the words of Master Humphrey, who narrates the early portions of the work: "There were suits of mail, standing like ghosts in armour, here and there; fantastic carvings brought from monkish cloisters; rusty weapons of various kinds. . . . The haggard aspect of the little old man was wonderfully suited to the place. . . . There was nothing in the whole collection but was in keeping with himself; nothing that looked older or more worn than he" (i).

His helplessness expresses itself further in his nighttime occupation, gambling at cards in the hope of gaining a fortune to support Nell in luxury. Not only does he never win, but also his very motivation for gambling is an admission of his incapacity to succeed at making life secure for Nell through any realistic course: "When was it that I first began?" he cries. "When I began to think how little I had saved, how long a time it took to save at all, how short a time I might have at my age to live" (ix). His gambling, prosaic vice though it may seem, thus is a natural expression of his inability to cope with time.

Nell, who sees her grandfather's unhappiness, suggests that they leave London for the country. Her desire to seek renewal away from the city derives in the most literal sense not from any understanding of the forces at work changing English society in the eighteenth and nineteenth centuries, but rather from her own recollections of recurring trips to the country in her childhood: "We often walked in the fields and among the green trees, and when we came home at night, we liked it better for being tired, and said what a happy place it was" (vi). Indeed, whether or not this statement qualifies as "the music of memory," the past Nell wants to revisit is her own.

In terms of the novel's thematic structure, nevertheless, the flight she and her grandfather make from the city is a flight from the cultural present into the cultural past. The London they flee, depicted time and again in the novel as a city of dark, endless streets and of the stream of life, is also the epitome of the worst of nineteenth-century goals, utilitarian commercialism, and the site of the squalid poverty that in the minds of many, including Dickens, was the inevitable result of such a cultural ideal. Quilp's preternatural evil often obscures the fact that he is chiefly a smuggler, moneylender, and slum landlord—a representative of the seamy side of commercial life. Moreover, the grandfather's most uneasy moment as he and Nell pass out of the city comes not when they encounter a gambling den or a gang of thieves but when they enter the city's commercial district (xv), for he, as a man solely of the past, fears most the modern economic system of contemporary London, a system in which he is unable to compete successfully and which has corrupted him to the extent that he considers Nell's happiness dependent on the wealth he is incapable of gaining. Nell's instinctive understanding of this corruption leads her to contrast the city and the country on the basis of what they demand in commercial terms: "Let us be beggars. . . . I have no fear but we shall have enough, I am sure we shall. Let us walk through country places, and sleep in fields and under trees, and never think of money again" (ix). Little Nell's version of Arcadia is a place where timeless nature reigns, rather than material values, a place, so she thinks, like the rural past, the past of her early childhood.

In succumbing to this desire to seek out a stasis of time and culture and to withdraw from the stream of temporal advance and the cultural present, Nell and her grandfather act out, as perhaps no other fictional characters of the period do, the essential plight of the individual when confronted by Victorian social change. Nell's craving for the security of the lost past grows to be not merely a desire to return to childhood but an expression of the sense of cultural loss common to the age; and her grandfather's distaste for the materialistic industrial towns is not merely a hatred of what he cannot understand or endure, but an example of the age's cultural shock of recognition at time and change. Their attempt to return to the past, finally, in its failure, signalizes one more truth, to Dickens a Christian one, that time cannot be evaded.

Much has been made of Dickens' lack of sympathy for the historical past, but I think that it is clear in *The Old Curoisty Shop* and in every work Dickens wrote subsequently that he was not so much against the past in itself as against attitudes toward the past which, in their spatialization of time, are morally, logically, and experientially indefensible, and yet which he saw around him as products of the age of flux in which he lived. The grandfather's inability to confront the present, for example, is to Dickens the ultimate result of immersion in the paraphernalia of the past, and Dickens reveals him as culpable, muddleheaded, and helpless. This is not to say, however, that Dickens was the champion of the historical present or of his age that some critics, strangely, have tried to make him. The horror of the Victorian cities that he presents consistently from *Oliver Twist* through *Our Mutual Friend* (and notably in *The Old Curosity Shop*), his consistent efforts for reform and attacks on abuses, his antagonism toward the blustering self-congratulation of the Great Exhibition and Podsnappery generally, and the social "darkness" of even his brightest works all belie his being a "proud Victorian" on the Macaulay model.[23] As I have commented earlier, Dickens' own attitude toward temporality simply precludes consideration of time in terms of periods or eras, except insofar as such consideration is linguistically convenient. To make him the enemy of one era and (sometimes as a result) the champion of another, misses or distorts what works such as *The Old Curiosity Shop* are about. Nell and her grandfather flee a Victorian present that is horrifying, but they fail in their attempt to return to the past, because such flight is impossible.

That their attempt is a failure is apparent practically from the beginning and for several reasons. First of all, Nell, who wants to go to the country and by so doing "never think of money again," finds very soon that worrying over how to get by on limited funds is one of her chief occupations. In addition, she discovers that the country is hardly as idyllic as she imagined. Misery and hardship are the everyday lot of the pair at every stage of their flight, not just in the industrial town. They meet, also, the vices of the city in the country in the form of the gamblers who get a hold over the grandfather and the social snobs at Miss Monflathers' school who abuse Nell. While not identical to the city they flee, the country shows all the signs of being just as exposed to the problems of the real world and just as susceptible to time and change as was London.

This susceptibility is evident from the attitudes toward time of the people Nell meets in the country, among whom temporality and evanescence are states of existence taken virtually for granted, whereas the timelessness she expects is conspicuous for its absence from their minds. The first man she meets outside of London strikes the chord that sounds again and again when he says that "it was nigh two-and-thirty years since he had been [in London] last" and he had heard "there were great changes. Like enough! He had changed himself, since then" (xv).

Nell's education in the inescapability of time rests in part on her observance of the attitudes of this and other characters, but it rests even more on certain striking scenes and events which impress her as she travels on and which make the major plot of the novel a progression to an understanding of the old church clock which, in retrospect, seems almost to have drawn her like a magnet to the place where she dies. The last and most important of these scenes—each marked by Nell's "thoughtful" contemplation—comes when Nell confronts the reality of the industrial town, a town epitomized most by the great furnaces in the mill at its heart. The imagery surrounding the mill itself is strongly suggestive of a hell on earth where men "moving like demons among the flame and smoke" are "tormented by the burning fires" (xliv). The central fire, however, by which Nell and her grandfather rest, stands apart from the others, and its chief characteristic is its eternality. It burns "by night and day," having "been alive," so its keeper remarks, all his life: "the fire nursed me—the same fire. It has never gone out" (xliv). Among the numerous symbolical ramifications of such a fire in such a place, the most pertinent is its perpetual continuance. Like the time measured by St. Paul's clock in *Master Humphrey's*

Clock, the eternal fire in the mill goes on inexorably, slowly consuming all that comes within its sphere.

That these temporal implications are not meant exclusively for the squalid urban present of the town, but for all environments, including the supposedly rural past, evinces itself, by no accident, in the nature of the isolated country village which marks the end of Nell's journey. Had Nell truly escaped into the past, the village would surely have been a vital, preindustrial center of agriculture, but instead it is described almost entirely in terms of decay, so that not timelessness or stasis, but age, death, and ruin, solemn emblems of temporality and change, greet Nell in the village churchyard, and when she sees them her education is complete. She knows at last that "time and chance happeneth" to all things and that no past exists into which she can retreat.

The newborn resolution with which she comes to face her own death (lii), while undoubtedly rooted in a belief of the immortality of the soul, is thus rooted also in the Christian acceptance of time that her travels have brought her. She flees the present no longer when she comes to the village, not because she can go no further or because she has reached the past, but because she has been educated in the inescapability of time along the way.

The old church tower bell which appears at the conclusion of Nell's part in the novel rings out its "unheeded warning to the living," but Nell, who once fled time, now listens to the tolling of this clock "with solemn pleasure almost as a living voice" (lxxii). That it rings its "remorseless toll" when she dies is only fitting, for her regard for it is the fruit of the temporal awareness that gradually comes to her as she progresses toward it. It symbolizes, in its chime, the meaning of her life and death.[24]

For Nell, the warning of time "to the living" is to learn how to die, but for Dick Swiveller, left behind in London and the present, its message is to use time well. Dick's "ordeal," if a thing so buried beneath his habitual cheerfulness can be given so serious a name, comes about in the novel because of his initial amorality and his potential for development, a potential that is denied Quilp and Kit, the moral polarities of evil and good pulling on Dick in the course of his trials.

Quilp, the pole of moral evil, stands in opposition to Kit in no way more significantly than in his attitude toward time. Whereas the clock associated with Quilp is an eight-day clock in his counting house "which hadn't gone for eighteen years at least and of which the minute-hand had been twisted off for a toothpick" (v)—a pungent symbol of his contempt for time—Kit's clock is almost certainly the clock of St. Paul's, that inexorable timepiece of *Master Humphrey's Clock* which marks the seconds of life with a sledgehammer beat. Kit's remark to Nell that "you can see a piece of the church-clock, through the chimneys [from where he lives], and almost tell the time" (xi), besides identifying St. Paul's as his special clock, provides a clue to his attitude toward temporal flow that is verified by his later actions: he does not need to see the exact hour on a clock because he is attuned to making the most of what time he has. His return to "work out" the shilling given him by Mr. Garland marks the respect Kit shows for time that stands in counterpose to Quilp's contempt for it.

That contempt appears most forcibly in Quilp's initial appeals to Dick on the subject of Dick's marrying Nell for the nonexistent fortune supposed to be hoarded by her grandfather. Falling in at once with Fred Trent's scheme to use Dick as a proxy to gain the inheritance, Quilp tells Dick that, with his added help, "You've both of you made your fortunes—in perspective." It is to his credit that Dick sees through this verbal juggling of time, replying that "these fortunes in perspective look such a long way off" (xxiii).

Dick's knowledge of time, in fact, has been attained in what for him has been a hard school—being a poor relation to a rich old aunt "who was going to die when [he] was eight years old, and hasn't kept her word yet" (vii). But, although he is well aware of the nature of time, he considers himself helpless to use that commodity even for his own good and allows himself, after a series of misfortunes, to be coerced by Quilp into taking a job as a law clerk under Sampson Brass. "Under an accumulation of staggerers," he remarks, "no man can be considered a free agent. No man knocks himself down; if his destiny knocks him down, his destiny must pick him up again" (xxxiv).

"Destiny" does little for Dick, in truth, but confirm him in the habit of doing nothing he is not forced to do. Nevertheless, two new influences enter his life at Brass's which, in the end, are the making of his character—Kit and the Marchioness, Sally Brass's nameless slavey. Dick, who earlier had recognized Quilp as an "evil spirit," not a "choice" one (xxiii), recognizes something distinct in Kit, too, on their first meeting, that makes Dick decide to "keep his own counsel" apart from the Brasses, who are Quilp's willing agents (xxxviii). The Marchioness, similarly, inspires Dick's secretiveness to the extent that he befriends her while the "Dragon," Sally Brass, is away. His growing revulsion for the Brasses and Quilp and his growing liking for Kit and the Marchioness lead him to "ponder" (xxxviii) and to fall "into deep cogitation" (lviii) over the "mysteries" of the latter pair, a practice which parallels Nell's "thoughtfulness" over certain occurrences during her travels and which leads, in the end, to Dick's gradual rejection of the concept of his own helplessness in the hands of fate.

His first act of personal initiative is to smuggle food and drink in to feed the Marchioness. Then, he offers to help Kit escape from Sampson Brass's clutches after Brass has contrived to make Kit appear a thief. Although Kit refuses his aid, he sends Kit beer in prison to cheer him up and takes Kit's family in hand after Kit's conviction:

> "Some friend will rise up for us, mother," cries Kit, "I am sure. . . . Oh! is there no good gentleman here, who will take care of her!"
>
> The hand slips out of his, for the poor creature sinks down upon the earth, insensible. Richard Swiveller comes hastily up, elbows the bystanders out of the way, takes her . . . and nodding to Kit, and commanding Barbara's mother to follow, for he has a coach waiting, bears her swiftly off. (lxiii)

Dick, once an amoral entity at the mercy of time, has become a "good gentleman" who acts on his own initiative to make use of time.

It is no mere idle whim of Dickens that makes him twice in *The Old Curiosity Shop* cause Dick's name to be mispronounced. Early in the novel, a servant girl, "with that quick perception of surnames peculiar to her class," addresses him as "Mister Snivelling" (vii). After his illness, in contrast, the Marchioness calls him "Mr. Liverer" (lxiv). Dick's ordeal, for all its external lack of seriousness, is in the end serious indeed, for it depicts his development from Mr. Snivelling—snivelling before destiny, incapable of using time—to Mr. Liverer—the "good gentleman" who has learned to act in time and, hence, truly to live. It is difficult to stress enough the fact that in this respect Dick Swiveller serves as a pattern for a great variety of Dickens' characters in subsequent novels—from Gabriel Varden in *Barnaby Rudge* to John Jasper in *Edwin Drood*—who reveal in their attitude toward time their immediate capacity for good or evil. The more clearly they understand that time is the continuum for the moral exercise of the will, the more they exhibit those features of goodness Dickens associates with Christian behavior. Man's temporal attitude is inextricably linked with his moral attitude, and time—to Dickens as to Bergson—is almost synonymous with life. Thus Dick Swiveller's ordeal brings him to a moral understanding of the temporal continuum, just as Nell's fool's errand leads her to a comprehension of death and eternity. To live in good acts and to die in peace of mind—these are the Christian lessons of time in *The Old Curiosity Shop*.

— *3* —

Pure duration is the form which the succession of our conscious states assumes when our ego lets itself *live*. . . . Nor need it forget its former states: it is enough that, in recalling these states, it does not set them alongside its actual state as one point alongside another, but forms

both the past and the present states into an organic whole.—Henri
Bergson, *Time and Free Will*

Dickens' essential view of time changes little after *The Old Curiosity
Shop.* What does change from work to work are the inadequate attitudes about time that Dickens opposes to his own through the central
form of each novel or story and the increasing adeptness of Dickens'
integration of the Christian temporal theme into the overall pattern of
character, symbol, and theme of each work. Although they have already been carefully scrutinized regarding their treatments of time by a
variety of critics, the works of the 1840s are worth additional attention
for what they reveal about Dickens' feelings toward several common
temporal attitudes. Whereas *The Old Curiosity Shop* treats the fallacies of
escape into the past and fatalistic inaction in the face of time, *Barnaby
Rudge* examines the belief in lack of change, *A Christmas Carol,* the
misapplication of time, *Dombey and Son,* dependence on the future, and
David Copperfield, absorption in the personal past. In the next few paragraphs my main concern will be to show how the treatment of these
problems relates to the form of each work.[25]

Barnaby Rudge is significant in its own right as an historical novel
about the Gordon Riots, and as such it involves a variety of temporal
considerations. But the temporal "message" the novel drives home is at
their heart: that to confront time is to confront change. Dickens bla-
tantly sets up the long description of the Maypole which begins the
novel in order to underscore this message, as he does also the character
of its landlord, John Willet. The Maypole is so old as to seem virtually
timeless, perhaps as old as it claimed to be and "perhaps older," and its
pride is the legend that Queen Elizabeth had once addressed the people there from a mounting block which "stood in the same place to that
very day" (i). The atmosphere of changelessness surrounding this inn,
so we are told, affects its keeper's attitude to the extent that he acts as if
time brings no change, sitting and smoking his pipe before the boiler
apparently for years on end (xxxiii), even unwilling to admit the man-
hood of his son, Joe, whom he regards as a timeless boy.

To understand the difference between Willet's belief in stasis and
that of Master Humphrey is to understand, I think, Dickens' compul-
sion to write *Barnaby Rudge* in spite of the obstacles that put off its inception for several years.[26] Whereas Master Humphrey seeks to escape
into stasis from time and change, Willet simply cannot conceive of
change. He formalizes time into a static present. The late 1830s, during
which Dickens was contemplating this work, were of course the years of
Carlyle's *French Revolution,* but perhaps more significantly, they
brought, with the railroad, the application of the Reform Bill, and the

new queen, the first *widespread* awareness that the contemporary social scene was significantly different from the previous make-up of England.[27] In *Barnaby Rudge,* Dickens is aiming his message at those who, like Willet, refuse to acknowledge such change. His long descriptions of the smallness, inconvenience, and danger of London in the 1780s should not be taken as attempts to glorify the present at the expense of the past, for they all are pointedly about change, the changes that have occurred between past and present: "Only six and sixty years ago a very large part of what is London now had no existence" (iv); "it would be difficult for the beholder to recognize his most familiar walks in the altered aspect of little more than half a century ago" (xvi).

These observations and their accompanying descriptions lead directly to the riots themselves and the despoiling of the Maypole, an event so shocking to John Willet that it drives him out of his senses and makes him wish he were dead: "The very Maypole," he cries, "stares in at the winder as if it said, 'John Willet, John Willet, let's go and pitch ourselves in the nighest pool of water as is deep enough to hold us; for our day is over!' " (lvi). Madness and suicidal impulses, Dickens implies, result when an unrealistic belief in a static present is forced to confront the temporal continuum with the changes it brings.

At the moral center of *Barnaby Rudge* is Gabriel Varden, whom Dickens creates as the antithesis of John Willet, both as a father-figure for Joe Willet and as a man who is temporally aware. Speaking to Mr. Haredale he makes the most significant statement on time in the novel and one that in its Christian acceptance of temporality links *Barnaby Rudge,* with its social and historical consciousness, to the works that precede and follow it: "We all change, but that's with Time; Time does his work honestly, and I don't mind him. A fig for Time, sir. Use him well, and he's a hearty fellow, and scorns to have you at a disadvantage" (xxvi).

The second half of this statement might serve further as Dickens' motto for *A Christmas Carol.* Robert L. Patten's exhaustive study of the *Carol,*[28] which details its emphasis on Christmastime as a special time and its manipulations of past, present, and future of Scrooge's consciousness, leaves but two remarks to add to the subject. First, the lesson Scrooge learns in his night of wonders is about the use of time. Marley makes this quite clear when he exclaims in disgust at Scrooge's obtuseness: "Not to know that any Christian spirit working kindly in its little sphere . . . will find its moral life too short for its vast means of usefulness. Not to know that no space of regret can make amends for one life's opportunity misused!" (i). The emphasis on Christmastime as a special time leads only to this awareness in Scrooge: "I will honour Christmas in my heart and try to keep it all the year!" (iv). As soon as he gains this awareness, Dickens tell us, "The Time before him was his own, to make amends in" (v). In no other work, except perhaps *Bleak House,* does Dickens connect Christianity so directly to the acceptance of time.

Second, when Scrooge says, "I will live in the Past, the Present, and the Future" (iv)—a phrase that echoes back to Gog and Magog in the "Giant Chronicles"—he is commenting, not on periods of time or life, but on the temporal continuum. When he goes on to say, "The Spirits of all Three shall strive within me," and "I will not shut out the lessons that they teach," he makes clear, perhaps more directly than Dick Swiveller, that one's attitude toward that continuum in its varying facets bears heavily on what he does from day to day. In this attitude Dickens' view of time again parallels Bergson's on an external level, for just as Bergson sees elements memoralized from the past as potent factors in man's consciousness,[29] so does Dickens believe that Christian behavior results from conscious consideration of existence as a temporal mode. What Dickens rejects is a dwelling on the past or future for their own sakes, because such dwelling leads to misuse of time in the present.

As, in fact, *Dombey and Son* and, later, *David Copperfield* show. In a study entitled "Dickens and *Dombey and Son:* Past and Present Imperfect," John Lucas suggests what is indeed the case, that the focal points of *Dombey and Son,* the Dombey house and the Wooden Midshipman, are centers of the present and the past in many of the attitudes which, through their inhabitants, they represent.[30] Nevertheless, overriding this juxtaposition in importance, I would argue, is the problem of incorrect attitudes toward the future. *Dombey and Son* is absolutely overrun with characters who depend wrongly on the future or make an incorrect assessment of what it will bring, from the master chimney sweeper in Staggs's Garden who plans to scoff at the failure of the railroad, to the members of Parliament who did make merry of it in advance; from Miss Tox, who angles for Mr. Dombey, to Mrs. Skewton, who thinks her daughter's marriage to Dombey will succeed; from Captain Cuttle, who projects a smooth future for Walter on the pattern of Dick Whittington, to Carker, who naïvely expects to complete his liaison with Edith Dombey in France. And the character who most seriously mistakes the future again and again throughout the novel is Dombey himself.

In Dickens' title for *Dombey and Son* lies the key to Dombey's estimate of time—that fulfillment comes in a spatialization of the future—a point Dickens drives home not only in Paul's innocently accurate identification of him—"He's Dombey and Son" (xii)—but also in his confrontations with others: " 'My son is getting on, Mrs. Pipchin. Really, he is getting on.' There was something melancholy in the triumphant air with which Mr. Dombey said this. It showed how long Paul's childish life had been to him, and how his hopes were set upon a later stage of his existence" (xi).

Paul's death does little to chasten Dombey in this attitude, his confidence in the future and in himself in future acts leading to his Soames Forsyte-like marriage and his financial ruin. Dickens reveals Dombey's self-delusive naïveté regarding both halves of his life in his major confrontation with his second wife: " 'Do you think you can degrade, or bend or break, *me* to submission and obedience?' Mr Dombey smiled, as he might have smiled at an inquiry whether he thought he could raise ten thousand pounds" (xl). In Dickens' eyes, he can do neither. His pride—Dickens' central theme [31]—and his lack of self-knowledge, both expressed by his dependence on the correct issue of future events, go simply and directly before his fall.

As in *Master Humphrey's Clock,* Dickens here uses a clock—the clock at Dr. Blimber's school—to underscore the correct attitude toward time which contrasts with that of Dombey and the other characters like him in the novel. In its perpetual question about Paul's health, "How, is, my, lit, tle, friend?" (xi), this clock establishes the uncertainty of the future and its dependence on what precedes it in the temporal continuum, an aspect of time Dombey fails to take into account. The sea, nondiscursive symbol for death, futurity, immortality, and the eternal; the temporal river that bears Paul to the sea; the delayed consumption of the last bottle of Madeira at the Wooden Midshipman; and the pointed quoting of the "for better, for worse," portion of the marriage service (xxxi), all combine with Dr. Blimber's clock to suggest that the message of the novel's last chapter, "to wait the fullness of time and the design," is the final, correct view of time and the future that Dickens opposes to Dombey's in *Dombey and Son.*

David Copperfield, the last novel of the 1840s and the first of the 1850s, follows logically on the heels of *Dombey,* insofar as it is Dickens' statement on time and the personal past. As Miller notes, in spite of its "remembrance of things past," it affirms "no Proustian doctrine of the transcendence of time through a merger of past and present," [32] for to Dickens, the past cannot be recaptured. All the same, the use of the past in *David Copperfield* is an important theme, one that Dickens develops in a variety of ways to reinforce the narrative approach of personal recollection that he uses extensively for the first time.

The most unusual of these ways is through Mr. Dick's Memorial. Stanley Tick has suggested that an important parallel exists between that document and the novel in which it appears.[33] Mr. Dickens, like Mr. Dick, is writing a sort of Memorial. Further, he, like his fictional character, seemingly cannot avoid bringing in his own "King Charles the First's head," his traumatic experience in the blacking factory as a child.[34] This, the "great disturbance and agitation" of Dickens' life, and also, in modified form, of David Copperfield's, seems thus almost to be parodied [35] by Mr. Dick's similar affliction.

The important point, however, is that Dickens, and David, get away with including their traumatic experience in their writings, whereas Mr. Dick does not, and they succeed, whereas he fails, because, unlike him, they are *not* trying to return to or recapture the past. In contrast, Mr. Dick's Memorial is continually spoiled precisely because he attempts to record a return to his own past within it. Such obsessive attempts, as Dickens knew, perhaps from personal experience, are signs of emotional disturbance, the nervousness and mild derangement that Mr. Dick evinces whenever he dwells on his past life. It is no accident that his growing self-control and happiness in the latter stages of the novel come because he keeps "King Charles the First at a respectable distance" (lx) by employing himself in the present, attuning his existence to the flow of time.

David's life, even as it is recalled, serves in a different way to undermine the idea that reliving the past is either feasible or desirable. That his life begins at the beginning (i), that he was born as the clock struck twelve (i), that when he and Emily were children "the days sported by us, as if Time had not grown up himself yet" (iii), that the holiday from Creakle's comes day by day "from the week after next to next week, this week, the day after tomorrow, tomorrow, today, tonight" (vii), that his idyllic childhood fantasies about being married to Emily and "never growing older" (x) fade so quickly—these and countless other elements of the narrative suggest that the dominant chord of "the music of memory" in *David Copperfield* is the inexorability of temporal flow. Mrs. Creakle sums up David's childhood when she says, "You are too young to know how the world changes every day . . . and how the people in it pass away. But we all have to learn it, David; some of us when we are young, some of us when we are old, some of us at all times of our lives" (ix).

Dickens reinforces this temporal motif through the figure of Mr. Omer, the not-so-grim reaper of Omer and Joram's Funeral Furnishers ("The way I look at it is, that we are all drawing on to the bottom of the hill, whatever age we are, on account of time never standing still for a single moment" [li]), and also through the inevitable clocks that lurk in the background of every Dickens novel: "He seemed to be the only restless thing, except the clocks, in the whole motionless house" (xi); "the rooks were sailing about the cathedral towers; and the towers themselves . . . were cutting the bright morning air, as if there were no such thing as change on earth. Yet the bells, when they sounded, told me sorrowfully of change in everything" (lii).

What good, then, is the past? That is the question Dickens asks in *David Copperfield,* and he finds its answer not in the music of memory or the recapturing of lost moments, but in the very passage of experience that time and change afford. Aunt Betsy Trotwood, who, more than Agnes Spenlow, is at the moral center of the novel, strikes the keynote of *David Copperfield* when she says, "It's in vain, Trot, to recall the past, unless it works some influence upon the present" (xxiii). And that is Dickens' fictional aim in having David write his autobiography: to find out whether or not he "shall be the hero of his own life" and to discover in his own experience a means to control his "undisciplined heart." David's retrospections, unlike Mr. Dick's, are not a symptom of illness but a diagnosis for health, and through them he overcomes the apparent "irreversibility" of external temporal flow, which many modern novelists and commentators, including Bergson, find conquerable only in the *durée* of the inner consciousness.[36]

As the last work of the 1840s, *David Copperfield* thus corresponds to the others in its examining of an attitude toward time through its central form. The fixity of consciousness of John Willet, the obliviousness to the portents of time of Scrooge, and the dependence on the future of Dombey find their completion, in a sense, in Mr. Dick's obsession with the personal past and the alternatives to it provided by David's narration. In the works of this decade Dickens comes full circle from Nell's attempt to escape into the past, and yet he remains consistent throughout to the ideal of the Christian acceptance of temporal flow that he sees as necessary for coping morally with the real world. In his next novel, *Bleak House,* he abandons the circle to depict, not merely a character or group of characters, but a whole society in moral peril and at odds with itself for want of a clear view of time and change.

— *4* —

Time is a more important dimension of fiction than space. A novel is a temporal rhythm made up of the movement of the minds of the narrator and his characters in their dance of approach and withdrawal, love and hate, convergence and divergence, merger and division.—J. Hillis Miller, *The Form of Victorian Fiction*

Whether it derives from satire, Renaissance allegory, the Puritan tradition, or all three, the threat and satisfaction inherent in time coming to an end stand in answer to an even less tolerable idea of historicism: the thought of time reaching endlessly before and after human life without stop.—Alexander Welsh, *The City of Dickens*

In *Bleak House* Dickens returns to the central image of the symbolic clock, but whereas in works like *The Old Curiosity Shop* timepieces serve to expose the attitudes of characters toward temporality and change, in *Bleak House* time is gauged by a cosmic or world clock manifesting much more profound and complex ramifications. *Bleak House* is Dickens' most truly religious novel, and in this regard it strongly parallels Tennyson's *In Memoriam,* the publication of which preceded the publication of *Bleak House* by two years. Just as *In Memoriam*, to paraphrase T. S. Eliot, is an impressively religious work because of the quality of its doubt, rather than the quality of its faith, so *Bleak House* is religious rather for its sense of life in a fallen state—what A. E. Dyson calls its "tragic world of Christian belief" [37]—than for its sense of joy in God and salvation. Philip Rogers has suggested that *Bleak House* may be a refutation of that novel of "prelapsarian" innocence, *Pickwick Papers*,[38] a suggestion which gains credence when one recognizes that the fog and mud of *Bleak House* are symbolic, in part, of a "post-lapsarian" world, not, I think, as Miller sees it, out of touch with God,[39] but rather, in nondogmatic terms, in dire need of redemption. This somber religious outlook in *Bleak House* and its themes of time and dependence on the past are not so much interrelated as they are different aspects of the same point of view, and therefore to understand any of them fully, one must understand them all.

Like almost any other discussion of *Bleak House,* this one must begin with its opening mud-and-fog description, the inexhaustible mine of images and themes taken up and developed in the rest of the novel. With reference to time that description is particularly revealing: London is so muddy that it seems "as if the waters had but newly retired from the face of the earth, and it would not be wonderful to meet a Megalosaurus, forty feet long or so, waddling like an elephantine lizard up Holborn Hill. Smoke lowering down from chimney-pots, making a soft black drizzle, with flakes in it as big as full-grown snow-flakes—gone into mourning, one might imagine, for the death of the sun" (i). This glance backward to the beginning—"the waters had but newly retired from the face of the earth"—and forward to the end of things—"the death of the sun"—places the world of *Bleak House* well within the boundaries of Christian time, with its continuum of temporal flow. The passage also suggests, in its Biblical allusion, a connection between time and religious meaning, and in its reference to heavenly bodies, what I will call the concept of the world clock.

The first of these, a connection between time and religious meaning, is not, from Dickens' point of view, undercut but supported by the geological reference to the "Megalosaurus . . . waddling like an elephantine lizard up Holborn Hill." The very title of the then-popular work on geology, Robert Chambers' *Vestiges of Creation* (1844), implies the widely believed hypothesis that fossil remains of dinosaurs and the like, whatever they might mean in terms of dating the earth, are firm evidence of God's work in the world and of man's at least potential superiority to beasts.

From a Christian standpoint, however, that superiority is most tenuous, for men must exist in a post-lapsarian state, trapped, so *Bleak House* implies, in the mud and fog of a fallen world: "losing their foothold at street-corners" and "slipping and sliding since the day broke" (i), unable to see clearly in the fog. In this respect, the Court of Chancery is representative of all mankind: "Never can there come fog too thick, never can there come mud and mire too deep, to assort with the groping and floundering condition which this High Court of Chancery, *most pestilent of hoary sinners, holds, this day, in the sight of heaven and earth*" (i) [my italics]. It is hardly surprising, in light of the perilously fallen state of the court, that Miss Flite, one of its petitioners, expects no judgment on her case until "the Day of Judgment" (iii). She, too, for all her apparent madness, makes the link between time and Christian belief that runs as an undertone from the opening paragraphs of *Bleak House* onward through the work.

Time in *Bleak House*, in addition, is measured by a world clock of cosmic progression. Dickens' use in the first paragraph of the novel of the origin of the earth and the death of the sun as images of alpha and omega, beginning and ending, besides indicating religious significance, presents time as a function of vast universal motions and events of inexorable occurrence and awful portent "in the sight of heaven and earth." The second chapter of the novel begins with further discussion of the concept of the world clock, as its workings apply to the sheltered sphere of the aristocracy:

> [The world of fashion] is not a large world. Relatively even to this world of ours which has its limits too (as your Highness shall find when you have made the tour of it, and are come to the brink of the void beyond), it is a very little speck. There is much good in it. . . . But the evil of it is, that it is a world wrapped up in too much jeweller's cotton and fine wool, and cannot hear the rushing of the larger worlds, and cannot see them as they circle round the sun. It is a deadened world, and its growth is sometimes unhealthy for want of air. (ii)

Like a delicate, expensive watch, the world of fashion is inactive, wrapped in jeweller's cotton; therefore it "cannot hear the rushing" of the world clock in motion through space. Mr. Boythorn later echoes this image when he likens Sir Leicester Dedlock to "one of a race of eight-day clocks in gorgeous cases that never go and never went" (xviii). Sir Leicester, like the world he represents, is static and therefore out of touch with the great temporal motion of the real world.

When examined in terms of time, in fact, not merely that part treating the aristocracy, but the whole of the novel, seems concerned largely with characters and institutions out of touch with the portents of time, and most of them are in this state because of their extreme age or their unhealthy association with things of the past. The Court of Chancery is "the most pestilent of hoary sinners"; the world of fashion

is a world of families, like Sir Leicester's, "old as the hills"; and "both
the world of fashion and the Court of Chancery are things of precedent and usage; oversleeping Rip Van Winkles" (ii) made unconscious
by their preoccupation with the past of the motions of the world clock.
As usual, Dickens connects moral capacity to temporal perception, so
that the Court is the worst of "sinners" because of this preoccupation,
and the "evil" of the world of fashion is its inability to see the "larger
worlds" as they "circle round the sun."

Not merely Chancery and the aristocracy suffer from their age and
association with the past, however; throughout *Bleak House* the evil of
oldness is a dominant theme. Tulkinghorn, that "old-fashioned old
gentleman, attorney-at-law," who threatens and terrorizes such apparently diverse characters as Lady Dedlock, Jo, the crossing sweep,
and George Rouncewell, "is of what is called the old school—a phrase
generally meaning any school that seems never to have been young"
(ii). His chief characteristic is his function as a "silent depository" of the
family secrets of the aristocracy, in which he rivals Krook, the parody
of the Lord Chancellor and a character who is also old and fond of the
trappings of the past (v). To Tulkinghorn and Krook, one can add old
Mr. Turveydrop, whose worship of the "deportment" of the age of the
Prince Regent of thirty years before incapacitates him for any meaningful task; Vholes, who, as a representative of the outworn legal system,
helps "to shore up some decayed foundation" of law through his outward respectability (xxxix); and the Smallweeds, a family that has had
"no child born to it" for generations, with the result that "the complete
little men and women whom it has produced have been observed to
bear a likeness to old monkeys with something depressing on their
minds" (xxi).

The Smallweeds, though perhaps less damaging in their activities
than Tulkinghorn or Vholes, are equally important as representatives
of evil in *Bleak House,* for through them Dickens restates and elaborates
his initial treatment of the themes of time and religious meaning. The
Smallweeds, indeed, embody three characteristics—age, animality, and
evil—in such a way that each becomes an expression of the other two.
The age of the Smallweeds antedates the age of the institutions and
most of the other characters in *Bleak House,* and it does so because of
the Smallweeds' collective animality. Young Bart is "a kind of fossil
Imp" (xx), and his sister Judy at times "appears to attain a perfectly
geological age, and to date from the remotest periods" (xxi). These references to the geological past, in recalling the opening description of
the waters "but newly retired from the face of the earth," recall as well
the Megalosaurus "waddling like an elephantine lizard up Holborn
Hill" and the often-times teleological geology of the day [40] which suggested that animals foreshadowed man's appearance in the temporal

continuum and that man superseded them on a higher moral level. Thus the Smallweeds, in their great age, on the one hand are "owlish," "monkeyish," grublike, "a horny-skinned, two-legged money-getting species of spider," "an animal of another species" (xxi); and on the other, comically diabolical, Grandfather Smallweed, in truth, being the "devil" to whom Nemo is supposed to have sold his soul (x); Grandmother Smallweed being addressed as a "brimstone scorpion" by her husband (xxi); the entire family inspiring George Rouncewell to use imagery of hell and the diabolical when he visits them; and their having as a group a "fiendish appearance" (xxxix). Their "perfect geological age" gives them the inferior moral stature of animals in human form, and the evil that results from this combination is diabolical, as it is for Mademoiselle Hortense, who is "feline" and "tigerish" (xlii) in her veritably Satanic pride, and for Vholes, who, as his name implies, is a human beast of prey, a ghoul or cannibal who devours Richard Carstone's vitality. Mademoiselle Hortense and Vholes, though not "old" in the same sense that Tulkinghorn or the Smallweeds are, all the same, are aligned with the evilness of oldness in their animal nature.

Three characters in *Bleak House* who are not evil and yet who have strong associations with the past—Mrs. Rouncewell, George Rouncewell, and Sir Leicester Dedlock—tend nevertheless to substantiate the theme which on the surface they seem to deny. Mrs. Rouncewell's character is laughable precisely at those points where—as when she remarks, "disgrace never comes to Chesney Wold" (vii)—she defends the institution of the aristocracy. Her son George is helpless in the hands of Grandfather Smallweed precisely because his life in the army's basically feudal social order has crippled his ability to act on his own initiative. And Sir Leicester is ridiculous precisely in those opinions he holds as to the importance and efficacy of institutions and the chaos of the "opening of floodgates" (xxviii) of society. What separates Sir Leicester, whose family, "old as the hills," is as ancient as the Smallweeds', from the evilness of oldness that blights so much and so many in the novel (and what by extension separates the two Rouncewells from it as well) are his qualities independent of his position: "His noble earnestness, his fidelity, his gallant shielding of [Lady Dedlock], his generous conquest of his own wrong and his own pride for her sake, are simply honorable, manly, and true. Nothing less worthy can be seen through the lustre of such qualities in the commonest mechanic, nothing less worthy can be seen in the best-born gentleman. In such a light both aspire alike, both rise alike, both children of the dust shine equally" (lviii). Sir Leicester is "honorable, manly, and true" almost in spite of his loyalty to the past and outworn institutions, certainly not because of it.

For this reason, he heads the list in *Bleak House* of those characters who are mixed or morally flawed. Besides Sir Leicester, the novel presents such potentially good characters as "Conversation" Kenge, Inspector Bucket, Mr. Snagsby, and Richard Carstone, the last of whom Dickens epitomizes as the victim of the outmoded legal system, all the more a victim because, unlike the victims of Kafka, he has the potential to escape. Though John Jarndyce—yet another flawed character—pleads with him to "trust in nothing but in Providence and your own efforts" (xiii), Richard, like so many other characters in the novel, casts his lot with the institutions of the past rather than with the efforts of the present.

In so doing he, like them, is guilty of "trifling with time" (xxiv), and in so doing, also, he contributes to the mud-and-fog climate of ethical paralysis and physical decay which permeates the world of *Bleak House* from the legal stagnation of Chancery and the "deadened" isolation of Chesney Wold, to the squalor of migrant laborers' huts and the infection of Tom-All-Alone's. Since so many are out of touch with the great temporal movement of the world clock, the smaller world of England has all but come to a halt.

This overriding climate of ethical paralysis expresses itself in almost every aspect of the novel but in none more forcibly than its characters who are admired and respected on moral grounds: Skimpole, Mrs. Jellyby, Mrs. Pardiggle, and Reverend Chadband. Without exception they are moral idiots, and Skimpole and Chadband are canting hypocrites as well. After listening to a barrage of Chadband's "abominable nonsense," Jo, the crossing sweep who has never "knowd nothink" about God or salvation, learning "not so much as one short prayer" from Chadband or anybody else (xlvii), "moves on" out into the street: "and there he sits . . . looking up at the great Cross on the summit of St. Paul's Cathedral, glittering above a red and violet-tinted cloud of smoke. From the boy's face one might suppose that sacred emblem to be, in his eyes, the crowning confusion of this great, confused city; so golden, so high up, so far out of reach. There he sits, the sun going down, the river running fast, the crowd flowing by him in two streams—everything moving on to some purpose and to one end—until he is stirred up, and told to 'move on' too" (xix). In London's moral paralysis, the Cross poised above the clock at St. Paul's remains high up, reserved for institutional worship, with the result that the field is abandoned to Chadband, who neither projects its Word nor epitomizes its message. Jo remains on his "dark benighted way" in the time continuum: "the sun going down, the river running fast."

The Christian light, nevertheless, does come upon Jo's "dark benighted way," if only at its end. His death and the seven other deaths in the novel sound an irregular litany across its "whirlpool" pattern of form,[41] a litany that underscores both its religious and its time-related themes and that sums up, more than anything else, what the novel is truly about.[42] The first of these deaths is that of Esther's "godmother." Esther's lamentable sense of her own unworthiness, which flaws her narration for many readers, comes as a result of unaccountable sin instilled in her by this woman. The stroke that fells her happens, so Esther tells us, in a peculiar fashion:

> I had come down at nine o'clock, as I always did, to read the Bible to her; and was reading, from St. John, how our Saviour stooped down, writing with his finger in the dust, when they brought the sinful woman to him.
> "So when they continued asking him, he lifted up himself and said unto them, 'He that is without sin among you, let him first cast a stone at her!' "
> I was stopped by my godmother's rising, putting her hand to her head, and crying out in an awful voice, from quite another part of the book:
> " 'Watch ye therefore! lest coming suddenly he find you sleeping. And what I say unto you, I say unto all, Watch!' " (iii)

Miss Barbary, discovering her own metaphoric stone-casting at Esther and her mother singled out for reproof, grasps at once in her remorse the Christian and temporal significance of her own behavior: time moves on and Christ in the form of death and judgment comes unannounced, like a thief in the night.

The three great death scenes in the novel, those of Krook, Jo, and Tulkinghorn, are also those with the most concentrated thematic relevance. Krook's death, the symbolic death of Chancery, comes at "the Appointed Time" (xxxii). It is "the death of all Lord Chancellors in all Courts, and of all authorities in all places under all names soever, where false pretenses are made, and where injustice is done." It comes at an "appointed time" because it is the inevitable outcome of evil, "the same death eternally—inborn, inbred, engendered in the corrupted humors of the vicious body itself, and that only" (xxxii); and it comes to Krook, the "hoary sinner" who rivals the Court in his worship of the past, his secretiveness, and his indifference to time, because these practices rot him unknowingly from within until at the "appointed time," he disintegrates into fiery darkness.

In contrast, Jo, worn away like Gridley before him and Richard Carstone after, ends not in darkness, but light. For all his ignorance Jo has "moved on" across "this little earth," "all round the clock" (xlvii) in hard endeavor until his journey in the time continuum comes to a close. His essential goodness is expressed in his temporal awareness: he knows that "it's time for me to go to that there berrying ground," and when he does so "the light is come upon the dark benighted way."

Tulkinghorn's death shortly after Jo's joins even more firmly the threads of time and death, for he, too, like Krook and Chancery, whom he parallels in age, evil, and secretiveness, has an "appointed time" for death. After threatening Lady Dedlock with the exposure of her past, he stops to check the time before a clock in the Dedlock house: " 'And what do *you* say,' Mr. Tulkinghorn inquires, referring to it. 'What do you say?' If it said now, 'Don't go home!' what a famous clock, hereafter, if it said to-night of all the nights that it has counted off to this old man of all the young and old men who have ever stood before it, 'Don't go home!' " (xlviii). Checking his watch, Tulkinghorn finds it two minutes wrong and remarks, "At this rate you won't last my time"; ironically, however, it is Tulkinghorn whose oldness and evil do not last, for soon in his chambers, in darkness—the two candles snuffed out—"Mr. Tulkinghorn's time is over for evermore" (xlviii).

After Lady Dedlock's tragic death comes the conclusive death in *Bleak House,* Richard Carstone's. Like those of Krook and Tulkinghorn, Richard's demise comes as a result of his turning away from the world clock to place his interests in the past; like Nemo he has isolated himself from his fellows; and like Miss Barbary and Jo, he sees the Christian light at his end, which Esther describes:

> A smile irradiated his face, as [Ada] bent to kiss him. He slowly laid his face down upon her bosom, drew his arms closer round her neck, and with one parting sob began the world. Not this world, O not this! The world that sets this right.
> When all was still, at a late hour, poor crazed Miss Flite came weeping to me, and told me she had given her birds their liberty. (xxv)

That Richard cannot begin again except in "the world that sets this right," and that Miss Flite, truly despairing of an earthly judgment, releases her birds to freedom, at once reorient the novel to the fallen Christian world of its beginning and suggest that although the "appointed time" may come for Krook and Tulkinghorn and even Chancery, the real evil of oldness is not rectifiable in this life. Institutions and attitudes imbued in the past are always outworn and no justice can be expected from them. By not trusting in "Providence and your own efforts" as measured by the world clock of the temporal continuum, but by trusting in the past, Richard negates his own promise and destroys himself. In light of this outcome, Esther's quiet family life of Christian deeds at the novel's close assumes added meaning as the course Richard could not follow but which, in a post-lapsarian, time-bound world of mud and fog, is the only way open to social and self-development, not to self-destruction.

All in all, *Bleak House* is Dickens' most complete and most complex transformation of his temporal attitudes into artistic expression. In the pervading symbol of the world clock, the network of characters whose moral status expresses itself through temporal associations, and the finely-drawn geological and institutional figures who dramatize the evil inherent in disregard for temporal change and in association with the past, he defines through what is almost a re-creation of the world and human society the Christian temporal issues which man either faces or avoids and the consequences of both forms of action.

On a smaller scale and yet an equally profound one, he traces two variations on the theme of time and man in the world in the last two novels I shall examine, *Great Expectations* and *Edwin Drood*. Although both of these works carry on from *Bleak House* the connection between moral and temporal attitudes and the image of the clock at the heart of their thematic development, they apply these to new problems,[43] the problems that most concerned Dickens later in his career: materialism (in *Great Expectations*) and evasion of reality (in *Edwin Drood*). The manner in which Dickens approaches these new subjects requires examination for a full understanding of his final view of time and human experience.

— 5 —

To stop the clock of busy existence at the hour when we were personally sequestered from it; to suppose mankind stricken motionless, when we were brought to a standstill; to be unable to measure the changes beyond our view by any larger standard than the shrunken one of our own uniform and contracted existence; is the infirmity of many invalids, and the mental unhealthiness of almost all recluses.— Charles Dickens, *Little Dorrit*

But all the clocks in the city
   Began to whirr and chime:
"O let not Time deceive you,
   You cannot conquer Time."
                    W. H. Auden, "As I Walked Out One Evening"

To turn from *Bleak House* to *Great Expectations* is to turn from Dickens' most perfect structure on a grand scale to his most perfect structure on a small one. It is also to turn from the pervasive, cosmic influence of the world clock and the socially blighting evilness of oldness to the apparently narrow sphere of the stopped clocks at Satis House and the folly of stasis for but one person. The narrowness of the significance of Miss Havisham's stopped clocks, however, is only apparent, not real, and the folly of stasis, in truth, lurks in the shadows not merely for her but for the bulk of her characters with thematic importance in the novel.

The relative spareness of plot line and theme in *Great Expectations* reveals its unity and coherence as a work of art immediately to anyone who reads it, something which cannot be said for the unity in complexity of *Bleak House, Little Dorrit,* and *Our Mutual Friend,* and that spareness extends as well into the novel's dominant symbols and images, which relate to characters and actions in what for Dickens is a very simple way. The stopped clocks at Satis House are a case in point with regard to this simplicity: Miss Havisham has stopped them on the one hand to memorialize the moment her heart was broken and on the other to signify that for her life has stopped. Their surroundings in Satis House—the crumbling wedding cake, the rotting beer casks, the decaying wedding dress and the aging woman clothed in it—all point to Dickens' Christian moral that temporal flow continues regardless of individual attempts at stasis and, hence, that such attempts are self-delusive folly. Even Miss Havisham, in one part of her mind, knows that for all her stopped clocks and closed shutters, time move on inexorably: " 'On this day of the year,' " she says to Pip on her birthday, " 'long before you were born, this heap of decay,' stabbing with her crutched stick at the pile of cobwebs on the table, 'was brought here. It and I have worn away together. The mice have gnawed at it, and sharper teeth than teeth of mice have gnawed at me' " (xi). Very little needs to be added to this statement to delineate completely the direct meaning of clocks and time in *Great Expectations.*

But, to go no further than this simple interpretation of the stopped clocks is to ignore a great portion of their symbolic meaning and their relationship to the conflict between material and human values which is the central issue of the novel. That the clocks are located at Satis House has to do not only with Miss Havisham's broken heart but with the far-reaching ramifications of the mansion where she lives, a mansion, so Estella tells Pip, which was given the name of Satis or "Enough" House to signify that "whoever had this house could want nothing else" (viii). It is a great symbol, in other words, of the materialistic ideal of happiness in possessions, which means that its clocks in metaphoric terms were always stopped, attuned to the static nature of satiety, of wanting "nothing else."

Of course, just as the decay of Satis House lays bare the folly of Miss Havisham's desire to stop time, so does Miss Havisham's own need of love lay bare the nature of the ideal of Satis House as unrealistic, not to mention harmful. Had Satis House been "enough" for her, she would not have fallen in love with Compeyson, nor would she have attempted to stop time when he jilted her. Nevertheless, her upbringing in Satis House, with its goal of stasis in material satiation, corresponds with her disappointment in love [44]: her overly violent reaction, to give up life itself in all but name and to take away from Estella every element of human feeling and desire, along with her stopping of the clocks, implies strongly that Dickens envisioned her as seeking a stasis in the satiety of love—a philosophy that whoever has *love* wants "nothing else"—paralleling the materialism of the mansion she inherited. After the satiety of love failed her, as had that of materialism earlier, she is meant to have stopped the clocks to create a sham stasis, all the more sham for her awareness of her own decay.[45]

Although the materialistic ideal is thus disparaged from the very first with regard to Miss Havisham, all the same it is the partial or entire motivation of an astonishing number of characters in *Great Expectations*. Mr. Pumblechook's interest in money and, through it, self-aggrandizement, colors his existence to the extent that he calls Pip "six-pennorth of halfpence" (iv) and contemplates monopolizing the corn and seed trade (xix); Wemmick's "guiding-star" is, "Get hold of portable property" (xxiv); Jaggers tells Pip, "I am paid for my services, or I shouldn't render them" (xviii), and confronts each of his legal clients with the question—"Have you paid Wemmick?"—before he will discuss anything else; the Pockets, with the exception of father and son, wait on Miss Havisham's death with expectations of inheritance; Wopsle wants the church "thrown open" to competition (iv); and even Abel Magwitch, Pip's convict-benefactor, thinks to turn Pip into a gentleman with nothing more than money and the things money buys.

The material values of all these people serve as a backdrop to Pip's own in the novel, and conversely, his gradual corruption by Satis House displays in concentrated, explicit form the inadequacy of their own less well-defined monetary goals. Pip's passion for Estella and his desire for wealth go hand in hand—a combining of the stasis in material satiation of Satis House and the stasis in love that once betrayed its owner, and Estella's attraction as an object of passion is inextricably linked to the jewels Miss Havisham puts in her hair, jewels signifying wealth and position.

The money of Pip's "great expectations," indeed, he regards at first merely as the means with which to purchase the social stature necessary to attract Estella, but the influence of incipient wealth, of the prospect of a stasis of material satiety, of, in short, the stopped clocks of "great expectations" realized, quickly changes his view. When he proposes that "the clergyman wouldn't have read that about the rich man and the kingdom of heaven, if he had known all" (xix), far from making the usual objection that, being rich, he will still be saved, Pip implies, on the contrary, that wealth itself is heaven—the old ideal of Satis House of timeless happiness in money and possession that stands opposed to the Christian view of temporal flow in a fallen world. When he

goes to buy a new suit from Trabb the local tailor, this vision seems to
be comfirmed, for, once Trabb hears of his good fortune, the tailor
treats him with obsequious respect, even to the point of ordering his
young helper to hold the door for Pip. Thus, Pip's "first decided experience of the stupendous power of money was, that it morally laid upon
his back Trabb's boy" (xix). The operative word in this comment is
"morally": in deriving from money the social and *moral* stature, apparently, to lay anyone and anything flat on their backs before him, Pip
seems to have everything he could want or need—"enough." He seems,
in fact, to be on the verge of attaining what all those with material motivations in the novel—Pumblechook, Wemmick, Sara Pocket, and so
on—indeed would like if their wants were more clearly defined: a temporal stasis of orgiastic happiness.

Dickens, naturally, is setting up Pip's misjudgment in order to
knock it down. Pip discovers in the course of time that, far from bringing happiness and content, money tends to increase one's problems and
to lower rather than raise one's moral stature. More importantly, perhaps, he learns to appreciate Joe Gargery, who, for all his blundering,
embodies a purely Christian attitude toward time and change and as a
result stands completely free from material values.

Dorothy Van Ghent argues that when Joe fails to communicate in
his confrontations with Miss Havisham and Jaggers, he merely typifies
the isolation of Dickens' characters from one another and their tendency to soliloquize,[46] but whether or not Miss Van Ghent's argument
is sound, she picked the wrong example to support it, for there is a
very good reason why Joe cannot communicate in those two instances:
Miss Havisham and Jaggers are using a language Joe refuses to speak,
the language of money.

"You expected," said Miss Havisham . . . "no premium with
the boy?"

"Joe" I remonstrated; for he made no reply at all. "Why don't
you answer—"

"Pip," returned Joe, cutting me short as if he was hurt,
"which I meantersay that were not a question requiring a answer." (xiii)

"But what," said Mr. Jaggers, swinging his purse, "what if it
was in my instructions to make you a present, as compensation?"

"As compensation what for?" Joe demanded.

"For the loss of his services." . . .

"Pip is that hearty welcome," said Joe, "to go free with his
services, to honour and fortun', as no words can tell him. But if
you think as Money can make compensation to me for the loss

of the little child—what come to the forge—and ever the best of friends!—"(xviii)

The people who really cannot communicate in these encounters turn out to be Miss Havisham and Jaggers, not Joe, for whereas Joe understands their questions, they are incapable of understanding his answers. His dissociation from material desires baffles them completely: not wanting to stop any clocks by accumulating "enough," but rather understanding and accepting the fact that time moves on and "life is made of ever so many partings welded together" in a Bergson-like duration of existence (xxvii), Joe remains *ever* the best of friends to Pip, so that when Pip's "great expectations" of stasis in money and passion come to naught, Joe, the true gentleman and the true "Christian man" (lvii), nurses him into a correct estimate of time, money, and human values. Later, as proof of his new awareness, Pip tells Joe and Biddy, "And when I say that I am going away within the hour, for I am to go abroad, and that I shall never rest until I have worked for the money with which you have kept me out of prison, and have sent it to you, don't think, dear Joe and Biddy, that if I could repay it a thousand times over, I suppose I could cancel a farthing of the debt I owe you, or that I would do so if I could!" (lviii).

Like Dick Swiveller in *The Old Curiosity Shop* and Richard Carstone in *Bleak House,* Pip in *Great Expectations* rises in moral stature by accepting the reality of confronting time. Just as Dick recovers to reject submission to destiny and just as Richard dies after rejecting allegiance to the past, so does Pip regain health to reject the imaginary stasis of materialism and the stopped clocks of Satis House.[47]

Because it is unfinished, *The Mystery of Edwin Drood,* Dickens' last novel, carries its protagonist to no similar ending of moral and temporal realization. All the same, many indications exist to suggest that its closing scene was to have been a confrontation between the two halves of John Jasper's divided personality,[48] a clash which could not—knowing Dickens—have but issued out in some resolution between Jasper, the symbolic enemy of time in the novel, and time itself. In a *Dickens Studies Annual* article entitled "Time in *Edwin Drood*," [49] Paul Gottschalk has pointed out many of the elements of this last treatment of time by Dickens, both in terms of its presentation of Cloisterham as an enclave of the outmoded and in its growing stress on Christian regeneration to oppose the outmoded. My purpose in the following paragraphs, thus, will be to show how these essential conclusions about the novel relate to its major motifs and to fit them into the pattern of Dickens' temporal thought generally.

Edwin Drood, as any number of critics have noted, is in most respects a new departure for Dickens, with its villain-protagonist, its detective-novel format, and its deep probings into the psychology of evil.[50] Regarding the subject of temporality, nevertheless, the work is at once a continuation from previous novels and a summing up, a last variation on the theme of time that instills the final meaning into those that precede it.

Time follows two apparently unconnected threads in *Edwin Drood,* threads which in reality are woven together from the beginning by the questions asked in its opening paragraph.

> An ancient English Cathedral tower? How can the ancient English Cathedral tower be here! The well-known massive grey square tower of its old Cathedral? How can that be here! There is no spike of rusty iron in the air between the eye and it, from any point of the real prospect. What is the spike that intervenes, and who set it up? Maybe, it is set up by the Sultan's orders for the impaling of a horde of Turkish robbers, one by one. It is so, for cymbals clash and the Sultan goes by to his palace in long procession. . . . Still, the Cathedral tower rises in the background, where it cannot be, and still no writhing figure is on the grim spike. Stay! Is the spike so low a thing as the rusty spike on the top of a post of an old bedstead that has tumbled all awry? (i)

Viewed in larger terms these questions are really about the connection between the novel's social analysis of Cloisterham society and its probing of Jasper's divided self—why are they in the same novel?—and the answer to it, as the completed chapters of *Edwin Drood* indicate, revolves around the question of time.

We soon learn that the ancient English Cathedral tower that appears in Jasper's fantasy is the tower of Cloisterham cathedral where Jasper is Lay Precentor, and we soon discover as well that Cloisterham itself, by way of its long centuries of association with institutional religion, epitomizes both the past, being "a city of another and a bygone time" (iii), and an attitude toward the past which is unrealistic: "A drowsy city, Cloisterham, whose inhabitants seem to suppose, with an inconsistency more strange than rare, that all its changes are behind it, and that there are no more to come" (iii).

Side by side with the ruins and decay of the cathedral in the novel are elements of new light and regeneration: "Children grow small salad in the dust of abbots and abbessess," we are told, and "the most abundant and the most agreeable evidence of progressing life in Cloisterham are the evidences of vegetable life in many gardens" (iii). Similarly, though the institution of the church is outworn and the cathedral usually dark, its deathless spirit on occasion reappears: "A brilliant morning shines on the old city. Its antiquities and ruins are surpassingly beautiful, with a lusty ivy gleaming in the sun, and the rich trees waving in the balmy air. Changes of glorious light . . . penetrate into the Cathedral, subdue its earthy odour, and preach the Resurrection and the Life. The cold stone tombs of centuries ago grow warm, and flecks of brightness dart into the sternest marble corners of the building, fluttering there like wings" (xxiii).

John Jasper, who sees only too well the immobilized decay of Cloisterham, seems not to see at all the vegetable and spiritual regeneration latent there. He even goes so far as to compare negatively his own dull life with the lives of the past in Cloisterham: "No wretched monk who droned his life away in that gloomy place before me can have been more tired of it than I am!" (ii).

A close inspection of his attitude reveals that Jasper's complaint about Cloisterham is distinctly different from that of the Dickens narration, for whereas Dickens objects to the town's willing association with and worship of the past and to its obliviousness to the Christian reality of temporal change, Jasper objects to the "cramped monotony" of his "daily drudging." His dislike of Cloisterham, in other words, is not really a dislike of the past but a dislike of everyday, temporal existence. His escapes into opium dreams are just as much escapes from time as are the lesser reversions into the past of Mr. Sapsea, the town mayor, who proposes as current a patriotic toast that was appropriate in his infancy (iv). Moreover, just as Mr. Sapsea, in his pride of the past, would "uphold . . . his clock against time" (iv), so would Jasper uphold his recurring timeless fantasies against "the distasteful work of the day" and "the wakeful misery of the night" (xix). Jasper, indeed, is the enemy of time, as his meeting with Rosa Bud in the garden of Nun's House makes clear: "he does not touch her. But his face looks so wicked and menacing as he stands leaning against the sun-dial—setting, as it were, his black mark upon the very face of day—that her flight is arrested by horror as she looks at him" (xix). As the enemy of time he is also the enemy of life, the murderer of Edwin Drood, and his fantasy at the beginning of the novel is intruded upon by the image of Cloisterham cathedral, symbol of the decaying town and its worship of the past, because his vision in its sham timelessness and the Cathedral in its association with a spatialized form of time stand equally in opposition to the temporal continuum and are equally delusive. The iron spike in the dream is the reality he hates and Cloisterham ignores, but it remains, a solid bedpost, when the Sultan and the Cathedral fade into nothing. The link between Dickens' social criticism in *Edwin Drood* and his analysis of Jasper, implied from the opening passage of the novel onward, resides thus in the essential similarity of moral conclusions, that attempted evasion of temporal flow by withdrawal either into the past or into fantasy is evil.

Juxtaposed to the elements of the decaying past in the work are "the Resurrection and the Life" of vegetable growth and spiritual truth. Similarly, juxtaposed to Jasper's escapism and murder are the forces of life that seem to be gathering toward the end of the completed portion of the novel—Crisparkle, Grewgious, Tartar, Datchery. Juxtaposed as well to Jasper in this last, incomplete novel is Dickens' final chilling use of a clock as symbol, the Cathedral clock whose hands are blown off in the storm the Christmas-Eve night that John Jasper murders Edwin Drood: "All through the night the wind blows, and abates not. But early in the morning, when there is barely enough light in the east to dim the stars, it begins to lull. From that time, with occasional wild charges, like a wounded monster dying, it drops and sinks; and at full daylight it is dead. It is then seen that the hands of the Cathedral clock are torn off" (xiv). To what use, one wonders, would Dickens have put this Cathedral clock in the (apparently) projected climax of the novel— a chase up the Cathedral tower stairs involving the forces of life and time—Tartar, Datchery, Helena Landless—and Jasper, time's enemy and the destroyer of life? [51]

Whatever the climax was to be, this clock and the fictional events surrounding it represent much not only in *Edwin Drood* but, by implication and circumstance, in all of Dickens' writing. Like Little Nell's clock, it suggests an "unheeded warning to the living" that in time men move inevitably on to death; like the world clock of *Bleak House,* it suggests the portentous cosmic nature of time and the Christian judgment of acts like murder that is to come when time halts; like Miss Havisham's stopped clocks, it suggests the evil inherent in attempts to circumvent temporal flow, be they made through worship of the spatialized past, or desire for materialistic stasis, or escape from reality; and like the sundial darkened by the shadow of John Jasper, it suggests the outrage to time and life perpetrated by time's enemy, a man who hates temporal reality and murders his own kin on the eve of Christmas, the season of celebration of earthly and heavenly love. By posing symbolically the Christian acceptance of time against attempts to evade or circumvent it, this clock without hands sums up Dickens' creative incorporation of time into his novels, and it expresses both the moral implications Dickens attributes to temporal attitudes and also the deliberate, intellectual affirmation of life that is Dickens' career-long response to the problems inherent in temporality.

— 6 —

The doctrine of continuous creation . . . was a medieval heritage, for it said that God provided continuity and structure—thus preventing disintegration and disappearance of the world and the self—by joining the separate parts of time and experience together in a continuous, invisible act of creation.—Hans Meyerhoff, *Time in Literature*

Human time . . . is intelligible only as duration, as a constant indivisible flow in which life will be a continuous, enduring unity of change, and the consciousness, by memory and desire, will completely merge any given moment of the present with the whole personal past and future. Such a formulation, essentially Bergsonian, belongs largely to a post–Victorian period. But its terms were freely anticipated by various philosophies current in the nineteenth century.—Jerome H. Buckley, *The Triumph of Time*

Dickens' view of time is expressed, not through dialectic, but through the unique artistry of his fiction, through its complex integration of symbol, theme, language, plot, and characterization, but to say that his temporal attitude has no metaphysical purport is to underestimate Dickens' intellect as well as to misunderstand the tenor of his creative genius. In work after work Dickens gauges his characters' moral stature by their acceptance or rejection of a temporal attitude that parallels Bergson's in form and complexity, that corresponds to the Christian reality of a fallen world, and that, in Dickens' fiction at least, reigns superior in direct confrontation to all other views of time. It stands, further, as an integral part—perhaps *the* integral part—of Dickens' world view, and, in its assertion of a tough-minded attitude about man's role in the external world, it reveals more about Dickens' religious outlook than any other element of his fiction, for if, as it implies, man is free to act with the temporal flow of past, present, and future as his guide, then he is, to Dickens, a type of Christian pilgrim traveling through time in a fallen world. And if, as it also indicates, the escape of time through spatialization of it into such forms as stasis or the personal past is impossible, and the attempt to do so evil, then Christian man's only means of overcoming the irreversibility of temporal flow is through his attention not to interior consciousness but to the lessons of time and change afforded to him in the world. And if, as Dickens' many symbolic clocks suggest, duration is the mode of time in the exterior universe as well as in the human mind, then that duration—to which man is free to conform and which he must confront to function for the good—must be an expression of the consciousness of a greater mind, the mind of God.

These conclusions may or may not be palatable, but they are hardly superficial or conventional, for they derive, in truth, from an understanding of time that bridges the gap between the complex modern reasoning of Bergson and the reasoning of that most admired of medieval philosophers, and the first to examine in detail the relationship between time and free will—Boethius.[52]

That Dickens expresses his view of time in a creative rather than an argumentative mode ought not to blind us to this fact.

Margaret Ganz

PICKWICK PAPERS

Humor and the Refashioning of Reality

GEORGE GISSING has said of Dickens that "to write of [him] at all, is
to presuppose his humour." [1] Unfortunately the assumption of later
critics (not only that one should take the humor for granted but that
discussing it is intellectual gaucherie), abetted by what Ada Nisbet calls
"the oversolemn preoccupation with the Existentialist, Kierkegaardian,
Jungian, Freudian, Marxian, Etceteran undertones in Dickens," [2] has
nearly consigned Dickens' humor to oblivion. Even in dealing with à
work like *Pickwick Papers,* the primary reason for its initial appeal has
been minimized or neglected in favor of the motifs of crime and rebellion in the interpolated tales; the work's failure to achieve the structure
of a *roman;* the pattern of its hero's engagements and withdrawals from
reality in the quest for identity; the "impulse towards transcendence." [3]
Beyond its susceptibility to critical fashions, the sobriety, disabusement,
and self-consciousness of the modern temper have inhibited its capacity
to relish the kind of humorous invention that is not morbid and world-
weary, but instead conveys "that sense of everlasting youth—a sense as
of the gods gone wandering in England." [4] To move from Chesterton's
exuberant celebration to J. Hillis Miller's projection of the threatening
implosion of reality on the questing Pickwick ("the world no longer
remains a passive scene. It is human, alive, and it threatens to force the
spectator to yield his secret") [5] is to measure the temperamental alienation that has contributed to the near-exile of humor from the Dickens
world of many critics. The very language used in denoting the experiences and reactions of the central character marks an estrangement
from certain premises of humor. And when language addresses itself
to language, the alienation seems complete: "Jingle is an approximation
of uninflected linguistic energy. He seems incoherent but he is not; his
speech proceeds rapidly and by associations; his syntactical mode is
abbreviatory and contracted; his logic is elliptical, abstractly minimal,
and apropositional." [6]

    If we care to redress the balance, we can hardly redress the temper. But we can stress the extent to which preoccupations with structure, theme, symbol—and more recently, language—have short-circuited our imaginative empathy with Dickens' most spontaneous gift. Ultimately we may even convince some critics that the strategies of humor, transcending mere buoyancy, traffic in subtle affirmations to allay the threats of pain and annihilation. Surely we are closer to a just assessment of Dickens' talent when, for instance, we worry less whether Jingle's speech pattern "repeats in miniature the disjointed quality and rapid pace of the novel," [7] but respond more viscerally to the impact of his telegraphic concoctions, an impact predicated on the kind of accommodation with life their creativity suggests. For the magic of Jingle's conversation, that "gift o'the gab wery gallopin'" (as Tony Weller, his first linguistic critic, puts it), derives precisely from its having no narrow structural or symbolic function in the work as a whole, while paradoxically seeming, in its affirmation of life's incongruities, at once more essential and more gratuitous than other elements. That Dickensian tendency to load a ludicrous idea or situation with a positive charge at the expense of structure or theme (from which many other characters beside Jingle profit) is brilliantly evoked in Orwell's familiar reference to Dickens' work as "all fragments, all details—rotten architecture, but wonderful gargoyles." [8] Abrogating that critical distance which in formalizing tends to reduce and simplify (how just is Barbara Hardy's contention that "it is much easier to see the structure and statement of *Pickwick Papers* at a considerable distance from the full text itself"? [9]), and taking a chance on the "gargoyles" can illumine the comic fecundity of Dickens' first novel while placing other elements in a juster relation to it and to each other.

Much of the novel's power is then seen to emanate not from the focus on a central fable, or the progressive maturing of a social vision, or the projection of a moral ideal, or the documenting of a geniune *Bildung*, but from the playful, erratic, and yet not unsubtle exercise of Dickens' imagination on the human dilemma that perpetually concerns tragedian and humorist alike: the ambiguous interaction or ideal and real, illusory and actual in the forging of human experience. Of course the spectacle of Pickwick's repeated encounters with the world and of his interpretation of what he sees gives the novel a relative coherence [10] and endows gratuitous creations like Jingle, Count Smorltork, and Bob Sawyer with a relevance denied to them by the episodic plot. But no such reassurance of thematic or structural sense is needed if one finds the novel's richness in the imaginative devices with which it challenges and affirmatively resolves (*seriatim*, as it were) the contradictions of experience.

Pickwick Papers is relatively so late a manifestation of the picaresque and addresses itself to a theme so centrally and persistently consecrated by art—the plight of deluded innocence buffeted by experience—that certain questions of originality become irrelevant. Critical comparisons between Pickwick and Don Quixote persist to this day, not to speak of references to Fielding's, Smollett's, and Sterne's successful adaptations of genre and theme to English fiction. Even the initial idea of the predicaments of ridiculous sportsmen (with Dickens to provide the texts and Robert Seymour the illustrations) was of course imitative.[11] Yet if he has not originated, Dickens may be said to have re-created his theme, refashioned it even as the peculiar nature of his humor conspired to refashion reality.

For the dilemma of innocence which Pickwick faces in his exploration of the world is illumined and made distinctive by the quality of Dickens' imagination. It is the special thrust of affirmation in this vision which gives his theme so transcendent a power. Smollett's bluntness, Fielding's humane vitality, and the fey subtlety of Sterne leave a wider scope for the farcical, the burlesque, the satiric, the ironic, to assert themselves in the treatment of a Humphry Clinker, a Parson Adams, or an Uncle Toby. Nor are these elements left out of *Pickwick Papers,* of course, but when the Dickensian imagination has best exercised itself on the incongruities of character and the ambiguous nature of reality, Pickwick's encounters not only transcend in comic power the farcical pitfalls initially projected by Seymour but vastly outdistance satirical exempla or even tragic revelations in the power to approximate the *experience* of taming experience. That few of the creatures in the world Pickwick explores seriously threaten his candor and kindness (even the villains are transfigured so as to seem appealing and vulnerable in the manner of the innocent hero) suggests a complex process at work whose goal (perhaps like the myopic struggles of life itself) is less the ultimate resolution of conflict so characteristic of the final outcome of comic fiction and drama than a sequence of intermittent victories over the threats of reality. The cumulative comic power of these victories informs the novel; even as it celebrates the principle of psychic defiance, humor stubbornly, if not lastingly, resists the threatened encroachment of darker and more didactic elements.

That in appraising the human condition Dickens' humor transcends the frivolity of farce, the judgments of satire, and the poignant reappraisals of the tragic view is especially clear in *Pickwick Papers* because it encompasses all these modes, allowing one to assess and contrast their impact. After all, the novel begins with a farcical assumption, flowers into a work of humor, and declines (as humor's resistance is muted) into a half-satiric half-tragic portrait of the pitfalls which the real world stores up for the innocent.

To understand the threat which the farcical, satiric, and quasi-tragic aspects of the novel pose to the humorous exploration of its theme is also to measure the quality and power of the humorist's vision.

To begin with, the farcical and the humorous—two modes whose intentions and effect are all too often confused—are sometimes at loggerheads here. Soon freed of the limitations of his initial assignment, Dickens was still saddled with the basic subject of the sporting club and with some intractably burlesque characters. Given the idiosyncracies of the Pickwick Club members, he felt compelled to involve them intermittently in ridiculous imbroglios provoked by their respective oddities. Though incongruity—so essential a principle of humor—is involved in the unmasking of Winkle and Tupman, Dickens only occasionally invests the Pickwickian foibles with the humorist's perception that eccentricity is a token of humanity, not merely a ridiculous propensity but a richly diverting, touching, and ultimately illuminating *modus vivendi*.

Accordingly the "P.C." members are most often figures merely driven by one particular obsession, one decisive "humour" in the Jonsonian sense (though even Jonson has his whimsical, unpredictable Sir Politic Would-be). Pickwick himself is sometimes simplistically depicted as the wide-eyed, naïve traveler who enters the wrong room at an inn or foolishly thinks he has made a valuable antiquarian discovery. In the attitudes of the characters, their behavior, and the situations they encounter, mechanical obstacles to understanding and quirky rigidities of reaction provoke laughter along sound Bergsonian lines. The errors, misunderstandings, and physical mishaps characteristic of farce are rehearsed here as Winkle proves a dangerous sportsman to trusting onlookers, Tupman an unwitting accomplice to the elopement which destroys his own romantic plans, Snodgrass an eager suitor awkwardly imprisoned in a sitting-room, and Pickwick himself the near victim of military maneuvers and a lady in yellow curlpapers.

A comparison between Winkle and Jingle demonstrates how the alchemy of Dickens' humor transmutes a subject, immortalizes a character, refashions a theme. While farce here depicts imposture—the distortion of reality—as an isolated protective gesture of vanity (Fielding's terms "to purchase applause" are certainly applicable to Winkle), humor celebrates it as a style of life. Winkle is a pedestrian creation because he is never more than a bungling sportsman who claims to be proficient and is doomed to have reality provokingly belie his pretense. But in Jingle, a humorous creation (and a humorist in his own right), we sense imposture as a total response of the imagination to reality. His claims to importance are transfigured by the burlesque poetic visions he evokes: Spanish donnas who pined for him, revolutions in which he functioned as warrior and poet, cricket matches played under a burning West Indian sun with Sir Thomas Blazo and the heroic Quanko Samba who "bowled on, on my account—bowled off, on his own—died, sir." [12] The combination of "high-spirited fantasy" and an "impish insight into the grotesque" [13] harnessed to counter threatening realities—

here rootlessness, indigence, and ultimately dissolution—endows Jingle with a dimension of vitality and consequent authenticity denied to a far more predictable figure like Winkle.

Yet the authenticity Jingle projects has little to do with conventional realism in fictional characters. He seems to live because his responses to the world, in one sense preposterous, are yet emblematic approximations of genuine strategies by which the human psyche tries to cope with the anomalous, paradoxical, threatening terms on which it exists. When the outrageous adventures fabricated by Jingle take hold of us with the same persuasive force as Falstaff's monstrous boast of fighting Hotspur "a long hour by Shrewsbury clock," we neither accept the authenticity of these impostors' claims nor feel impelled to condemn them by a disdainful laughter as fabrications of vanity. We hail them as reassuring responses to universal longings and fears, modes of promoting well-being and assuaging anxieties about our present state and ultimate condition familiar, if not to our conscious, to our unconscious selves. Our suspension of doubt credits the imaginative leap, not the actual contention.

While the vitality of the humorous character so largely derives from the life of his imagination, figures of farce too often subsist on the barest minimum of traits needed to exploit simplified comic situations. (The travails of Winkle, Tupman, and Snodgrass are short-lived, superficial sources of amusement, for, beyond the display of some very obvious signs of vanity, their predicaments give no clues to their own natures.[14]) Not only do these characters lack an inner life but they are often denied the power of *expression*, that attribute of a humorous creation which most richly reveals his mode of taming experience. Dickens is perhaps the humorist in fiction most adept at fashioning conversation whose grotesque inventiveness unpredictably provides a pleasure of recognition at once psychological and aesthetic. Whether a character exploits incongruity (Jingle discoursing on the headless lady hampered in consuming her sandwiches) or illustrates it (Tony Weller voicing his scheme to rescue Pickwick from prison),[15] the language of humor authenticates personality and conveys the transposition—in reassuring terms—of the facts of experience. While farce, revealing the limitations of its scope, indemnifies our discontent as it bestows punishment on folly (like satire it is often merely an instrument of castigation), humor, with its whimsical verbal splendors, reconciles us to the failings of our nature and condition by arousing a laughter of indulgence, tenderness, and most of all complicity.

Yet one is lenient with the farcical treatment here when one remembers the origin of the novel or is momentarily diverted by the high spirits with which the sportsmen's blunders are often portrayed. Far more disappointing are the flaws which can be traced to the conflict between a humorous and somber vision of reality. That this conflict would be more pronounced in a sustained piece of work was inevitable (while in *Sketches by Boz,* separate stories could very naturally embody contrasting views, the interpolated tales in *Pickwick Papers,* despite the critical claims made for them, cannot really exorcise any intimations of anguish in the central story).[16] Yet no one could have guessed that the intrusion of seriousness upon high spirits, the clash of satire with humor, in the latter part of *Pickwick Papers* presaged Dickens' entire development. The conflict was never resolved; the darker view encroached more and more on the humorous perception of the world. "In Dickens's mind," Cockshut says, "fantasy fought against detailed reality, and reality won after a long struggle. Gay irresponsibility fought against moral seriousness, and seriousness won eventually." Yet that victory surely involved not only the overwhelming of fantasy by the details of reality but the loss of its capacity to enlist these details in its transfigurations; much more than "gay irresponsibility" was forfeited in such a loss.[17]

Ambivalence already threatens the humorous balance of Dickens' first novel. Precisely because *Pickwick Papers* appeals mainly to the sense that incongruities can liberate an affirmative laughter (a laughter negating the threats of despair and dissolution), the bitter indictments, the pleas for social reform, the stark or pathetic depictions of human misery, all so pronounced in the latter part of the book, strike us as particularly disturbing intrusions. They entail a drastic shift in consciousness without adequate preparations. They force us to exercise the moral judgment humor had allowed us to suspend and to become aware that the flaw in the novel is not the absence of sound construction but the abrogation of the humorist's vision of man's predicament.

It is the characters who prove to be the most immediate victims of this fragmentation. By making Jingle weep and repent toward the novel's conclusion, Dickens endows with moral assumptions a creature essentially conceived in aesthetic terms, who tends to "convert" the vicissitudes of existence "into his own nature," [18] whose impudence, dishonesty, and resourcefulness imagination had transformed not just into a mode of expression—into style—but, as we have suggested, into a mode of existence, a style of life that transcends ethical considerations. The magic of humor is destroyed, along with Jingle's original *raison d'être* as a representative not only of the anarchic, reason-negating attributes of humor, but of its capacity to fend off threats to the psyche (Freud would say to the ego) by trafficking in affirmative illusions. To the grand lies told in the face of degradation and despair can hardly be applied the judgments morality passes on standard breaches of honesty. Nor for that matter can trustfulness, when humorously conceived, be assessed by conventional moral standards. Thus the grotesqueness of Pickwick's innocence, the comforting paradox of the "angel in tights and gaiters" is disturbingly inadmissible when we are faced at Fleet prison with an earnest and thoughtful humanitarian, when we move from a largely aesthetic mode to a didactic one without any clear artistic motivation on Dickens' part. That Auden considers the change in Pickwick the centrally significant experience of the novel does not prevent him from acknowledging the drastic alteration of modes and its ultimate impact; of Pickwick and Don Quixote he notes that "in becoming ethically serious, both cease to be aesthetically comic, that is to say, interesting to the reader, and they must pass away." [19]

Some early critics, already aware of the change in the novel before its conclusion, interpreted the alteration of Pickwick's behavior (and that of the other Pickwickians for that matter) as evidence of a failure to devise complex and consistent characters.[20] Such strictures have continued to the present, not to speak of lively arguments about the nature, scope, and lasting effect of Pickwick's transformation. Yet one must realize that Dickens incurred some of these complaints and encourages these contentions because his novel incorporates two different modes of coming to terms with reality, two distinctive conceptions of action and passion.

It has often been noted that all comedy is essentially artificial, thriving on the invulnerability of characters who always rebound after they have seemingly been annihilated: the inhabitants of the animated cartoons are a case in point. Because (to use Susanne Langer's terms) they function as emblems of the seemingly indestructible "comic rhythm . . . of vital continuity" as opposed to the tragic rhythm of human existence delimited in a "unique, death-bound career," [21] and serve the viewpoint that incongruity can be a source of joy rather than a threat, comic characters cannot be permanently affected by the destructive accidents of existence without forfeiting their function. Physical injury for instance can only be a passing obstacle, most often a source of additional laughter for the observer. (Don Quixote is pummeled into insensibility, starves himself, is hung by the arm for hours, but must inevitably recover to undertake another ludicrous quest. Pantagruel and Panurge are bound to escape the perils of drowning or destruction by monsters to continue their exotic and amusing travels in search of the Oracle of the Bottle.) But if all comedy tends to invest its characters with a *physical* invulnerability to threatening elements—and indeed at times with a concomitant emotional buoyancy—humor, as we have seen, adds a dimension of *psychic* invulnerability as well. The handling of reality that secures it has the transfiguring power of the process of art. Thus Falstaff's role as an inspired wit and buffoon depends not just on his physical but on his mental immunity to blows, insults, and the dangers of war, an immunity predicated on his creative strategies for dealing with reality, his "power to transform accident into essence, as it were" (in John Killham's terms) through the verbal felicity which exploits what Hillis Miller in a different context calls "a self-generating web of meaning." [22] The ability to rebound in mind as well as in muscle endows humorous figures with the very permanence of existence their strategies are calculated to insure. That reassuring sense of immortality which they infectiously convey makes it hard to think of them as doing anything but what they always do; that they should have stopped doing anything is inconceivable. They are perceived and hailed as the exemplars of the destruction-defying, creative affirmation which is the permanent business of their lives.

The rejection of Falstaff by Hal is perhaps the clearest example of what happens when serious or tragic considerations enter into the humorous conception of a character (who, in addition, like Jingle, is a humorist in his own right). When the world of reality—and its tragic implications—encroaches upon the seemingly indestructible universe of humor, the godlike illusion is destroyed; pity and contempt replace admiration and joy; anxiety overwhelms assurance; incredulity may even attempt to reason away the intrusion of sorrow. For what has really been rejected or rather negated, beyond Fallstaff the man, or that frivolous anarchic spirit of his which threatens the political health of the kingdom, is the larger idea which he champions: the possibility of vanquishing through wit and humor the threats of destruction.

The same feeling of betrayal which is experienced at Falstaff's rejection greets the spectacle of Jingle taken to Pickwick's bosom. (Job Trotter humbled and shrewish Mrs. Weller on her deathbed discoursing on the duties of women are violations on a simpler level of the humorous norm regarding moral fallibility.) By failing to be consistent, by not always keeping his characters invulnerable, Dickens was bound to arouse criticism which might never have been levelled at fully sustained humorous creations. Perhaps when the *Westminster Review* reproached him for not "developing character in action," it was precisely because he had made a few inappropriate attempts to do so. Had the humorous mood of the work been sustained, no one might have challenged his emphasis on "peculiarities of manner" rather than on "the minute shades of character." [23]

Doing justice to the achievement of *Pickwick Papers,* therefore, precludes the demand that humorous characters in their psychological makeup should reflect the precariousness of human life, its infinite potential for tragedy; their destiny is precisely to counter or deny what makes us vulnerable. Purveyors of illusions, who promote the transfiguration of reality on the assumption that incongruity is food for laughter, they own an experience that is necessarily circumscribed even if its effect is subtly far-reaching. Yet they need not be one-dimensional

morality-play figures. If the humorous idea which their speech and behavior expound is sufficiently inventive, it is bound to endow them with
complexity and concreteness, with a kind of super-reality. They will
indeed seem to grow even in their sameness as the humorist plays variations on his theme, illumining his perception with imagination and
humanizing it by sympathy.

It is not only the humorous approach to character which allows
Dickens to transmute the dilemma of an ignorant traveler at odds with
the world into a paradigm of the refashioning of reality according to
the dictates of illusion. Rather the stuff of reality—scenes, situations,
social attitudes—is viewed in humor's ambiguous light as felicitous
source material for creative, Count Smorltorkian exercises. Robert Sur-
tees' Jorrocks is never much more than an amiable bourgeois whose
naïveté and uncouthness make him cut a silly figure on the sporting
field, at Ramsgate, or in Paris, the places themselves being merely the
settings for his *faux pas* and foibles. Pickwick is in some ways as concrete
as Jorrocks, but the humorous assumptions in action and language
make not only his nature and predicaments emblems of the universal
dilemma of innocence but the world itself (even if in some ways Ro-
chester, Bath, and London are described with graphic fidelity) a concat-
enation of incongruities that defies comprehension by the enlightened
reason. Though Pickwick is a latter-day Everyman propelled into a for-
bidding world to assimilate experience, his richest and safest discoveries about experience come not from seeing and knowing *things as they
are,* but rather from intuiting reality through *things shaped into being* by
the imagination of his humorous guide Sam Weller. Only the creative
realist can provide Pickwick with an antidote to the malady of experience.

The necessity for Pickwick to yoke himself to an expert trafficker
with reality to encompass its ambiguous, refractory nature and to
triumph over its threats reflects in an actual relationship the power of
humor as a life-protecting principle: to cope with reality one must
acquire the saving vision of its dangers which can annihilate them; according to one's imaginative power one must learn to see it as a humorist (Weller) or through the eyes of one (Pickwick). On a more subtle
level, Pickwick's need illustrates the psychological verity about aspects
of the self brilliantly suggested by Freud: the possible dependency of
ego on super-ego to minister to and preserve it through the exercise of
humor.

When Dickens embodies contrasting perceptions of the universe in
a master-servant relationship, perpetuating the great comic tradition of
such interactions,[24] as a humorist he can transcend the farcical and satirical potential of the theme (exemplified, for instance, in works as different as Marlowe's *Doctor Faustus* and Molière's *Tartuffe*). For he mod-

ulates the theme by modifying the values traditionally attached to the vantage point of each of the two protagonists and to the obstacles— human and material—which they confront.

As, with the heart of a Parson Adams or an Uncle Toby and an innocence as circumscribed, Pickwick follows the picaresque pattern of clashing with the world and getting into a variety of grotesque scrapes through lack of experience, the very spectacle itself of Pickwick's pure, fearful, and tender nature attempting in utter bewilderment to satisfy the demands of a selfish, coarse, and cynical society allows Dickens a certain richness of comic effect. But that effect is invariably intensified when Pickwick's predicaments place his intentions in a suspicious light. Then begins the process of liberation through humor: we laugh not only in contemplating ideal ludicrously enmeshed in reality but at a real world expressing in its monumental obliviousness to ideal goodness, not just its moral myopia but the pursuit of its own psychological obsessions and the cultivation of its irrationalities. The failure of communication between Pickwick and the ladies of the boarding school, as two assumptions about human behavior clash whimsically, has the ultimate effect of reconciling us to the threats of social opprobrium. Because it has been made to seem so irrationally, viscerally, erratically, we might almost say vulnerably suspicious, the condemning social voice which greets Pickwick's "Hear me. I am no robber. I want the lady of the house" with "Oh, what a ferocious monster! . . . He wants Miss Tomkins" (223) has been defused of the power to harm.

In a world where kissing one's hand to a lady evokes the jocose epithets of "wicked old rascal" and "wenerable sinner," the misjudgment of Pickwick is likely to recur and the humorous reverberations to multiply. When, at Bob Sawyer's party, Mrs. Raddle (indirectly discharging her anger at her improvident lodger) rebukes Pickwick with the incongruous judgment: "Old enough to be his grandfather, you willin! You're worse than any of 'em" (171, 446), the comic effect produced by such views of Pickwick transcends the Bergsonian assumption that rigid, mechanical deviation from a flexible social norm evokes castigation in the form of laughter. Our laughter here is finally an antisocial gesture compounded of negative and positive reactions. We do laugh *at* rigid limitations—here of members of society judging according to their narrow, corrupt, unimaginative lights—and we laugh expansively because these weaknesses have been made to seem tokens of vulnerability, to unreason for example. We also, however, laugh in sympathy *with* this social outsider, and with the reverberations for us of his incongruous plight. For humor has made him the vicar for the travails our illusions and ideals endure at the hands of the world. That world may superficially seem to be having the best of it in these interchanges, but at a deeper level its authority and assumptions are being undermined, not the least because they are shown to be tainted by irrationality and moral blindness.

It is when Sergeant Buzfuz deliberately juggles fact and delusion to paint an outrageously false picture of the character and intentions of Pickwick that the humorous effect of society's failure to assess Pickwick correctly can be fully plumbed.[25] For, as we shall see, Buzfuz's technique approximates that of the humorist refashioning reality; his misunderstanding is willed artifice. Curiously enough, the humorist Sam Weller does temporarily misunderstand Pickwick's intentions toward Mrs. Bardell, yet does not rely solely on appearances, commenting "I didn't think he'd ha' done it, though—I didn't think he'd ha' done it!" Unlike those other representatives of the world of reality who judge the unfamiliar mostly by their own standards, Sam Weller possesses the imaginative insight into both worlds which allows him not only to straddle them but to transcend their lures. Only he, accordingly, can guide Pickwick through the perils of his pilgrimage. By yoking himself to Pickwick, he testifies to his respect for the claims of the ideal; by enlightening him (in his own special, relative fashion) about reality, he asserts the need not just to know the world but to reach an accomodation with it in order to survive. Thus the blending of imagination and sympathy characteristic of humor transforms the clever servant into a sophisticated, benevolent, and playful dealer in realities. Like Jingle, Sam provides us with suggestions for such trading, reassuring options cast in sometimes bizarre but invariably diverting forms—humor's oblique modes of taming reality. In so doing, Sam is fulfilling what amounts to a vocation, a comic destiny, for was he not, as he himself says, "first pitched neck and crop into the world, to play at leap-frog with its troubles"? (209). (It is in such humorous acrobatics that Weller best exemplifies the reaction of the ego when, as Freud says, it "refuses to be distressed by the provocations of reality, . . . insists that it cannot be affected by the traumas of the external world, . . . shows, in fact, that such traumas are no more than occasions for it to gain pleasure" or, more subtly, the specific strategy of the super-ego which "tries, by means of humour, to console the ego and protect it from suffering." [26])

While Pickwick's innocence and optimism blind him to Winkle's incompetence, Tupman's interest in Rachael Wardle, Jingle's rascality, and the matrimonial schemes of Mrs. Bardell, Sam, who has long gauged the pervasiveness of human weakness, most often shrewdly detects what appearances hide. It is not surprising that he greets his discoveries mostly without anger and always without smugness; a humorist has the gift of defusing life by the transformations of comic art. Thus the spectacle of self-deception and hypocrisy which might provoke misanthropy or moral outrage in another fires his imagination, his sense of incongruity, and his indulgent tenderness; even as he anatomizes the behavior of man, he transforms it by versatile juxtapositions of truths and delusions that arouse not anger but a mellow laughter. Unlike the more predictable response of standard *farceurs,* his very approach to his subjects varies with the variety of their foibles. He calls Winkle's bluff by whimsical indirection as he points out that Winkle is floundering on the skating rink not because he has, as he claims, "very awkward skates," but because "there' a orkard gen'l'm'n in 'em" (411), yet when Mr. Stiggins hypocritically calls alcoholic beverages "vanities," Sam calmly cut through the figurative impasse by inquiring which "partickler wanity" he "like[s] the flavour on, best" (634). He triumphs over the pompous Bath servants at their "swarry" not by indignation but by revelling imaginatively in their ludicrous pretensions. Vanity is here reduced to absurdity not by direct mockery but by weaving the materials of the servants' boasts into a humorous declaration of the indignity of class envy, greed, and the distortion of roles. When "the favoured gentleman in blue," who has just implied that the daughter of the house has a secret passion for him, inquires of Sam whether he has "any little thing of that kind in hand,"

> "Not exactly," said Sam. "There's no daughters at my place, else o' course I should ha' made up to vun on 'em. As it is, I don't think I can do with anythin' under a female markis. I might take up with a young 'ooman o' large property as hadn't a title, if she made wery fierce love to me.—Not else." (524)

Sam here ironically annihilates the servants' values by creating an imaginary persona that carries such assumptions to their ultimate consequences. But in negating their threat, in disarming them, he disarms us in a different sense, not the least by the whimsical picture of fortune-hunting he has fabricated to expunge distasteful realities.

It is because Sam's creative interactions with reality function as subtle protective devices against the anguish of deception, humiliation, and cynicism that he projects the sense we have earlier associated with Falstaff—that he is heroically invulnerable. At the trial of Bardell vs. Pickwick only he is strong enough to cope with Dodson and Fogg, not merely because he is wily, resourceful, and knows about their bullying tactics but because his sense of humor is attuned to the absurdity of extracting truth through falsehood and violence. Winkle is the born victim of rascally attorneys but Sam is bound to offset Winkle's victimization, winning at least a partial victory through the strategic weapon of humor.

"You rayther want somebody to look arter you, sir, wen your judgment goes out a wisitin' " (310), Sam justly tells Pickwick. Seemingly untouched despite his age by the stark facts of human experience, Pickwick is to be enlightened and, most important, protected by the youthful yet maturely wise Sam. The exchange of roles, here perhaps more absolutely than in Smollett, Fielding, or Sterne, negates the generational threats characteristic of New Comedy (with the representative of the older generation here being anything but "the opponent to the hero's wishes," [27] whether as father or father-surrogate). Sam's assumption of the paternal role has far more complex reverberations, in view of Freud's suggestion that "the humorist would acquire his superiority by assuming the role of the grown-up and identifying himself to some extent with his father, and reducing the other people to being children. This view probably covers the facts, but it hardly seems a conclusive one. One asks oneself *what it is that makes the humorist arrogate this role to himself*" (italics mine).[28] If, as is natural to speculate, Dickens is through Sam exorcising his own generational conflict (was he not, in fact, betrayed into playing leapfrog with the world's troubles by parental abdication of responsibility?), the willed transfiguration of that world *to offset the capitulation of authority* must surely be a central impulse of the humorist.[29] Since, in the process by which guide and follower exchange places, humor must cover the tracks of that capitulation, in the relationship of Pickwick and Sam, no dignity is to be forfeited on the one hand, no power abused on the other. The dialogue that takes place after Sam has informed Pickwick of the arrival downstairs of "a couple o' Sawbones" though not of the "reg'lar thorough-bred" variety aptly illustrates the subtle terms of the relationship:

> "In other words they're Medical Students, I suppose?" said Mr. Pickwick.
> Sam Weller nodded assent.
> "I am glad of it," said Mr. Pickwick. . . . "They are fine fellows; very fine fellows; with judgments matured by observations and reflection; tastes refined by reading and study. I am very glad of it."
> "They're a smokin' cigars by the kitchen fire," said Sam.
> "Ah!" observed Mr. Pickwick, rubbing his hands, "overflowing with kindly feelings and animal spirits. Just what I like to see!"
> "And one on 'em," said Sam, not noticing his master's interruption, "one on 'em's got his legs on the table, and is a drinkin' brandy neat, vile the t'other one—him in the barnacles—has got a barrel o' oysters atween his knees, wich he's a openin' like steam, and as fast as he eats 'em, he takes a aim vith the shells at young dropsy [Joe], who's a sittin' down fast asleep, in the chimbley corner."
> "Eccentricities of genius, Sam," said Mr. Pickwick. "You may retire." (406–7)

Here the juxtaposition of contrasting viewpoints is mellower than in other Pickwickian encounters since Pickwick's incurably optimistic generalizations are neither misunderstood nor denounced but steadily counterpointed by Sam's concrete and yet inventively detailed ("openin' like steam") assessment of what the realities of behavior are. Moreover Pickwick is allowed a momentary triumph over enlightenment even if he trembles on the brink of it. He owes his well-being, however, to the fact that Sam does not always "retire" but assists him not just with tangible problems like the machinations of Jingle or Dodson and Fogg, but with the larger more elusive ways of the world. To say that Pickwick "is not really taught by the education which Sam Weller tries to give him," as Miller does,[30] is in one sense to render an accurate verdict, in another to ignore the humorous terms on which the education is undertaken. Though psychologically authentic, it abides in the realm of aesthetic illusions, as Pickwick himself remains immune to real change and suffering as long as the humorous spirit is sustained.

In keeping with that spirit, Sam's revelations and instructions are not serious moral indictments of corruption but playful excursions—grotesque anecdotes for instance—in which the transforming fancy, casting knowingly an indulgent light upon unpleasant fact, reassuringly bridges the gap between the world as it is and as one would like it to be, between the assumptions of Dodson and Fogg and those of Pickwick. The shady trickery of the license touters at Doctor's Commons becomes diverting impudence in Sam's story as Tony Weller embarks on matrimony merely to satisfy the touter's insistence that he purchase a marriage license. The irrelevant exchanges between Tony Weller and the touter sustain the burlesque mood of this improbable anecdote and conspire to make us ignore moral *content* (legal corruption) in our visceral amusement at the celebration of *style* (the power of salesmanship). The same principle is at work as Sam lifts the veil from the production of veal pies, chronicles the perils of manufacturing sausages, and establishes an inextricable bond between poverty and oysters. To see a story like that of the convenient tossing of the voters in the canal as an instance in which Sam "*very slowly* forces grim reality on to his master's hasty demand for comic reassurance," his "instinct" being "decidedly anti-comic, both here and in his dark similes" [31] is to discount the textual hints of a humorous exchange in the anecdote and to miss the defusing of reality by imaginative play at the heart of the "Wellerisms." Just as Sam's response to Pickwick's inquiry about the fate of the voters negates the reality of disaster: "I rather think one old gen'l'm'n was missing'; I know his hat was found, but I a'n't quite certain whether his head was in it or not" (168), so his quaint comparisons comically exorcise the dangers of disease, boredom, poverty, marital incompatibility, suicide, death.

In devising these oddly terse and memorable comments which ubiquitously punctuate Sam's conversation, Dickens was not completely original.[32] He was remarkably inventive, however, in yoking together the commonplace statements of responses (the starting point of the Wellerisms) with the seemingly incongruous characters and circumstances best calculated to liberate a perceptive commentary on human behavior while taking the sting of censure or pain out of the discovery. Thus, as Sam asserts that his carefree behavior toward his father derives from "the wery best intentions, as the gen'lm'n said ven he run away from his wife 'cos she seemed unhappy with him" (364), man's almost endless capacity to rationalize is at once whimsically revealed and excused by one who is beyond such self-deception (note that the gentleman has comfortingly transposed his breach of loyalty into selflessness).

Many of Sam's whimsical sayings, like his stories, suggest why the macabre is so important an element of humor. If we contrast Dickens' impudent treatment of this subject in the Wellerisms with his morbid descriptions of death in the *Sketches by Boz* and in the interpolated tales of *Pickwick Papers,* we realize the capacity of the humorous viewpoint not only to allay the threats of pain and sorrow (as we have seen earlier) but to triumph over the ultimate threat: annihilation. For most of Sam's comments, in the tradition of the lighthearted and invulnerable *picaro* of fiction, embody the principle of *Galgenhumor,* at the heart of which, as Freud so clearly realized, is the negation of change and destruction. In fact, as he wheels Mr. Pickwick in a barrow, Sam transforms the ridiculous situation by a warning to Mr. Wardle's servant that embodies the classic reality-denying assertion of this type of humor: "If you walley my precious life don't upset me, as the gen'lm'n said to the driver when they was a carryin' him to Tyburn" (254). But that negation is the product of some very subtle interplay with the forces of darkness in which the counterpointing might seem at times to violate happy commonplaces: "Avay vith melincholly, as the little boy said ven his school-missis died" (623); "There's nothin' so refreshin' as sleep, sir, as the servant-girl said afore she drank the egg-cupful o' laudanum" (211); "Proud o' the title, as the Living Skellinton said, ven they show'd him" (207).[33] The ultimate effect, however, of wrenching such platitudes from meaningless banality by yoking them with macabre suggestions is a positive one. An aggressive but not satiric triumph over destructive forces—not the least of them authority—is achieved: the servant-girl has ultimately denied her plight by gulping laudanum ostensibly as if it were an integral part of the temporary process of sleep; the school-miss is equated with the sentiments she aroused and dismissed, the melancholy of boredom here substituted for the melancholy of despair. The context of course heightens the impact: it is when Pickwick calls for his "servant" that Sam invokes the Living Skellinton who has transformed defect into distinction.

Juxtapositions of all sorts in fact enrich Dickens' exploration of the traffic between illusion and reality: Sam's lower-class world with the staid bourgeoisie of the Pickwickians, the Wardles, and their circle of friends; the rarefied atmosphere of family gatherings, picnics, sports and excursions with the coarser one of imbibings in the Marquis o' Granby's back parlor, of perorations at the Brick Lane Branch evangelical meetings, of dabblings in legal mysteries in the Portugal Street public house. As in *Sketches by Boz* Dickens' expert knowledge of the lower classes allows him to forge humor out of what is incongruous in their susceptibility to cant and falsehood, their vulgarity, their ignorance. Moreover he enriches the relation between Pickwick and Sam by juxtaposing them with a figure that encompasses characteristics of both; for the slickness and impudence Tony Weller shares with his son are tempered by a mellowness and capacity for sentiment reminiscent of Pickwick.

The natural parent and the spiritual father have indeed much in common. Like Pickwick, Tony Weller is the perpetual victim of his emotions and his suggestibility, and thus also a most likely prey for ambitious "widders" bent on remarrying. His grasp on reality is at times as unsure as that of Pickwick—witness the zany schemes for smuggling Pickwick out of prison in "a pianner forty" with "no vurks in it," his admiration for a shabby and dishonest lawyer, his faith in the efficacy of such arcane legal weapons as an "alleybi" and a "have his carcase." Just as Pickwick is unspoiled by introspection, so Tony Weller can be "quite unaware that his solemn profundity is irresistibly banal," [34] and majestically bestow absurd advice on Sam—warning him against the "unnat'ral" art of poetry practiced only by "a beadle on boxin' day, or Warren's blackin', or Rowland's oil, or some o' them low fellows" (452), or recommending "pison" as an efficient forestaller of marriage guaranteed to make Sam "glad on it arterwards" (315).[35]

Yet, despite his resemblance to the befuddled and warmhearted Pickwick, Tony Weller comes, as we have suggested, rightly by his paternity. Even the naïve schemes and advice function like Sam's conscious refashionings of reality to annihilate threats humorously: the law is not quite so heartless, prison so dismaying, poetic clichés so irritating, marriage so formidable, once Tony has propounded his remedies, suggestions, and assessments. Even the mystifying intricacies of finance are put in their place by Tony's whimsical conception of "the funds" as "them things as is alvays a fluctooatin', and gettin' theirselves inwolved somehow or another vith the national debt, and the checquers bills, and all that" (736).[36] (Tony in fact is not beyond his own exercises in *Galgenhumor,* envisaging death as a providence at work in assisting undertakers.)

Because he too possesses, in paradoxical combination with his innocent enthusiasm, something of Sam's sophistication and cynicism, of

his shrewd eye for detecting not only "gammon" but subtler incongruities in people's behavior, Tony Weller can also provide Pickwick with
the modified enlightenment that is the province of humor. Yet his reactions are perhaps ultimately the most wisely humorous, tempered as
they are by sentiment. For he greets humbug, not with Pickwick's indignation, nor Sam's lively impudence, but with a monumental mellowness
that is conveyed in irrepressible laughter or more frequently in a
quietly amused resignation. His conscious excursions into humor are
understated triumphs for such resignation. Like the "gen'l'm'n" who
nobly deserted his wife, Tony is adept at recasting the terms of a relationship, but he is not unaware that some of the comic effect is at his
own expense when he shares with Sam the conviction that his shrewish
wife who has "been gettin' rayther in the Methodistical order lately . . .
and . . . is uncommon pious, to be sure," is "too good a creetur for me,
Sammy. I feel I don't deserve her" (297).

In the conception of Pickwick and the Wellers, humor demonstrates its capacity to reconcile us to man's predicament in a world inexorably demanding that he curb by reason the promptings of his imagination, that he reconcile reality with his idealistic yearnings. Yet its
power is even more evident in Dickens' treatment of objectionable
characters. Just as reality is made bearable for Pickwick because Sam
can bridge the gap between real and ideal through his imaginative
projection of the ways of the world, so human error is tempered for us
by Dickens' inventive treatment of it. As we have already suggested,
Jingle's capacity to lead an imaginative life markedly affects our judgment of him. This seeming representative of reality cannot threaten
Pickwick's innocence because, like Pickwick (though in a different way),
he is vulnerable to the claims of fancy; the gratuitous inventiveness of
his mind charms us into suspending our moral judgment of his sordid
behavior and his parasitical schemes. Moreover, since he has been let in
on the secret of the humorist's perception, part of the author's temper
lives on in him, sustaining his appeal, and he can, like his creator,
transfigure reality. After Jingle has regaled the Pickwickians with his
fantastic stories, Pickwick is, on one level, laughably in error when he
declares him to be "a close observer of men and things" (14). Yet, in a
comic sense, the term "close observer" is entirely appropriate; only the
sharpest perception of appearances can allow their successful transformation into humorous truths. It is because Jingle has piercingly assessed Tupman's ridiculous aspirations as a lover that he can enshrine
them in a whimsical portrait: "Rather fat—grown up Bacchus—cut the
leaves—dismounted from the tub, and adopted kersey, eh?" (16). The
silly ostentatiousness of the Pickwick Club uniform has never struck us
so forcefully as when Jingle, musing on the initialled club button, diag-
noses the whole enterprise: "What does 'P.C.' stand for—Peculiar coat,
eh?" (18).

Jingle is probably the most striking instance in *Pickwick Papers* of the power of humor to mitigate the impact of reality by transmuting reprehensible behavior. Bob Sawyer (the forebear of the whimsical Dick Swiveller in *The Old Curiosity Shop*) also exemplifies the process by which humor negates the moral viewpoint, as vice becomes mere eccentricity. Slovenly, ruthless, and improvident like Jingle, Bob Sawyer arouses sympathetic laughter rather than indignation because, as the grotesqueness of his macabre conversation and his shifts to fend off insolvency testify, he too is not immune to the charms of the imaginative life and not incapable of offering some hints on how to deny with its help anguish and deprivation. His odd schemes to recruit patients and his reduction to abstractions of the threatening figures of his creditors are a case in point, as when he confesses to Winkle that he had mistaken him for "the King's taxes," and goes on to elucidate this cryptic statement: "I did, indeed, . . . and I was just going to say that I wasn't at home, but if you'd leave a message I'd be sure to give it to myself; for he don't know me; no more does the Lighting and Paving. I think the Church-rates guesses who I am, and I know the Water-works does, because I drew a tooth of his when I first came down here" (532).

Just as humor forestalls the condemnation of characters by emphasizing their eccentricities and illusions at the expense of their vices, their mental life rather than their actions, it can function more widely to minimize if not to exorcise the threats of negative social behavior—appealing to our sense of what is in effect its saving grace: its perennial absurdity. In emphasizing the paradoxical and the irrational in social assumptions, humor charms us into tolerating the disconcerting pedestrian realities of man's vanity, hypocrisy, and greed. The depiction of the *"fête champêtre,"* the Eatanswill election, and the Muggleton cricket match shows evidence of an approach to human frailty that makes a playful defusion of social pretensions often possible. Though Dickens is far more serious when he attacks religious cant, sheer buoyancy and a delight in incongruities can override moral indignation and satiric intentions (treating us, at the Brick Lane Branch, to the absurd testimonials of the Shepherd's followers).

That humor transcends didactic condemnation is particularly evident in Dickens' attack on the law. The Bardell vs. Pickwick trial shows humor successfully and memorably robbing the vices of mendacity and hypocrisy of their destructive power. We are far less likely to recall the painful story of Mr. Ramsay which acidly illustrates the heartlessness of the clerks of Dodson and Fogg and the corruption of their employers than the trial scene which likewise denounces the "mean, rascally, pettifogging robbers," but in humorous terms. Though Dickens begins in a satiric vein (sardonically exposing the petty pride of brief-carrying lawyers—and the pretensions of those without briefs—the gruffness of the Judge, and the hypocritical attempts of Dodson and Fogg to sway the jury), he restores us to the assumptions of humor when he proceeds to denounce the mishandling of evidence through the distortions of Sergeant Buzfuz. A perception of incongruity similar to that which forged Sam's Wellerisms, Jingle's tall tales, and Bob Sawyer's shifts is at work here, with effects equally diverting as, on the reality of Pickwick's innocence, the resourceful Sergeant Buzfuz superimposes his fantastic conception of villainous intent ("The serpent was on the watch, the train was laid, the mine was preparing, the sapper and miner was at work"). Indeed, as he proceeds to assign sinister meanings to the homey terms "warming pan" and "Chops and Tomata sauce" in Pickwick's notes to his landlady, anger and indignation at such chicanery become irrelevant. We feel that so inventive a villain under challenging circumstances ("Chops and Tomata sauce. Yours, Pickwick! Chops! Gracious heavens! and Tomata sauce! Gentlemen, is the happiness of a sensitive and confiding female to be trifled away, by such shallow artifices as these?" [37]) cannot be wholly irredeemable, the very reaction Jingle provokes. Moreover, we find it hard to take Pickwick's plight seriously because the manner of the misinterpretation removes its menace.

Just as the humorous trial scene remains the most striking aspect of the whole Bardell vs. Pickwick episode, so the most memorable moments of the whole novel are born of the application of humor to characterization and to social criticism. *Pickwick Papers* allows us to perceive that, by transcending moral indignation and the concern for specific reform (the frequent impulses of satire), humor affords us a wide and generous criticism of life. By bringing imagination and an appreciation of incongruity to bear on personal and social failings, it frees us from anguish through laughter yet allows us to remember ubiquitous frailty so vividly that we may accept the unmendable and be divertingly shamed into reforming what we can. But the widest, most universal, timeless appeal of the humorist's vision is its capacity to cultivate in us the illusion that we can triumph over reason, eclipse authority, ultimately negate annihilation.

Of course Dickens was not always capable of sustaining his comic vision. It is not, however, as Edmund Wilson would have it, that Dickens' humor is but an intermittent escape from "the prison of life" to which "gloom and soreness must always drag it back." [38] Such a point of view vastly minimizes the breadth of vision of the humorist. Far from seeking refuge from the prisonlike aspects of life, that vision denies them significance as it perceives and comes to terms with existential perplexities through the accommodations of art. What we do have in Dickens is the conflict between two modes of encompassing the paradox of the human condition. When man's delusion and weakness provoke in him anger and sorrow, life indeed seems not an exhilarating if complex experience but a threatening specter (as it so often does in the later novels). Then the prison gates enclose him as he responds to reality with very different weapons: sentimentality, satire, or moral righteousness—the palliatives for the merely mortal state. When "gloom and soreness" do not overcloud his vision, life seems anything but a prison; he does not seek to escape it but weaves its contradictions and grotesqueries into the humorist's celebration of immortality.

Pickwick Papers owes much of its greatness to its embodiment of a vision almost unmarred by anguish or indignation. The work not only reveals a whimsical understanding of quirks and foibles and a tolerant amusement at the shifts and deceits of folly and vanity—the comic writer's basic equipment—but the special gift of transforming observed incongruities. As his talents were brought to bear on the central dilemma of coming to terms with experience (a dilemma his own youth had so poignantly plumbed), Dickens largely affirmed man's capacity to overcome the gap between the actual and the desired, between life as it is and what we think it is or would wish it to be. In that sense his first novel had, even more fully than Dickens himself could realize, earned the term "TRIUMPHANT." [39]

Steven V. Daniels

PICKWICK AND DICKENS

Stages of Development

PICKWICK PAPERS was, as Steven Marcus has recently argued, an "activity of self-creation," [1] for, after the novel's at best unsteady beginning, what emerged through the process of composition was not only the Mr. Pickwick readers remember, but also Charles Dickens the novelist, a writer far different in range and intentions from the young man who, with high hopes and limited goals, undertook to write the letterpress for a proposed series of sporting plates. Robert Seymour's plan for the project was altered even before his suicide while working on the illustrations for the second monthly installment; though his death allowed Dickens more freedom than he had already assumed, it was not followed by immediate changes in design or conception. The changes—changes that helped establish the course of Dickens' career—came, not as the result of sudden inspiration or the sudden release of creative energy, but rather through the gradual recognition and exploration of possibilities already implicit in the work. And in learning who Mr. Pickwick was and why his adventures mattered, in bringing his own values and experience to bear on stock characters and a conventional comic pattern, Dickens discovered who he was and who, despite the darkening of the later novels, he was in large measure to remain. The real story of Mr. Pickwick is not merely the story of what that character learns in his confrontation with the world (his success, as I hope to show, is dependent upon his not learning, his not adapting himself to the way "the world runs," but the story of what Dickens, too humane and creative to limit himself to hackneyed formulations, learned and taught as the novel's pattern took shape and in turn gave shape to his own imagination.

— *I* —

For a book that begins by heading nowhere in particular, *Pickwick Papers* starts out, once the burden of the ill-conceived initial chapter is

[56

overcome, with remarkable rapidity. And what is remarkable is not only the rapidity of the action and the motion but also, and more importantly, the rapidity with which the incidents begin to shape themselves into a pattern. What is especially striking is that the pattern, the traditional comic pattern of innocent good-nature followed by deception followed by recovery (so that further deceptions and recoveries may ensue), seems to be implicit in the action before Dickens himself recognized it and set about to develop its potentialities.

Since the development of this pattern proceeds in stages parallel to the development of the character of Mr. Pickwick, it seems possible and, I think, fruitful to regard the changes in Mr. Pickwick's character as accommodations to the pattern, as an attempt on Dickens' part to make the pattern more apparent and more pertinent. At any rate, no one has ever been satisfied with Dickens' own account of how those changes came about and of what they consisted in. His remarks about the genesis and development of Mr. Pickwick are limited to two: one, the cryptic and tantalizing "I thought of Mr. Pickwick, and wrote the first number"; [2] the other, his response to critics who commented upon Mr. Pickwick's unnatural metamorphosis from caterpillar to butterfly, from pompous comic butt to "angel in tights and gaiters." To this criticism his reply was the ingenious and somewhat disingenuous, "I do not think this change will appear forced or unnatural to my readers, if they will reflect that in real life the peculiarities and oddities of a man who has anything whimsical about him generally impress us first, and that it is not until we are better acquainted with him that we usually begin to look below these superficial traits, and to know the better part of him." [3] This does seem to characterize rather aptly a method of presentation frequently employed by Dickens, in, for example, Newman Noggs in *Nicholas Nickleby,* Wemmick in *Great Expectations,* perhaps Miss Flite in *Bleak House.* And it is true that Dickens was always fond of having a character make his initial and often indelible impression in terms of his "peculiarities and oddities" of dress, appearance, or speech. But the explanation does not seem an entirely adequate description of the reasons for the change in Mr. Pickwick. Some have suggested that the change stems from an alteration in Dickens' intentions, from "a normal evolution in his conception of the novelist's art, when the growing number of his readers enhanced his feeling of moral responsibility and his hope of exerting a beneficial influence." [4] No doubt there was such an evolution, but to speak of it as "normal" begs the question: the most popular authors do not always distinguish themselves by their moral responsibility. Inadequate as it is, there may after all be something to Dickens' own explanation, if not directly as the basis for Mr. Pickwick's change, then perhaps as a factor in Dickens' own evolution. It may be that what Dickens became "better acquainted with," or rather more aware of, was not Mr. Pickwick's character, but Mr. Pickwick's plight in the world.

The presentation of reports and observations is at the outset Mr. Pickwick's only program and, but for one other factor, Dickens' own. That other stipulation is that the observations be amusing, a stipulation that takes us from the observations themselves to the principal observer. Mr. Pickwick himself, equipped with "gigantic brain" and "beaming eyes"(2), is, through his foolishness and gullibility, to assure the amusement. And so, in the earliest stages of the novel, while his eyes do occasionally beam, it is the waywardness of his "gigantic brain" that receives the most attention. The charming waywardness of his confrontation with the cabman at the outset of his journey and of his first encounter with Jingle, and the rather appalling waywardness of his only reported journal entry, his description of the "conviviality of the military."

> "It is truly delightful to a philanthropic mind, to see these gallant men staggering along under the influence of an overflow, both of animal and ardent spirits; more especially when we remember that the following them about, and jesting with them, affords a cheap and innocent amusement for the boy population. Nothing can exceed their good humour. It was but the day before my arrival that one of them had been most grossly insulted in the house of a publican. The barmaid had positively refused to draw him any more liquor; in return for which he had (merely in playfulness) drawn his bayonet, and wounded the girl in the shoulder. And yet this fine fellow was the very first to go down to the house next morning, and express his readiness to overlook the matter, and forget what had occurred." (14)

Fortunately, there is no more of this, and even here, as is not true of the other incidents, Mr. Pickwick is presented as being outside the action, as an observer and a reporter of hearsay, not as a participant. It is, I think, important that Mr. Pickwick's worst moment, his only really bad moment after Chapter i, comes in such a way. Dickens can force Mr. Pickwick to misconstrue so grossly and so callously only when he can conceive of him as an uninvolved observer, as someone withdrawn from the action and untouched by it. When Mr. Pickwick is involved, as with the cabman or Jingle, his wits may fail him quite as badly, but they fail him in a different manner and with a different result. Here he, at the very least, misinterprets; in his other confrontations and involvements he is the victim of his gullibility and of circumstances, not the originator of his misconceptions.

And it is obvious that Mr. Pickwick's traveling companions, Messrs. Tupman, Winkle, and Snodgrass, cannot offer him the kind of support in the outside world that they represent in the clubroom. On the contrary, they are quite as vulnerable as he is, as is immediately evidenced in the aborted Winkle-Slammer duel in the first and second monthly numbers, and in Tupman's loss of Miss Rachael Wardle in the third and fourth. They, too, are defenseless against Jingle's mischief and the force of circumstances. But how, then, do they differ from Mr. Pickwick? In one very basic and very simple way: Mr. Pickwick is the center of our attention, and so, with lapses, we see him move rapidly from misadventure to misadventure; the others engage our interest and attention only in discrete and widely-separated incidents. In other words, their stories lack the kind of continuity we have in his. And this affects our perception—perhaps, in the early stages of composition, Dickens' own—of their characters. Mr. Pickwick, simply by acceding to the demands of his comic role, simply by virtue of his resiliency in bouncing from one adventure to the next (as he, at the outset, bounces from the cabman to Jingle, and as he, a bit later, will make a significant leap from Jingle into the protective "arms of Sam"), acquires resiliency as a character trait. And this resiliency, which becomes not only a character trait but an issue in the novel as well, perhaps the significant issue in the period of Mr. Pickwick's incarceration and release, separates him from his companions and establishes him as a figure worthy of the author's attention and our own. And in this effort to determine how the term "the immortal Pickwick" (1) came to be an appropriate epithet rather than the ironic label it is in its original usage, it is important to note that resiliency is a trait that Mr. Pickwick acquires rather than one inherent in him, or rather that it is a trait that he, with his creator looking on, gradually acquires as inherent in him.

It is in Chapter xi, which follows immediately after the chapter in which Mr. Pickwick is "caught in the arms of Sam" and precedes the one (published in the next monthly number) in which he hires Sam and befuddles Mrs. Bardell, that Dickens seems to announce his own recognition of resiliency as a matter of character and not simply a necessity of the comic pattern. The announcement is muted, and its presentation is descriptive rather than analytic, but it is, I think, significant that Dickens includes in this one chapter two very similar reawakenings. The first begins the chapter with the morning after the return of Mr. Pickwick, Wardle, and Miss Wardle from the White Hart Inn and the disclosure of Jingle's treachery. It should perhaps be juxtaposed with the final paragraph of Chapter x:

> Slowly and sadly did the two friends and the deserted lady, return next day in the Muggleton heavy coach. Dimly and darkly had the sombre shadows of a summer's night fallen upon all around, when they again reached Dingley Dell, and stood within the entrance to Manor Farm.

> A night of quiet and repose in the profound silence of Dingley Dell, and an hour's breathing of its fresh and fragrant air on the ensuing morning, completely recovered Mr. Pickwick from the effects of his late fatigue of body and anxiety of mind.

Complete recovery from both exhaustion and depression is the product less of the atmosphere than of Mr. Pickwick's resiliency, his ability to be unchanged, untainted, by unpleasantness. Later in the chapter, there is another cheery morning, this one following a night darkened by Mr. Pickwick's solitary perusal of "A Madman's Manuscript," a grim tale of insanity and selfishness and a "gray cell, where the sunlight seldom comes": "The sun was shining brilliantly into his chamber when he awoke, and the morning was far advanced. The gloom which had oppressed him on the previous night had disappeared with the dark shadows which shrouded the landscape, and his thoughts and feelings were as light and gay as the morning itself" (147).

These are not the first sunrises to greet Mr. Pickwick, nor are they to be the last. But coming when they do and as they do, they are especially revealing. If we look back to the previous mornings, at the beginning of Chapter ii and at the beginning of Chapter vii, we discover as much brightness and even in one instance the picture of Mr. Pickwick bursting "like another sun from his slumbers" (6), but we find nothing comparable to Chapter xi's explicit association of the sunrise with Mr. Pickwick's capacities for recovery and renewal. If we look back even further, we may discover in the novel's first sentence, an exercise in parodic orotundity, a retrospective interest in "the first ray of light which illumines the gloom and converts into a dazzling brilliancy that obscurity in which the earlier history of the public career of the immortal Pickwick would appear to be involved."

This resiliency, though it begins as a neutral characteristic, acquires a positive significance as it comes to be more frequently called into play. For, though Mr. Pickwick is capable of intellectual pretension even as late as his discovery of the "strange and curious inscription of unquestionable antiquity" in Chapter xi (the chapter in which he has his two reawakenings), it soon ceases to be simply, or even primarily, Mr. Pickwick's self-importance and the other qualities associated with his "gigantic brain" that are threatened by his contact with the outside world; it is his cheerfulness and his openness to new experiences, only hinted at first in his "beaming eyes" and impressively, though not yet decisively, demonstrated in the springtime festivities at Dingley Dell (vi), that are most endangered. His naïveté, in a world in which wisdom is too often the worldly wisdom of the Jingles and, later, the Dodsons and Foggs, becomes more a virtue to be preserved than a foible to be laughed at; and the laughter comes to have as its source less the absurdity of that naïveté, that innocence, than the triumph of its preservation.

It is not until the fourth monthly number that Sam Weller makes his first appearance. As the bootblack at the White Hart Inn, a colorful "original," he is distinguished principally by his self-possession and his imperturbability and by his remarkable verbal resources, all characteristics that he shares with Jingle. In the expression of these verbal resources, apparent in everything he says, but particularly in the "Wellerism" and the comic anecdote, he achieves a prominence out of proportion to his relative insignificance in the action. In the next monthly number, he is transformed from an incidental character into a major participant in the novel's plot and theme, when he, as yet more concerned about the benefits of his employment than about the needs of his employer, is installed as Mr. Pickwick's manservant.

What prompted Dickens to this fortunate transformation is a matter for speculation. He was, no doubt, moved by the applause and advice of William Jerdan, the editor of the *Literary Gazette,* who urged him to develop Sam's potentialities "to the utmost" and who, by printing passages from the Weller monologues in his weekly magazine, was at least partially responsible for the great increase of sales of the fourth number.[5] From this point of view, providing his hero with a non-Pickwickian companion might simply have been Dickens' easiest and most acceptable means of integrating Sam into the action, at least as an onlooker, and assuring frequent opportunities for his verbal displays. But Dickens might have been moved as well by his developing realization of who Mr. Pickwick was, of what he might represent, and of his need for a guide and protector. Mr. Pickwick himself when he decides to hire Sam speaks of him as a person possessed of "a considerable knowledge of the world, and a great deal of sharpness . . . which may be of material use to me" (151). And though there is nothing in the fourth monthly number that clearly indicates the role that Sam is to play, there is, at least in retrospect, surely something symbolic in the tableau that follows the unmasking of Jingle: "Mr. Pickwick was a philosopher, but philosophers were only men in armour, after all. The shaft had reached him, penetrated through his philosophical harness, to his very heart. In the frenzy of his rage, he hurled the inkstand madly forward, and followed it up himself. But Mr. Jingle had disappeared, and he found himself caught in the arms of Sam" (131). There is still the facetious view of Mr. Pickwick's "gigantic brain" and "philosophical harness," but there is also a new emphasis on his vulnerability and his "heart." And just as Jingle, who disappears only temporarily, had been the perfect irritant to his brain and his self-importance, Sam, a safe and notably sane refuge in an often treacherous world, is to be the perfect complement to his heart and his better nature. The very terms of the final sentence seem to pose Sam as an alternative to Jingle: it is as though Dickens is only too anxious to fill the void left by Mr. Pickwick's disappointment in his first non-Pickwickian companion with a new and worthier presence. But though Sam is a fit companion for his employer, the precise terms of that companionship are, for Dickens, still to be worked out, or rather, as is so frequently the case in *Pickwick Papers,* to be recognized and developed.

— 2 —

The sixth monthly number is the first in which the reader is apt to get a strong sense of Mr. Pickwick as a coherent and engaging character rather than as a kind of split personality torn between the claims of "gigantic brain" and "beaming eyes," and an equally strong sense of Dickens' control of his materials and his tone. The last of the number's three chapters is devoted almost entirely to an interpolated story (but even it includes a paragraph interesting in the study of Dickens' presentation of Mr. Pickwick); the first two seem designed—for design, at last, appears to be the appropriate word—to establish, for both author and reader, the true nature of Mr. Pickwick, and to call attention to the issue already latent in Mr. Pickwick's adventures, the issue, that is, of self-preservation in a threatening or disappointing world.

The installment begins with what is, in a sense, a chapter of negation: Mr. Pickwick, through authorial will and not, of course, psychological development, is stripped decisively of his self-importance. It is almost as though he willingly surrenders it rather than compete with a new group of characters who obviously have him far outdistanced. The change is signaled when Mr. Pickwick is invited to one of Mrs. Leo Hunter's fancy-dress "feasts of reason." To the suggestion that he costume himself as Plato, Zeno, Epicurus, or Pythagoras, "all founders of clubs," he responds, rather surprisingly considering his earlier displays of intellectual pretension, "as I cannot put myself in competition with those great men, I cannot presume to wear their dresses" (195).

It is not really Plato and Pythagoras who provide the competition, however, but Mr. Pickwick's host and hostess—or rather, to put things in their proper place, his hostess and host. The aptly named Leo Hunters seek Mr. Pickwick's acquaintance because of his fame, but it is their arrogance and outrageous self-esteem that are the objects of ridicule, and not his "greatness"; beside his hostess, who is pictured "in the character of Minerva, receiving the company, and overflowing with pride and gratification at the notion of having called such distinguished individuals together," Mr. Pickwick, who makes himself "universally agreeable," is the model of humility. Add to the offensiveness of the Leo Hunters the charming presumption of "so great a man" as Count Smorltork, who has assembled in a fortnight all the materials he needs for his study of all aspects of English society, and it is clear that the quality of "greatness" is not simply being drained from Mr. Pickwick, but is being transfused into many of those he comes into contact with.

These are not, it should be noted, the first examples of non-Pickwickian self-importance. What is new in the sixth monthly number is not the presence of such characters, but what seems to be a clear sense on the author's part of Mr. Pickwick's difference from them. What we have is, once again, not so much a change as a recognition: the recognition that Mr. Pickwick is most satisfactory as a contrast to these self-important characters rather than as a companion for them, that others might bear the full satiric burden and that Mr. Pickwick might be left only in possession of his more amiable characteristics. At any rate, there is in the remainder of the novel a decided emphasis on Mr. Pickwick's good nature and warm heart, a steady stream of "great men," and a notable decline—to two references by my count—in the number of times "greatness" is attributed to Mr. Pickwick.

The latter of these two references comes less than halfway through the novel. Mr. Pickwick is speaking to Peter Magnus, a man whose name itself announces his "greatness," when the narrator comments upon "the profound solemnity with which the great man could, when he pleased, render his remarks so deeply impressive" (323). It is a reference that is at most incidental, one that does nothing to revive the by then late and unlamented former Mr. Pickwick. The other of the two references is more interesting, coming as it does when least expected, in the same monthly number as that in which Mr. Pickwick, having been likened to the Greek philosophers, rejects the claim to "greatness." Two chapters after his attendance at the Hunters' absurd affair, and the morning after a trying day, we are told: "But although the bodily powers of the great man were thus impaired, his mental energies retained their pristine vigour. His spirits were elastic; his good humour was restored. Even the vexation consequent upon his recent adventure had vanished from his mind; and he could join in the hearty laughter which any allusion to it excited in Mr. Wardle, without anger and without embarrassment" (227). Taken alone, the first of these sentences seems an ominous indication of a reversion in Mr. Pickwick; "great man" has all along been used to mock his "mental energies." But in the context of the passage as a whole, another and quite explicit example of Mr. Pickwick's capacities for recovery and renewal, "great man" loses all its former sting: his vigorous "mental energies" consist, it appears, not in any intellectual pretensions, but in the elasticity of his spirits and the restoration of his good humor, qualities more relevant to his "beaming eyes" than to his erstwhile "gigantic brain." And surely, in his joining in Mr. Wardle's laughter, we have, not self-importance, but its opposite.

If Chapter xv is a chapter of negation, a chapter, that is, in which Mr. Pickwick gives up his claims to "greatness," Chapter xvi is a chapter with more positive implications. For in this chapter "Too full of Adventure to be briefly described" (as its title declares) much that has thus far been latent in Mr. Pickwick's character, in his relationship with Sam, and in his experience in the outside world, in—at least in comparison with the artificial world of the clubroom—the real world, begins to come to the fore in more or less explicit fashion.

The chapter begins with the pursuit of Jingle to Bury St. Edmunds, where Mr. Pickwick hopes to expose him again and prevent any further deceptions on his part, but where, instead, it is Mr. Pickwick himself who is deceived. Just as Mr. Pickwick has acquired Sam, Jingle has acquired a no less resourceful and, as it later appears, no less loyal companion in Job Trotter; and, in this first confrontation between the two, Job scores a victory over Sam and, consequently, over Mr. Pickwick. Acting the role of the appalled servant, Job "reveals" his master's latest fraud and convinces Mr. Pickwick that upon his willingness to hide himself in the back garden of a girl's boarding-school rests all hope of preventing an innocent and misguided heiress from eloping with the fortune-hunting Jingle. To the credit of his head, Mr. Pickwick twice announces his dislike for the plan, but, to the credit of his heart, he reluctantly consents to it.

After being drenched by the rain and embarrassed by the ladies of the boarding-school, Mr. Pickwick, in a rare moment of genuine depression, declares himself to have been "deceived, and deluded, . . . the victim of a conspiracy—a foul and base conspiracy," and vows vengeance on the two imposters. The vengeance is to be pursued, when knowledge of the culprits comes through the unlikely source of Sam's father, but something more important happens first. On the morning after his misadventure, Mr. Pickwick awakens with an attack of rheumatism and, more significantly, a renewal of his good humor. We are told, in a passage I have already had reason to quote, that "even the vexation consequent upon his recent adventure had vanished from his mind; and he could join in the hearty laughter which any allusion to it excited in Mr. Wardle, without anger and without embarrassment."

More than a means of sustaining the variety of incident in the narrative, more even than an anticipation of the dissolution of resentment in a later confrontation between Mr. Pickwick and his deceivers, this is, I think, a critical moment in Mr. Pickwick's history. It is now—now that Dickens has resolved his earlier uncertainties and now that, as a consequence, Mr. Pickwick has acquired a self worth preserving and acquired it as innate—that the resiliency Mr. Pickwick has already displayed begins to qualify as self-preservation. Mr. Pickwick has suffered, as he will continue to suffer, because of his vulnerability: his innocence of guile and his lack of suspicion, his "innate good-feeling" (218) and his benevolent disposition. These are his weaknesses, but these very qualities are also his strength: they attract the author to him; they attract the reader to him; and they already have begun to attract to him that mediator between the author and the reader, a kind of surrogate in the narrative for both, the keen-witted and ostensibly unsentimental Sam Weller. And whatever advantages, pecuniary or otherwise, Sam has in his new employment, the real gain is all on Mr. Pickwick's side. Not only in relation to the story itself, where he acquires a stalwart defender and ally, but also in the reader's imagination, where the admirable Sam's loyalty and praise make Mr. Pickwick seem all the more estimable. And, in the final analysis, Sam serves less as an effectual protector of Mr. Pickwick—in the episode of the supposed elopement, in particular, it is his being outwitted by Job Trotter that results in Mr. Pickwick's discomfort—than as an assertion by the author that Mr. Pickwick, in his travels in the world, not only needs a protector, but also merits one. It is, I think, an assertion that the reader comes to agree with.

Mr. Pickwick, in traveling through his limited world, must, in a sense, remain impervious to that world, must, that is, refuse to learn certain lessons that circumstances and adversaries would seem to be intent upon teaching. Having finally acquired, through the will of the author, "innate good-feeling," and along with it innate good nature, good humor, perhaps innocence, he must preserve those qualities in the face of disappointment and adversity. From being the substance of farce, his life, though farcical elements remain, becomes a demonstration, a kind of "realist fairy tale" [6] designed to please and support readers and to encourage them in the preservation of their own "better nature." "Oh, dear, dear! How adversity does change people!" remarks one of the disappointed widows in pursuit of the recently bereaved Tony Weller (734). And earlier, Sam and Tony join together in a seemingly irrelevant aside to Mr. Pickwick in which, in considering the motives of turnpike-keepers, they characterize the usual nature of the change:

> "They're all on 'em men as has met vith some disappointment in life," said Mr. Weller senior.
> "Ay, ay?" said Mr. Pickwick.
> "Yes. Consequence of vich, they retire from the world, and shuts themselves up in pikes; partly with the view of being solitary, and partly to rewenge themselves on mankind by takin' tolls."
> "Dear me," said Mr. Pickwick, "I never knew that before."
> "Fact, sir," said Mr. Weller; "if they was gen'lm'n you'd call 'em misanthropes, but as it is, they only takes to pike-keepin'."
> (302)

Shades of Miss Wade and Miss Havisham in the later novels! And relevant also to those characters—early, middle, and late—from Mr. Pickwick and Oliver Twist through Esther Summerson and Amy Dorrit and Arthur Clennam and Lizzie Hexam, who do not respond in this manner to the unavoidable or man-made disappointments they encounter. This latter group, the self-preservers, constitutes the staple of Dickens' fiction, and Mr. Pickwick, though he began as a conventional figure of fun, is the first among them. The members of this group, who sometimes offend modern taste on the grounds of sentimentality, also pose another problem: they jar against the taste, perhaps prejudice, for character development in fiction. But, it ought to be noted, their failure to develop is, in fact, an intuitive or conscious refusal to develop, a preservation of inherent merit. And, given the conditions of existence in the Dickens world, in which character is often challenged by circumstances, and Dickens' notion, as demonstrated in the novels, that character does not simply change, but becomes either better or worse, it is simply the more praiseworthy course to persevere in "innate good-feeling" than to become a misanthrope or a pike-keeper.

There is one passage in particular that seems to epitomize Dickens' new attitude toward his protagonist. It describes, to be sure, not a threat, but a moment of absolute joy. And if we share Dickens' pleasure in Mr. Pickwick's exuberance and good nature as he slides on the ice with his friends at Dingley Dell, we may, along with Dickens, take special delight in Mr. Pickwick's refusing to allow his being knocked down to deter him from resuming his place in the joyful enterprise. Even when there is no real threat, the capacity for recovery may be an invaluable asset.

> It was the most intensely interesting thing, to observe the manner in which Mr. Pickwick performed his share in the ceremony; to watch the torture of anxiety with which he viewed the person behind, gaining upon him at the imminent hazard of tripping him up; to see him gradually expend the painful force he had put on at first, and turn slowly round on the slide, with his face towards the point at which he had started; to contemplate the playful smile which mantled on his face when he had accomplished the distance, and the eagerness with which he turned round when he had done so, and ran after his predecessor: his black gaiters tripping pleasantly through the snow, and his eyes beaming cheerfulness and gladness through his spectacles. And when he was knocked down (which happened upon the average every third round), it was the most invigorating sight that can possibly be imagined, to behold him gather up his hat, gloves, and handkerchief, with a glowing countenance, and resume his station in the rank, with an ardour and enthusiasm that nothing could abate. (414)

Clearly, this is, for Dickens, Mr. Pickwick at his best; and the very best of the best is his refusal to stay down and his enthusiasm in getting up again. To watch Mr. Pickwick slide is "the most intensely interesting thing," but the superlatives of the final sentence far outdistance even this. In a sense, the whole of the novel has become a glorification of Mr. Pickwick's "ardour and enthusiasm," but along with that glorification, indeed as a result of it, comes the question of whether, in fact, "nothing could abate" those qualities. There is implicit in this absolute assertion a challenge: Mr. Pickwick, it is true, rises when he falls in his boyish participation in a winter sport; but will he rise with equal enthusiasm and regularity when, in the course of his adventures, he is tripped up by circumstances or adversaries? And if it is "the most invigorating sight that can possibly be imagined" to see Mr. Pickwick "resume his station in the rank" in this situation, how invigorating and reassuring it may be for readers to see him resume his better nature after other, more troublesome, disruptions. There is farce in seeing a fat man fall, but there may be a kind of moral triumph in seeing him rise again. Without artificially darkening this moment of absolute joy, one may notice its bearing on the rest of the novel: it serves not only as a contrast to the threats to Mr. Pickwick's better nature, but also, in a sense, as a definition of those threats and their significance.

The sliding occurs during the Pickwickians' Christmas visit to Dingley Dell, and that visit occurs when the most serious and sustained threat to Mr. Pickwick's equanimity, the Bardell vs. Pickwick law suit, has already been initiated. In fact, the Christmas number, during which Mr. Pickwick allows no fears for himself to darken his own enjoyment or that of his companions, is surrounded by installments in which the reader is reminded of the problem emanating "not only from the force of circumstances, but from the sharp practice of Dodson and Fogg to boot" (363). Dickens' practice in the presentation of the law suit, from the precipitating incident in Chapter xii to the trial in Chapter xxxiv, is to introduce every month or so a chapter relating to the litigation into the narration of Mr. Pickwick's other, more miscellaneous, adventures. This process of suspension has generally been seen as an attempt on Dickens' part to husband his materials or to sustain a variety of incident or to preserve a realistic juridical chronology. Whatever Dickens' reasons and aims—and he does succeed in these three— the process has one other significant effect. In providing a background for Mr. Pickwick's episodic adventures, it also provides, at least occasionally, a perspective on Mr. Pickwick's actions and attitudes, that is, Mr. Pickwick's participation in, for example, the Christmas festivities exists, not in isolation, but in the context of his legal difficulties. Viewed in this manner, what might otherwise be seen as simple forgetfulness on the part of Mr. Pickwick or manipulation on the part of his creator becomes instead an impressive display of an essential self-preservation: in not allowing the law suit to depress him, to alter his actions or his attitudes, Mr. Pickwick shows a strength of character as admirable as his adventures may be comic. And while these adventures are in themselves episodic, they acquire, as the result of the sustaining of this background, a continuity for the reader. In the earliest incidents, which are played out against no significant background, the reader's focus tends to be on the individual situation; now, whether the scene is set in Magistrate Nupkins' makeshift court or at Mr. Wardle's glowing hearth or in Bob Sawyer's lodgings, at least part of the focus is consistently on Mr. Pickwick and the problem of how well he manages to prevent his impending trial from casting a shadow over his activities.

It is immediately after the trial, in which chicanery has the upper hand and the jury finds for the plaintiff, that Mr. Pickwick is most seriously tested. Having opted for a principle and refused to pay costs and damages, he must now await further legal action on the part of his adversaries. The wait of two months, until the court's next official term, is obviously necessitated by Dickens' desire to conform in his monthly installments to the actual legal calendar. But whatever the author's reasons for sending Mr. Pickwick off again on his travels, he uses the moment to good advantage.

Despite his unwonted sternness and determination in refusing to accede to the court's decision, Mr. Pickwick remains essentially unchanged. And while his ability not to change is earlier left as a matter for the reader to admire if he should happen to notice it, as in his recovery of good humor after his incarceration in Captain Boldwig's pound, now the issue is brought clearly into the open: in Mr. Pickwick's response to his lawyer's assessment of the legal difficulties that await him two months hence, even the other Pickwickians find "heroism" and reason for reassurance. " 'Very good,' said Mr. Pickwick. 'Until that time, my dear fellow, let me hear no more of the matter. And now,' continued Mr. Pickwick, looking round on his friends with a good-humoured smile, and a sparkle in the eye which no spectacles could dim or conceal, 'the only question is, Where shall we go next?' " (489). Where they go does not really matter. What does matter is that, after being misjudged and maligned in court and compromised by his unwitting friends' testimony, Mr. Pickwick responds in this generous and self-effacing manner and, to use words I quoted earlier, resumes "his station in the rank, with an ardour and enthusiasm that nothing could abate."

This is one of those moments—and there are, admittedly, not very many—when the problem of self-preservation emerges fairly clearly. More often, during this second stage in Mr. Pickwick's narrative, the issue is implicit, sometimes, as I have indicated, in the contrast between the legal threats that tend to remain in the background and the hero's attitudes and actions in the episodes that occupy the foreground, sometimes in his response to incidental discomforts. It is when he is imprisoned in the Fleet, the most trying and triumphant period of his adventures, that what began as comic recovery most emphatically achieves the status of self-preservation.

— *3* —

For all of the darkening of atmosphere and setting in the installments devoted to Mr. Pickwick's imprisonment, these chapters include for the reader three instances of a type of excitement, an almost euphoric joy, rare in the literature of any language. And rather than give exclusive attention or exaggerated importance to the darkness, we ought, I think, to see it as the necessary background for the moments of triumphant joy, moments in which *Pickwick Papers* comes closest to achieving the "transcendence" that Steven Marcus attributes to it.[7] If that "transcendence" is present anywhere in *Pickwick Papers,* it is present in what Mr. Pickwick gives to Jingle and Job; in what he receives from Sam; and in his release, in which, as Dickens says in his chapter title, "Mr. Pickwick's Benevolence proves stronger than his Obstinacy" (xlvii). All three of these incidents are also related most closely to the issue of self-preservation, the first and the last representing Mr. Pickwick's response to his most serious challenges, the second an embodiment of his fortitude's reward.

Number XV begins depressingly enough, with the relief provided by Sam's anecdotes and the antics of Messrs. Smangle and Mivins being inadequate to brighten Mr. Pickwick's spirits in "this place which was never light"; for Mr. Pickwick is, to use Sam's categories, one of "t'other vuns as gets done over, vith this sort o' thing" (576). But it is when things approach their worst, when Mr. Pickwick enters the section of the prison reserved for "the most miserable and abject class of debtors" (595), that there is something of a turn in the action, a break, not in the darkness, but in the depression. For in the middle chapter of the monthly number, through the unexpected reappearance of Alfred Jingle, Mr. Pickwick is able to lighten the reader's burden, if not his own.

His nemesis has returned, but under greatly altered circumstances. And really, if an objection is to be raised against this sudden reappearance after an absence of some seventeen chapters, amounting to nearly one-third the length of the novel, it is to be raised, not on the grounds of coincidence, but on the more basic grounds of the extreme unlikeliness of that radical change in circumstances. That Mr. Pickwick and his old enemy should be in debtors' prison at the same time is nothing to Jingle's being in debtors' prison at all. Jingle's fall is at least as unlikely as Mr. Micawber's rise in Australia at the end of *David Copperfield,* and if it were used to as little advantage, if, that is, it were made to stand as an end in itself, a morally appropriate punishment, it would probably be as much an awkwardness and distraction in the novel. But the end, when it is an especially welcome and admirable end, may justify the means, may at least disarm, if not disqualify, criticism.

After speaking briefly with Jingle, who at last finds himself "wholly unable to keep up appearances any longer" (his mastery of appearances and disguises had all along been, for better or worse, his major achievement), Mr. Pickwick, at last in a position of power over his adversaries, calls upon the still faithful Job Trotter:

> "Come here, sir," said Mr. Pickwick, trying to look stern, with four large tears running down his waistcoat. "Take that, sir."
> Take what? In the ordinary acceptation of such language, it should have been a blow. As the world runs, it ought to have been a sound, hearty cuff; for Mr. Pickwick had been duped, deceived, and wronged by the destitute outcast who was now wholly in his power. Must we tell the truth? It was something from Mr. Pickwick's waistcoat-pocket, which chinked as it was given into Job's hand, and the giving of which, somehow or other imparted a sparkle to the eye, and a swelling to the heart, of our excellent old friend, as he hurried away. (598)

The first of these paragraphs is intended less to deceive the reader—who has already been informed that "Mr. Pickwick was affected; the two men looked so very miserable"—than to present him with two possible courses of action, the normative, as expressed in Mr. Pickwick's words, and the Pickwickian alternative, as expressed in his "four large tears." The reader is offered the two possibilities simultaneously, but, while he may be puzzled by the words, it is unlikely that they will obscure the significance of the tears. The explanation of what Mr. Pickwick means by "Take that, sir," comes less as a surprise than as a relief and a confirmation: a relief in that it is an indication that the reader has, indeed, not erred in placing his confidence in Mr. Pickwick's generosity; a confirmation in that it reassures the reader that neither depression nor the opportunity for revenge can alter in the least Mr. Pickwick's better nature.

But if the reader is reassured in his evaluation of Mr. Pickwick's character, he is also obliged to recognize that he values Mr. Pickwick precisely because Mr. Pickwick acts in a non-normative manner, because he does not intend "the ordinary acceptation of such language" and does not act in accord with the way "the world runs." Here again we are dealing with the matter of foreground action juxtaposed with a contrasting background, for the moment a background far more pervasive than the individual threats that challenge Mr. Pickwick. But, like those threats, the background of conventional behavior is not introduced to darken the prospect or the perspective; instead, in calling attention to the rarity of Pickwickian good nature and generosity, it heightens the issue and makes Mr. Pickwick's self-preservation all the more urgent and impressive. It does more even than this, for if at the end of the passage the reader, like the author, accepts Mr. Pickwick as "our excellent old friend," Dickens has succeeded not only in asserting the value of Pickwickian good nature, but also in challenging that more conventional and vindictive sort of behavior (a kind of behavior exemplified in many of the earlier interpolated tales) that Mr. Pickwick deviates from. Mr. Pickwick's good nature becomes more than what it is for much of the novel, more, that is, than simply a personal eccentricity; it becomes a genuine alternative to less admirable, if more common, attitudes and actions.

Having acted generously with Jingle and Job, Mr. Pickwick immediately attempts another act of kindness and generosity, the release of Sam from his attendance on him in the Fleet, but this second act, in bringing his unservile, even defiant, servant closer to him than ever before, backfires to Mr. Pickwick's great benefit. The desire to release Sam precedes the confrontation with Jingle and Job, but, for strategic emotional purposes it is not broached until after that confrontation. In reconstructing the chain of events, we may discover a continuity not immediately apparent: Mr. Pickwick goes to the poor side to find a substitute for Sam; he discovers Jingle and Job (the substitute-designate) and befriends them; and now he is prepared to offer Sam his freedom. Without the desire to free Sam there would have been no meeting with Jingle and Job; without the offer of freedom there would have been no such dramatic assertion of loyalty and concern as Sam's response embodies.

When we move from the chain of events to the chain of effects, an actual causality becomes a symbolic causality. In what might be called the logic of the situation, a logic that transcends rather than circumvents normal cause and effect, Sam's decision serves as an appropriate reward for Mr. Pickwick's good deed, as a satisfying response not so much to his proposal as to his generosity to "the destitute outcast who was now wholly in his power." In fact, Sam's decision has nothing to do with that act of generosity, since Sam knows nothing of it, does not even know that Jingle and Job are in the Fleet. The sense of causality here rests in the organization of the materials rather than in any cause and effect governing the events: Mr. Pickwick ought to be rewarded and then—but not, strictly speaking, as a result—Mr. Pickwick is rewarded. And the rightness of it all is compelling. Had there been no meeting with his former enemies, no striking example of Mr. Pickwick's self-preservation, Sam's act of loyalty, his voluntary imprisonment for a bogus debt to his father, would still have constituted one of the novel's finest moments. Because that meeting does occur and because Mr. Pickwick's proposal to Sam follows immediately after it, Sam's decision has the impact of more than a mere incident, albeit a moving one, and achieves the status of something like a metaphysical statement: not all is, to be sure, right with the world, but in unexpected and seemingly unconnected ways good deeds done without thought of recompense may be rewarded by other equally disinterested acts of kindness or loyalty. The moral world of Dickens' novels is less a world of apparent cause and effect than a world of mysterious, perhaps providential, relationships among events as well as among people.

Sam's emphatic words and gestures when he presents himself to Mr. Pickwick as a prisoner are a fitting end to the installment, a satisfying point at which to leave the reader. In a sense, Mr. Pickwick is no better off than he was when the installment began; but, in another sense, his problem seems less pressing, his distress less overwhelming. In the course of the number's three chapters, the reader, along with Mr. Pickwick, has moved from depression to the satisfactions of the meeting with Jingle and Job to doubt in Sam's abrupt departure from the Fleet and, finally, to something very like exhilaration in Sam's defiant return. The darkness has not been dispelled, but it has, if only temporarily, been superseded by a moment of joy.

The three chapters of Number XVI do not establish so neat a pattern, but, in the balance struck between light and dark, the emphasis is much the same. There are no events equivalent in emotional significance to the meeting with Jingle and Job or to Sam's assertion of loyalty; there are, however, at the outset and at the conclusion, preparations for such an event, for Mr. Pickwick's eventual release.

Chapter xliv follows immediately from the preceding number. The scene is the same as Mr. Pickwick asks Sam for an explanation and gets instead an anecdote, perhaps a lesson. One of the most appealing things about Sam is that his loyalty extends not only to his getting himself imprisoned, but also to his trying to get Mr. Pickwick to secure his own release. Demonstrating his sound judgment and his sense of practical priorities, the very qualities for which Mr. Pickwick hired him, he loses no time in suggesting that his own imprisonment has a bearing on—may be an only slightly distorted image of—Mr. Pickwick's noble, but perhaps misguided, gesture in suffering imprisonment for the sake of a principle. This may not have been part of Dickens' scheme when, in Number XV, Sam arranges for his own arrest, but by the beginning of Number XVI, whether as the result of planning or as an instance of improvisation, it—the representation to Mr. Pickwick of the nature and consequences of his own course of action—has become an important element in Sam Weller's thinking.

Mr. Pickwick, made uneasy by Sam's obstinacy in refusing to allow his debt to be paid, begins "rubbing his nose with an air of some vexation," at which "Mr. Weller thought it prudent to change the theme of the discourse": "I takes my determination on principle, sir, . . . and you takes yours on the same ground; wich puts me in mind o' the man as killed his-self on principle, wich o' course you've heerd on, sir." But it is less "the theme of the discourse" than the form of the lesson that Sam changes; his meaning is, if anything, made more apparent now that the issue shifts from his own imprisonment to the broader matter of actions based upon an obstinate adherence to principle.

Mr. Pickwick, protesting legal sham and an unjust court ruling, is ensnared by an ideal far loftier than the "great principle that crumpets wos wholesome," but he, like the crumpet-loving man of Sam's story, is ensnared, and Dickens here reveals that his hero's quixotism has less than his full approbation. Mr. Pickwick has acted nobly, but, in deciding to act on principle and, if necessary, to "spend the rest of my existence in a debtors' prison" (487), he has, it appears, begun to forget about people and to lose his sense of priorities. We have been given dramatic evidence, in his kindness to Jingle and Job and in his offer to Sam, that he has retained his generosity, but, in wilfully sacrificing the potential diversity of experience in the outside world for the sake of an idea, he has severely—and pointlessly—limited the range of his good influence. His sacrifice, though it indirectly results in his good works in the Fleet, can in itself do no good: it can neither correct legal inequities nor bankrupt Dodson and Fogg, but can only serve to endanger his own good spirits and well-being and to distress those who take pleasure in his company.

Chapter xliv moves on to the Chancery prisoner's recital of how he was ruined by a bequest, and ends with his death: "but he had grown so like death in life, that they knew not when he died"; Chapter xlv, which is devoted largely to another incident in the Weller saga, ends with a new determination on Mr. Pickwick's part: " 'I have seen enough,' said Mr. Pickwick, as he threw himself into a chair in his little apartment. 'My head aches with these scenes, and my heart too. Henceforth I will be a prisoner in my own room.' " The chapter also includes some lighter moments, as when Tony Weller suggests that Mr. Pickwick escape to " 'Merriker" in a hollowed-out "pianner-forty," and when Sam discovers his master's kindness to Jingle and Job and exhibits similar good nature himself. Despite these moments, if the installment ended when the chapter ends, we would have here a decidedly depressing monthly number, one that closed with Mr. Pickwick at his lowest point in both health and spirits. But the installment goes on to Chapter xlvi, which introduces a new and most significant element into Mr. Pick-wick's situation.

Three months have passed and the scene shifts, first to Mrs. Bar-dell's boarding house and then to a picnic at the Spanish Tea-Gardens in Hampstead. But the chapter and the installment end by returning us to the Fleet prison, with the unwary Mrs. Bardell, the latest victim of the unscrupulous Dodson and Fogg, detained for a failure to pay the legal costs she believed herself freed from when her case was taken on speculation. The reader is not let in on how this turn in events may work to Mr. Pickwick's benefit, but, in the normally imperturbable Sam's excitement and in his announcement that "I see some good in this," he is assured that it will have some beneficial effect. Though the matter remains a mystery, Sam's delight is not to be lightly shrugged off, and the installment ends, not with the depression that figures so largely in it, but with, for the reader, a heightened sense of expectation as to the good that is to follow.

It is all resolved—not only the significance of Mrs. Bardell's impris-onment, but also the larger issue of Mr. Pickwick's release—in the first chapter of Number XVII, in which "Mr. Pickwick's Benevolence proves stronger than his Obstinacy." For now the conflict between the rigid ad-herence to a principle and the best interests of people becomes more than a conflict between contending ideas, becomes one in which the claims of an abstraction—albeit a high-minded one—are challenged by the needs of particular individuals in particular circumstances. It is Mr. Pickwick's most challenging test, for it is a test in which there is a degree of right on both sides, a test in which the issue is less which ac-tion is the right action than which action is the one that will signal the preservation of Mr. Pickwick's most valued qualities.

Mr. Pickwick, who has already shown himself to be most compas-sionate when in a position of power in his treatment of Jingle and Job, is again placed in such a position by Mrs. Bardell's imprisonment: his accuser's fate, as Perker, his attorney, points out, is in Mr. Pickwick's hands. Perker itemizes the considerations, as Mr. Pickwick, at first in-dignant at the suggestion that he aid the woman who brought him to trial, is, at last, "evidently roused by his friend's appeal."

> "You have now an opportunity, on easy terms, of placing your-self in a much higher position than you ever could, by remain-ing here; which would only be imputed, by people who didn't know you, to sheer dogged, wrongheaded, brutal obstinacy; nothing else, my dear sir, believe me. Can you hesitate to avail yourself of it, when it restores you to your friends, your old pursuits, your health and amusements; when it liberates your faithful and attached servant, whom you otherwise doom to im-

prisonment for the rest of your life; and above all, when it enables you to take the very magnanimous revenge—which I know, my dear sir, is one after your own heart—of releasing this woman from a scene of misery and debauchery, to which no man should ever be consigned, if I had my will, but the infliction of which on any woman, is even more frightful and barbarous." (661–62)

Circumstances, which had earlier victimized Mr. Pickwick, now provide him with a choice between a principle and an "opportunity," as much an opportunity for his own recovery and renewal after a self-imposed solitary confinement of three months as a chance to do good to others. But before Mr. Pickwick can respond to Perker's entreaty, another element is added to the amount of good that can be done "for the paltry consideration of a few pounds" and a principle. The plea of Arabella Winkle, that Mr. Pickwick free himself so that he may reconcile the former Miss Allen's brother to her recent secret marriage to Nathaniel Winkle, supported by Perker's suggestion that Mr. Pickwick might be a suitable emissary to Winkle's supposedly implacable father, is the straw that breaks Mr. Pickwick's bondage.

It is, as Dickens narrates it, a joyful and triumphant moment, the equivalent at least of Mr. Pickwick's victory over the way "the world runs" in his generosity to Jingle and Job. And what is so very satisfying for the reader here is not only Mr. Pickwick's restoration, but also the sense that a danger has been averted. Principles, noble or otherwise, may be useful, but, for Dickens, people are more important; even noble principles become dangerous or inadequate when they become so central that they obscure the claims of individuals. When Sam Weller, Mrs. Bardell, and the newly-married Winkles make their appearance in the Fleet, when, in other words, Mr. Pickwick's world in its variety and concreteness challenges Mr. Pickwick's abstract principle, that principle, though it may be a good one, must be put aside. This is, for Mr. Pickwick, not so much a lesson he must learn as it is an "opportunity" he must take advantage of. Later, for Mr. Dombey and, more explicitly, Mr. Gradgrind, who through adversity discovers the value of "bending his hitherto inflexible theories to appointed circumstances" (*Hard Times*, III, ix)—two men guilty less of wickedness than of the blindness that springs from single-mindedness and inflexibility—it is something in the nature of a great, if belated, awakening.

And so, Mr. Pickwick secures his release, but not to engage in a life of social agitation. The reformist aspect of the debtors' prison episode coexists with, but differs from, its dramatic function: if such were not the case, our final impression of Mr. Pickwick, comfortable and surrounded by friends in his snug retreat, might be a less favorable one, might be tainted by the sense that he has simply run away from what ought to appeal to his social consciousness. But for reformist purposes Mr. Pickwick is merely a convenience, his imprisonment merely a means of introducing into a work of fiction an assault on an offensive institution. For Mr. Pickwick himself the issue is less what he sees and suffers than how well he survives and, most importantly, preserves those qualities of good nature, good humor, and benevolence that have come to constitute his most prominent characteristics. As Edgar Johnson remarks of Nicholas Nickleby, another Dickens hero who, though ostensibly engaged in the process of acclimatization and accommodation, is actually involved less in learning and development than in self-preservation, "Dotheboys Hall gives Dickens the chance to expose the [Yorkshire] schools, but Nicolas's life would have been little different had he never seen the place." [8] Similarly, Mr. Pickwick's life would have been little different had he never entered the Fleet prison; what would have been different—significantly less clear and vivid—is the reader's sense of Mr. Pickwick's life, of the values he represents and of the struggle for self-preservation that he, not entirely wittingly, is engaged in. Because this struggle, essentially a moral one, is the focus and dramatic center of the action, it is enough that Mr. Pickwick does persevere; his later adventures and his retirement are not an escape from social responsibility, but a reward, like that of Oliver Twist—in whom Dickens "wished to shew . . . the principle of Good surviving through every adverse circumstance, and triumphing at last" [9]—for a fight well fought and a victory won.

If we follow the developments in Dickens' art and purposes, along with the changes in Mr. Pickwick's character and characterization, we may discover that *Pickwick Papers* is a far more coherent novel than it has generally been believed to be. And along with this, we may gain a stronger sense of just what it is that makes *Pickwick Papers* so exhilarating a book. High spirits and fertility of imagination do not alone account for the sense of joy so many readers have experienced. But add to these a seriousness of purpose and a continuity of perspective, and the book's strange and lasting success becomes less inexplicable.

The book is exhilarating, rather than simply entertaining, and pertinent, rather than merely ephemeral, because the comic tale, for all its episodic organization, has a serious meaning. And that meaning, which is not hidden by the comic manner, but rather reenforced by it, is a triumphant one, one that encourages the reader to recognize and share in the triumph implicit in Mr. Pickwick's adventures. For Mr. Pickwick, though no youthful knight in shining armor, does triumph, not over enemies—at the end, Jingle, Job, and Mrs. Bardell have profited from his benevolence and generosity; Dodson and Fogg are none the worse professionally and something the better financially for having pros-

ecuted and persecuted him; even minor figures, such as Captain Boldwig and Magistrate Nupkins, have abused him with impunity—not over
enemies, but over common and persistent temptations. The essential
drama of the story lies not so much in the way in which Mr. Pickwick,
as Dickens' conception alters and solidifies, becomes increasingly a better person, but rather in the fact that, once "the immortal Pickwick" is
fully realized about a third of the way into the novel, he resists threats
and temptations and by virtue of his moral self-preservation refuses to
become worse. The process for Mr. Pickwick is scarcely a self-conscious
one; but the absence of psychological tension, while it simplifies the situation, does not nullify the reality of the problem. What Dickens dra-
matizes in his first novel remains a central issue in all of the novels that
follow: not so much *the matter of how* an individual preserves his better
nature and finer instincts in a largely hostile or indifferent environ-
ment as *the assertion that* an individual can preserve his humanity under
those circumstances.

Anne Humpherys

DICKENS AND MAYHEW ON THE LONDON POOR

EVEN THOUGH Henry Mayhew and Charles Dickens wrote in completely different media, one is still likely to think of Dickens when reading Mayhew's *London Labour and the London Poor,* and vice versa, if one knows Mayhew's work well. Reviews of Peter Quennell's selections from *London Labour* frequently drew parallels between the two. To date the only full studies of the two men's work have been concerned mainly with the influence of *London Labour and the London Poor* on Dickens' novels.[1] There are other interesting questions which grow out of a comparison of the two, however. Both writers tried to give a picture of lower-class life which was full, convincing, and true to life. Dickens, of course, had a larger and more comprehensive view of the Victorian world than Mayhew did. If we limit ourselves to the one subject they did have in common, however—the life of the Victorian lower classes at mid-century—we will find in a comparison of the two men's works that the same powerful results are achieved by two opposing methods of rendering the truth. The force of the opposition is particularly evident when one compares their journalism.

Dickens tends to distance himself from his subject and create an impressively generalized picture of London life. Sometimes his distancing results in a humorous whimsicality or sentimentality. On the other hand, Mayhew's compulsive search for details renders him adept in particularizing the facts of slum life, although, because of his obsession with minutiae, his picture is not inclusive and occasionally fails to converge into a coherent whole.

This opposition between Dickens and Mayhew is not simply attributable to the different genres in which they principally worked, although the broad reference of the novel and the emphasis on temporal immediacy in journalism do play some role in creating the differences in their pictures of lower-class life. Dickens did his best work as a novelist and Mayhew as a journalist *cum* sociologist, but both their methods of description are a mixture of the two disciplines: details seen by a

[78

keen eye and then presented by differing artistic means, Mayhew's sociological journalism, like the work of the late Oscar Lewis,[2] partakes of the drama, extension by example, and even the narrative unity of fiction. Dickens' novels in their turn frequently have a journalistic base in contemporary events.[3] Moreover, when Dickens changed genres, from fiction to journalism, his method of depicting lower-class life did not change, nor did Mayhew's when, after writing *London Labour and the London Poor,* he tried his hand at another novel.

The following discussion suggests some of the reasons that their methods remained opposed no matter what the genre, as well as some of the results. After analyzing the elements of Dickens' generalization and Mayhew's particularization in descriptions of the lower classes, we will find in their journalism similar oppositions in their methods of collecting material and in the resulting experience of the poor which they project for their readers. The tendency to generalize as well as that to particularize is also related to Mayhew's and Dickens' divergence of opinion on social questions after 1850. Finally, despite the inherent weaknesses in both methods of rendering the "truth" about lower-class life, the two authors found ways to suggest in their partial visions the larger picture.

Answering charges against the naturalness of Nancy's devotion to Sykes, Dickens said he found it "useless to discuss whether the conduct and character of the girl seems natural or unnatural, probable or improbable, right or wrong. IT IS TRUE." [4] Although he never denied that he "purposely dwelt upon the romantic side of familiar things" (Preface to *Bleak House,* p. xiv), Dickens insisted on the factual base of the familiar and the romantic. For entirely different reasons, Mayhew also insisted on his adherence to fact: "My vocation is to collect facts and register opinions," he said in his second article for the *Morning Chronicle* series on "Labour and the Poor" in 1849.[5] To romanticize the familiar and collect the facts, they both spent many hours of their lives prowling around London, particularly through the slums of St. Giles and Seven Dials, down the wretched alleys off Rosemary Lane, in Jacob's Island and other notorious districts where the poor lived.

When they came to put these similar direct experiences into words, however, their artistic methods were directly opposed, although in no way contradictory. The differences shed light on more than their artistic methods. Take, as an example which could be multipled, the two descriptions of Jacob's Island. Dickens wrote:

Crazy wooden galleries common to the backs of half-a-dozen houses, with holes from which to look upon the slime beneath; windows, broken and patched, with poles thrust out, on which to dry the linen that is never there; rooms so small, so filthy, so

confined, that the air would seem too tainted even for the dirt
and squalor which they shelter; wooden chambers thrusting
themselves out above the mud, and threatening to fall into
it—as some have done; dirt-besmeared walls and decaying
foundations; every repulsive lineament of poverty, every loath-
some indication of filth, rot and garbage. (*Oliver Twist*, p. 382)

This powerful description has been frequently pointed out as an example of Dickens' realistic portrayal of the details of the slums. Dickens
himself insisted on its accuracy in his preface to the novel. The nature
of its realism, however, is quite different from that in Mayhew's corresponding description, which, though written some ten years later, depicts a place little changed.

> The striking peculiarity of Jacob's Island consists in the wooden
> galleries and sleeping-rooms at the back of the houses which
> overhang the dark ditch that stagnates beside them. . . .
> Across some parts of the stream, rooms have been built, so that
> house adjoins house; and here, with the very stench of death
> rising through the boards, human beings sleep night after
> night, until the last sleep of all comes upon them, years before
> its time. Scarce a house but yellow linen is hanging to dry over
> the balustrade of staves, or else run out on a long oar, where
> the sulphur-coloured clothes hang over the waters, and you are
> almost wonderstruck to see their form and colour unreflected
> in the putrid ditch below. . . . In it float large masses of green
> rotting weed, and against the posts of the bridges are swollen
> carcasses of dead animals, almost bursting with the gases of pu-
> trefaction. Along the banks are heaps of indescribable filth, the
> phosphoretted smell which tells of the rotting fish, while the
> oyster shells are like pieces of slate from their coating of mud
> and dirt.[6]

The two descriptions begin in a similar fashion with a generalized
description of the way in which the galleries hang over the ditch. After
the opening clause, however, their methods diverge. While Dickens'
description remains generalized, Mayhew's becomes increasingly more
particularized, especially in regard to colors: yellow linen hung out to
dry is unreflected in the ditch, while the ditch itself is described in persistent sensory detail. In Mayhew's description, the reader responds to
the repulsiveness of the details of the scene which are conveyed
through such unrelentingly visual figures as "sulphur-colored clothes"
and oyster shells "like pieces of slate."

Dickens' description stimulates a similar negative response, not,
however, through a direct visualization of Jacob's Island. Partly the effect is achieved by the rhythm of his rhetoric. The pounding repetition
of sound patterns in the last sentence builds up to a climax that does

more to move the reader and convince him of the vileness of the place than do any of the imprecise details. The details themselves, by the simple device of removing the definite articles from "crazy wooden galleries," "windows," "rooms," and "dirt-besmeared walls," are transformed by a form of personification into representative elements of all slums everywhere in London. The adjective "crazy," moreover, does not attempt to render a visual image, as do Mayhew's adjectives. Instead, while vaguely suggesting both position and shape, "crazy" gives the slum itself the connotations of insanity.[7]

The opposing but complementary styles evident in these two passages are consistent throughout the work of the two men. Dickens, in both novels and journalism, repeatedly used personification. These personifications in turn frequently verge on symbolic extension, as we have seen in the piece on Jacob's Island and is implied in Dorothy Van Ghent's essay "The Dickens' World: A View from Todgers." Dickens' world is one where things imitate the human while people take on the characteristics of inanimate objects, a kind of reverse personification.[8] Although the passage on Jacob's Island does not demonstrate it, frequently the personifications of slums and low life contain an element of humor, as Kathleen Tillotson and John Butt remark.[9]

Mayhew, on the other hand, seldom uses either personification or metaphor in his own descriptions, although the reported speech of his informants can be highly metaphorical. He usually structures his descriptions around a selection of precisely worded observations, beginning with a general view and introducing one by one a series of details arranged so that the last one is the most shocking. (In his description of a group of vagrants waiting for the doors of the Asylum for the Homeless to open, his last descriptive detail is of their feet, "blue and livid-looking as half-cooked meat" [*LL&LP,* III, 428].) When Mayhew wants some sort of expression to render his scene more precisely and more effectively, he most frequently uses a simile, thereby choosing the one figure of speech which verbally reinforces the logical separation between the two objects compared. His similes are brought into his descriptions in order to increase the sharpness of a physical perception and not to extend the significance beyond the particular scene, as Dickens' figures tend to do. Mayhew also tried to use comparisons in his similes which would draw attention only to the physical details under view and not to the emotional responses of the reporter (oyster shells "like pieces of slate").

In addition to these artistic variations, reflections of Dickens' generalized descriptions of lower-class life and Mayhew's particularizations can be seen in their respective journalism both in the methods by which they collected material and in the nature of the experience they give their readers in their reports. As a reporter Mayhew set out to detail individual experiences of the poor; as a result, he consistently tried to find ways to experience poverty, albeit vicariously. In an escorted tour of a prison, he insisted upon doing his stint on the treadwheel; [10] he visited an illegal gambling game and reported on the watch set for the police (*LL&LP*, I, 17–18); he climbed alone into a deserted building to seek a bone-grubber he had met in the street the day before (*LL&LP*, II, 141). He went on rounds with a turf cutter (*LL&LP*, I, 156) and conducted an interview with a blind man in the dark (*London Characters*, p. 349). He avoided third parties who might inhibit a free exchange, tried to interview the poor in their homes, or wandered around the slums alone or with his brother, or had a surgeon, priest, or resident introduce him.[11]

Dickens, on the other hand, although he walked a great deal over the same ground, appears to have preferred a more generalized contact with the poor. He liked to tour with the police; in his journalistic accounts of his adventures, he is closer in sympathy to the officers than to the poor. He stands by Inspector Field while he and his men run through their job with severe and condescending efficiency, disturbing the sleep of people in asylums for the homeless and bullying the inhabitants of low lodging houses. (Inspector Bucket in *Bleak House* acts with the same brutality toward Jo. The effect is rather disconcerting since Dickens wants us to admire Bucket, whose attitude toward Jo seems violently at odds with our own.[12]) Dickens' identification with the police and separation from the poor sometimes results in a tone of delight in the cowering awe which the presence of the detectives evokes from the residents of the lodging houses. In one tour with Field, for example, Dickens describes the Inspector at work in a cellar which the reporter calls Rats' Castle:

> Inspector Field's hand is the well-known hand that has collared half the people here, and motioned their brothers, sisters, fathers, mothers, male and female friends, inexorably to New South Wales. Yet Inspector Field stands in this den, the Sultan of the place. Every thief here cowers before him, like a schoolboy before his schoolmaster. All watch him, all answer when addressed, all laugh at his jokes, all seek to propitiate him.[13]

The narrative distance here does more than establish a tone of condescension. In generalizing the inmates of this low lodging house by suggesting they are all blood relations with the whole criminal class, Dickens symbolizes in one broad reference all that is rotten and threatening in society, and thus evokes from the reader a response of outrage against the existence of the lodging houses.

Mayhew, for his part, avoided the police while interviewing the inhabitants of the slums. (When he held a meeting of ticket-of-leave men, he prohibited a single constable from attending [*LL&LP*, III, 430].) In his tours of the lower-class neighborhoods, although we do not get the scope of Dickens' vision of London's underworld, Mayhew does succeed in projecting a surprising, because unexpected, impression of the individual humanity of the men and women who live there. Mayhew reports one fifteen-year-old pickpocket saying, among many other things:

"I can pick a woman's pocket as easy as a man's, though you wouldn't think it. If one's in prison for begging, one's laughed at. The others say, 'Begging! Oh, you cadger!' So a boy is partly forced to steal for his character. I've lived a good deal in lodging-houses, and know the ways of them. They are very bad places for a boy to be in. Where I am now, when the place is full, there's upwards of 100 can be accommodated. I won't be there long. I'll do something to get out of it. . . . I can neither read nor write. In this lodging-house there are no women. They talk there chiefly about what they've done, or are going to do, or have set their minds upon, just as you and any other gentleman might do. I have been in lodging-houses in Mint-street and Kent-street, where men and women and children all slept in one room." (*LL&LP*, I, 411)

Mayhew makes this boy live for us by quoting all his remarks however irrelevant. In his aside that the people in lodging houses talk about business "as you and any other gentlemen might do," the boy is vividly present in all his self-importance, swaggering, and vitality.

The symbolic extension of Dickens' piece on the low lodging house and the detailed interview in Mayhew's evoke a similar emotional response of indignation. The difference for the reader lies in the role the low-life inhabitants play in creating our feelings of anger. In Dickens' piece, the inhabitants are part of the threat to morality and order which the lodging houses offer to society. In Mayhew's article, on the other hand, although we feel threatened both by the existence of the lodging house and by the lawless individuals who inhabit it, we are also concerned about the welfare of the boy thief who lives there because Mayhew has made him exist for us as a unique human being.

The reader's generalized response to the poor also exists in pieces where Dickens is sympathetic and even when he uses Mayhew's journalistic form of the personal interview. In the 1860s Dickens made a number of visits to the more destitute areas of the East End of London, an area Mayhew had haunted almost daily while writing his articles for the *Morning Chronicle* in 1849–50, and which he had returned to during the next two years and again in 1856. Dickens' sense of himself in these

walks through the East End was that of a detached commentator; he
tended, as he said himself, "to regard my walk as my beat, and myself
as a higher sort of police-constable doing duty on the same." [14] Like
Mayhew, he made a series of visits to the "homes" of people living in
the tenements, talking with them about their work and lives and re-
porting his interviews for the reader.

In his recounting of the dialogue, he repeats not only his questions
but also his feelings about the answers. " 'God bless you, sir, and thank
you!' were the parting words from these people,—gratefully spoken
too,—with which I left the place." [15] The quoted dialogue rings true
and does not differ from that found in Mayhew's interviews; the paren-
thetical reflection on its sincerity, to be found only in Dickens' interview, draws our attention away from the subjects and toward the narrator. Dickens also shifts his report from dialogue into indirect discourse,
and thus carries on an implied dialogue with the reader rather than the
actual one with the poor.

> But, you see, it come to her through two hands, and, of course,
> it didn't come through the second hand for nothing. Why did it
> come through the second hand at all? Why, this way. The sec-
> ond hand took the risk of the given-out work, you see. If she
> had money enough to pay the security deposit,—call it two
> pound,—she could get the work from the first hand, and so the
> second would not have to be deducted for. (*The Uncommercial
> Traveller,* p. 323)

The use of the third person here distances the lower-class woman from
us, but it also moves the interview onto a symbolic level. The tone of
the indirect discourse suggests the typicality of the situation and the
narrator's feelings about it; the woman becomes important because her
experience is that of all distressed needlewomen in London, and her
suffering is increased because it includes theirs. We in turn share the
narrator's outrage.

Mayhew's interviews are constructed in order to bring the reader
into direct contact with the poor person in all his individual complexity.
Mayhew removes not only his own responses but even his own questions from his reports. As a result the interview unfolds as a kind of autobiography told by the individual poor person directly to the reader.
The interviewer fades into the background, though his presence is
always deducible, and the specific woman in the following account ab-
sorbs all our attention.

> "Ah, its wonderful how a poor person lives—but they don't
> live. My clear gains are about 1s.6p. a week. In the summer
> time it's better, because I don't want no candle light. I work

second-handed for the piece master. I don't know what he makes. I've done the basting of the Sappers at 3d. a coat; the pockets are fully made, and the shoulder straps fully made, and for the basting of the trowsers I get 1d., and two button-holes worked in the waistband. Why they baste up only I don't know. Them I work for doesn't know. It would puzzle me to tell you how I do manage to live. I have nothing than a cup of tea and a bit of dry bread twice a day, for the week round; and if I can get a red herring (three or four a penny), why it's as much as I can get. If I've got a bit better work, I may chance to get a bit of meat—2d. or 3d. a pound. I've got no home at present. I was turned out—told I must leave—as I couldn't pay my rent, 'cause I've had no work, and had nothing to pay it with. I'm living now with a neighbor in the same house where I had my room. She has allowed me to stop with her till I got a bit of work; for I can't pay any rent, and she gives me a little food—part of what she's got, poor woman." [16]

The oppositions in Mayhew's and Dickens' social realism in their descriptions and in their journalism are also related to an apparent divergence in attitude on social questions which develops after 1850. Mayhew's commitment to reform remained steady after 1850, especially in regard to issues about the working class, while Dickens' reformism weakened and in some cases all but disappeared. During the first half of their careers,[17] Dickens' and Mayhew's publicly expressed attitudes on specific aspects of the Condition-of-England question were nearly identical. In regard to education they both condemned the practices of rote learning and corporal punishment,[18] and had mixed feelings about the Ragged Schools.[19] Their attitudes on philanthropy (they both attacked self-serving "philanthropy"), sanitation reform, and the hypocrisy and corruptness of some elements of officialdom, were also similar. In one case, pointed out by Philip Collins in *Dickens and Crime*,[20] their very subject of attack was identical. This target was a notorious magistrate, one Laing, pilloried by Dickens as Fang in *Oliver Twist*. Under Mayhew's editorship,[21] *Figaro in London* also criticized Laing and claimed full credit when he was removed from the bench in January 1838.

Victorian public opinion became more conservative about social questions after mid-century, and Dickens' journalism, as Collins demonstrates, reflects this shift. After 1850 Dickens was sometimes openly repelled by the non-criminal lower classes. Although he could be intelligently sensitive with the prostitutes he and Miss Coutts set about to reform at Urania Cottage, when he met an ordinary eighteen-year-old lower-class girl in Hyde Park and the girl swore at him, he tried to have her sent to prison in spite of the resistance of the police and the magistrate. "Do you really wish this girl to be sent to prison?" the incredulous magistrate asked Dickens, who reports himself "grimly" answering, "If I didn't, why should I take the trouble to come here?" [22]

Mayhew's attitudes, on the other hand, did not change. During the years in which Dickens was apparently reversing his position on the abolition of capital punishment, Mayhew still addressed the committee which advocated an end to the penalty.[23] Although Dickens, perhaps following Carlyle, called for the reinstitution of flogging in prison and the perpetual imprisonment of "ruffians," Mayhew denied that making prison more deterrent would reduce crime [24] and also conducted meetings of ticket-of-leave men ("parolees") in order to publicize their grievances and to help them get work (*LL&LP*, III, 430–39). In fact, Dickens' increased respect for Carlyle after 1850 and Mayhew's reiterated disgust with the author of *Latter-day Pamphlets* [25] demonstrate the increasing divergence between two men who only a few years earlier had expressed many opinions in common. In addition, at a time when public opinion was concerned over the "coddling" of prisoners, Mayhew wrote *The Criminal Prisons of London,* [26] which, although uneven, contains many sympathetic observations about criminals and prison management.[27]

The reasons behind this difference in attitude between two observers of the lower classes who began with such a wide range of similarities are complex, but a part of the answer is connected to the source and the effects of their differing methods of social realism. It begins in biography. Mayhew's relationship with his father was almost the exact reverse of that of Dickens with his, and this partly determined the stance Mayhew took vis à vis the lower classes. Joshua Mayhew had none of the amiable irresponsibility of Mr. Micawber; instead he was a stiff and tyrannical middle-class father. His influence loomed over his seven sons all their lives: his disapproving person in the front row of a lecture caused Henry, a grown man, to leave the platform in confusion.[28] In his will he ranked his heirs according to their fulfillment of his expectations; Henry received £1 a week from the £50,000 estate.

Easy-going and financially careless, Henry Mayhew had immersed himself in a world of newspaper reporters and farce writers in direct opposition to his father's wish that he become a solicitor. A struggle against his middle-class heritage may have given Mayhew an unconscious identification with the outcasts of respectability—particularly with the lively, footloose, financially irresponsible, semi-lawless street folk.[29] This response in turn may have helped him break down the barriers in class between himself and his subjects. Dickens, too, tried to erase the past, though like Mayhew he never succeeded completely. His attempt to deny the inheritance from his father's failures may have helped determine his generalized narrative method, for by distancing himself as narrator in this way he is able to reinforce a separation between himself and the poor.

The two men thus began with opposing tendencies in the way they responded to the lower classes. As they developed, the differing methods of expression which resulted also influenced how they responded to changes in public sentiment. From 1849 Mayhew's journalistic survey subjected the experiences and positions on reform which he had shared with Dickens to the test of multiple specific observations. He consciously thought of his survey as a kind of "scientific experiment,"[30] the data of which were the details given him through the "lips of the people themselves" (*LL&LP*, I, iii). Although he insisted on his role as a collector of facts, there did come a point after 1849 when the evidence he had accumulated seemed to necessitate a challenge to some of his own attitudes.[31] He spoke in favor of the Trade Unions (*LL&LP*, III, 222) based on his favorable experiences of their meetings; in 1851 he declared that what he had learned from individual encounters with working men forced him to renounce the tenets of laissez-faire.[32] The details in the many personal stories which lay behind both this about-face and his other conclusions about the causes of low wages and the nature of the poor provided Mayhew with a firm anchor in the wake of changes in fickle public sentiment after 1850.

Dickens did not render his experiences of the lower classes in Mayhew's particularized way. Even when recounting the most specific of his adventures, he projected the overview rather than the individualized experience. His generalized narrative responses created a powerful poetic vision of Victorian England which did not exclude the lower classes, but it weighted Dickens with no burden of stubborn specifics which would countervail the shift from a liberal and reform-oriented 1840s to a conservative and smug 1850s.

Both methods of portraying the truth about the lower classes, moreover, had inherent difficulties. The more precise and detailed Mayhew's picture became, the more circumscribed it was, and the more fragmented the overall pattern of slum conditions and the causes of poverty became. The week-by-week development of *London Labour* unfolds a project always expanding. In the middle of Volume II Mayhew decided that he wanted to consider street cleaning as part of the classification of street work and so the volume digresses into over one hundred pages on the intricacies and merits of various ways of picking up and disposing of the garbage of London, a discussion which itself modulates through remarks on casual labor among rubbish carters into a passage on the general means of decreasing wages by overwork. Although Mayhew began *London Labour* with the intention of covering all branches of the subject,[33] the more precise he became about the street folk, intended originally only as a fill-in while he collected statistics on the skilled trades,[34] the vaguer and more undefined the overall picture became. Hence the disparity between title and content noted by Gertrude Himmelfarb.[35]

Mayhew does overcome the weakness of limited scope to some degree by artistic means, although he is less successful in projecting a unified vision. In his surveys, quantity comes to look like scope. His canvas seems crowded and large because of the amount of information present; the statistical details are as crucial to this artistic extension of the specific as are Mayhew's descriptions of persons and places, and the array of seemingly gratuitous human particulars given by each informant. (Oscar Lewis achieves the same effect. His intense and detailed study of a single Mexican family in *The Children of Sànchez* leads the reader to feel that he is learning something about the whole of the Mexican poor.) Although Himmelfarb is right to caution against using only the street folk in *London Labour* as a basis for our sense of artistic extension of Mayhew's work, if we add the *Morning Chronicle* articles and *The Criminal Prisons of London,* our sense of the breadth as well as the depth of Mayhew's vision of the lower classes is more justified.

Dickens' tendency to generalize lower-class life creates a different set of difficulties, some of which were seen in the report of his tour with Field. His own ambivalence about the lower classes [36] helped determine his generalized approach. At times this resulted not only in a failure of sympathy as in the low lodging house, but it also is responsible for what Gissing labeled a "misrepresentation of social facts" about the lower classes.[37] Dickens' generalizations can dehumanize the lower classes through either humor or sentimentality. Although we have seen how he counteracts this tendency through symbolic extension, in his journalism his distancing and generalizing devices of whimsy and sentimentality about the lower classes do frequently distort the grimmer realities of slum life as well as project an unpleasant tone of narrative superiority. In a gay scene where the overt and hidden misery is not necessarily relevant, as in "Meditations on Monmouth Street" in the *Sketches,* Dickens' imaginative and whimsical personification literally brings the Old Clothes Exchange to life. The same tone used in the description of a brutal street corner in "Seven Dials" (*Sketches,* pp. 69–73) is both misleading and dehumanizing.

Before the *Morning Chronicle* articles, the Brothers Mayhew [38] had tended toward similar kinds of distortion. The street sellers in *The Greatest Plague in Life* are patronized by humor, and in *Whom to Marry* when the heroine visits a poor seamstress, the woman is a distressed gentlewoman who came to such a pass by marrying beneath her station. Mayhew came to distrust such sentimentality, for experience taught him that reduced gentlefolk were frequently the least "deserving" of the poor (see his remarks in "Answers to Correspondents," 28 January

1851). When Henry and Augustus wrote a novel after their survey of 1849–52, the humor and the sentiment disappear, and the lower classes are particularized in a manner consistent with Mayhew's nonfictional surveys. In *Paved with Gold*,[39] the picture of the lower classes is deliberately anti-sentimental as well as objectively precise in the descriptions of low-life neighborhoods and activities. In the scenes depicting the antics of the crossing sweepers the tone is carefully controlled to prevent the reader from laughing at the boys. Several of the passages are reprinted verbatim from *London Labour* without interrupting the dramatic narrative of the novel. Other scenes, such as that of the market at Farringdon, are simple dramatizations of Mayhew's descriptions in *London Labour*.

Mayhew's experiences also led him to see where Dickens' weakness lay. In 1851, he described the novelist as "one of the most minute and truthful observers" (*LL&LP*, II, 24), but years after he had abandoned his own survey of the poor, he was more discriminating about the novelist's achievement. "If Mr. Dickens had been but wise enough to eschew the fatally-facile trick of sentiment; if he had never written the profound rubbish of 'The Chimes,' nor the fatuous drivel of the 'Cricket on the Hearth,' nor the Adelphi rhodomontade of the 'Tale of Two Cities,' *et id genus,* he would beyond doubt have been as great a literary genius, after his kind—as fine a painter of the broadly marked characteristics of human life and out of the way places—as England has seen for centuries." [40]

Personification and symbol are not the only ways Dickens overcomes the limitations of whimsy and sentimentality. In his novels particularly, Dickens arouses the reader's sympathies for an oppressed class rather than for any individual poor person by his uncompromising attack on the hypocrisy, complacency, and smugness of the middle classes. In *The Chimes* (1844), for example, Trotty Veck, an impoverished porter, and his daughter Meg, a slop seamstress, are both sentimentalized and Trotty is additionally dehumanized through humor. Though Trotty and Meg may have brought tears to the eyes of Dickens' readers, the picture of lower-class life is, as Mayhew said above, "profound rubbish"; nothing brings forward the complicated details of vacant squalor and violence which Mayhew discovered in his interviews for the *Chronicle* series and which many other investigators, including Charles Booth later in the century, verify. *The Chimes* does fully and legitimately engage our concern for Meg and Trotty, however, through Dickens' bitter attack on the impeccable representative of middle-class morality, Alderman Cute (modeled on an actual magistrate: Sir Peter Laurie [41]). Even in *Bleak House,* when we first meet the brickmakers, the most realistic lower-class characters Dickens ever drew, we are more concerned about the ugliness of Mrs. Pardiggle's middle-class philanthropy than about the details of their lives. We come to sympathize with the brutalized male brickmakers, moreover, through their wives, whose maternal feelings are emphasized to assert their symbolic connection with humanity.

Mayhew also found it difficult to sympathize with brutalized lower-class men, but through the detailed "life histories" which emerge from his interviews with them, he succeeds in individualizing and hence humanizing them. By letting a hostile and ignorant cesspool sewerman talk at length, and by repeating what he says, Mayhew manages to portray sympathetically a stupid, threatening, but thoroughly human individual (*LL&LP*, II, 448–49). When taken together, Dickens' brickmakers and Mayhew's sewerman, as well as all the other parallels and analogues in their work, give a picture of lower-class life in mid-century London at once sharply detailed and of extraordinary scope. For this reason Mayhew's articles are an enlightening corollary to Dickens' journalism and novels as well as an impressive achievement in their own right.

Lawrence Frank

"THROUGH A GLASS DARKLY"

Esther Summerson and Bleak House

"You are further to reflect, Mr. Woodcourt . . . that on the numerous difficulties, contingencies, masterly fictions, and forms of procedure in this great cause, there has been expended study, ability, eloquence, knowledge, intellect, Mr. Woodcourt, high intellect. For many years, the—a—I would say the flower of the Bar, and the—a—I would presume to add, the matured autumnal fruits of the Woolsack—have been lavished upon Jarndyce and Jarndyce."—Conversation Kenge

BLEAK HOUSE has attained the status of a classic in the sense in which Frank Kermode speaks of the classic nature of *King Lear*. This is not to equate the two works, but to confront the fact that *Bleak House* asserts a pressure upon the modern imagination which cannot be ignored. The novel, like Shakespeare's play, *survives* through those readings of it which make it comply with what Kermode calls those "paradigmatic requirements for a classic" in our time.[1] Recent changes in the attitudes of modern readers toward Esther Summerson reflect both the pressure the novel asserts and the paradigms we find satisfying. For these reasons Esther's "case" remains, like those of so many others in the novel, in Chancery. The legacy of her written progress has yet to be exhausted by the critics, with all their "study, ability, eloquence, knowledge, intellect." The current, and I think the legitimate, emphasis on Esther's story as a complex psychological study reveals not only the needs of the modern reader, forever in search of such tales to engross his attention, but that element of Dickens' art, his psychological awareness, which seems still to be the least readily accepted part of his achievement. And in a time of sexual politics, we can perceive, in retrospect, the audacity, if not the sheer masculine arrogance, of Dickens' decision to have an illegitimate child, now a woman, tell her own story in her own words. We can agonize over Jane Austen's Fanny Price or Charlotte Brontë's Jane Eyre without feeling the need to deal with this other fact, a male writer trying to imagine himself into the consciousness of an Esther. These concerns become increasingly important as

Esther's responses to the world she encounters, the fictive world of
Bleak House, grow more inadequate, evasive, faintly self-righteous in
their persistent humility and self-negation.

The existence of the double narrative in the novel complicates
matters. Esther may be seen to exist as a foil played off against the verbal and imaginative virtuosity of the present-tense narrator. The presence in the novel of a consciousness so different from Esther's, whether
we call this consciousness Dickens' or the narrator's, serves to emphasize the limitations of Esther's perspective, and the inevitability of such
limitation for every character in the novel. Neither Mr. Bucket nor
Esther, in mounting the high towers of their minds, can imagine the
full complexity of the murky world in which they live. But Esther's
"silent way of noticing what [passes] before" her is peculiarly her own.
The silence which so often accompanies the retelling of her story
suggests, not simply a coyness bordering on the vacuous, but a failure
to understand, a failure not fortuitous, but, in some way, willed. As
early as her first visit to Krook's rag and bottle warehouse, it becomes
clear that Esther's silences create an aura of mystery as important as
any of the mysteries in *Bleak House.* As Krook ticks off the names of the
families involved in Jarndyce and Jarndyce, "the great suit," he men-
tions the name Barbary—and nothing happens. Esther remains dis-
creetly silent. There is no shock of recognition on her part at the mention of the surname of her aunt, the woman who has perhaps done
more to define her being than even the mother whose "disgrace" she is.
Like the letters which the illiterate Krook chalks upon the wall and
then rubs out, leaving each one in a state of isolation and meaningless-
ness, until someone joins them to form the name, Jarndyce, "Barbary"
is left in suspension, unintelligible by itself until some consciousness is
brought to bear on it to give it meaning. Krook's eccentric gesture is
one emblem for the novel as a whole: only at the end will all the mysteries be brought together to reveal a meaning inherent in apparent
chaos. If Esther ignores, consciously or not, the signs which might provide a clue to her identity, she will remain a mystery to herself, and
radically incomplete.

Dickens, as always, understands fully what it means to deny the
past. Lady Dedlock, "bored to death" behind the mask of her acquired
self, undergoes a process of disintegration, of internal combustion, as
fatal as that experienced by any other figure in the novel, including
Captain Hawdon, who has chosen to acknowledge his own annihilation
through the pseudonym, Nemo. Lady Dedlock believes in the story of
the Ghost's Walk because she knows the past inevitably asserts itself.
Like the Lady of Sir Morbury Dedlock whose history she relives, she
never speaks "to any one of being crippled, or of being in pain," but
she is as deeply maimed psychically as her ghostly predecessor was

physically.[2] In part, Esther's silence about the name, Barbary, is her attempt to deny the past, to shut out memories of her aunt's denunciations and bitter resentment. She seeks to bury the past as she buried the doll which was her only real companion in her childhood. But the past cannot be buried, as her aunt's unexpected stroke reveals. With a rather curious innocence, Esther implicitly challenges and condemns her aunt by reading from St. John, "He that is without sin among you, let him first cast a stone at her!" (iii). Miss Barbary's response is her desperate attempt to justify herself, and to warn Esther: "Watch ye therefore! lest coming suddenly he find you sleeping. And what I say unto you, I say unto all, Watch!" (iii). The lines from St. Mark remain forever ambiguous. Perhaps Miss Barbary has been found "sleeping," culpable, in her treatment of Esther. But Esther herself may one day be found "sleeping," under far different circumstances. The ambiguity must be unresolved because Miss Barbary's paralysis becomes her refuge. The years of oppression take their toll; she chooses, or she is reduced to, immobility, and silence.

Dickens is working here, as in other novels, with a full awareness of the psychological predicaments of his characters. Miss Barbary's stroke is rooted in her own response to Esther's muted accusation. It is Dickens' knowledge of such experiences, reinforced by the objectivity potentially inherent in the double narrative, which permits him to maintain, through much of *Bleak House,* a remarkable detachment toward Esther. On that first night in London, as Ada sleeps and Caddy Jellyby rests her head in her lap, Esther's situation becomes clearly defined:

> At length, by slow degrees, they [Ada and Caddy] became indistinct and mingled. I began to lose the identity of the sleeper resting on me. Now it was Ada; now, one of my old Reading friends from whom I could not believe I had so recently parted. Now, it was the little mad woman worn out with curtseying and smiling; now, some one in authority at Bleak House. Lastly, it was no one, and I was no one. (iv)

Esther is not only a social "no one" because of her illegitimacy. She tends to perceive herself as a "no one," and her dilemma is, in part, to become a *some one,* to say, with some kind of confidence and authenticity, either I or Me, as she apparently does in the final pages of the novel. If she fails to define, or redefine, herself in some viable way, she will run the risk of following in the steps of her father, Captain Hawdon, whose sign she encounters in the window of Krook's shop on the morning after her premonitory dream.

John Jarndyce and Bleak House provide Esther with an opportunity to define herself, to create an identity. She accepts the housekeeping keys and the names conferred upon her: Old Woman, Little Old Woman, Cobweb, Mrs. Shipton, Mother Hubbard, Dame Durden.[3] In the process, her "own name soon [becomes] quite lost among them" (viii). She participates in a communal fantasy which, in part, alienates her from herself, from her own name. She is submissive and eager to earn the love of others, on their terms. And she finds comfort in thinking of herself as "a methodical, old-maidish sort of foolish little person" (viii). She seeks to deny or to evade the consequences of her illegitimacy. She fixes herself psychologically in a "time" safely beyond that in which her own mother dealt, unsuccessfully, with the fact of her sexuality. For a Dame Durden, a Little Old Woman, a Mother Hubbard, there seems no threat of another dashing captain's appearing to set in motion a painful reenactment of her mother's fate.[4]

Esther is also trying, however inadequately, to reconcile herself to her own humanity in a more general sense. All people inevitably feel, as Esther feels in her childhood, both "guilty and yet innocent." This has nothing to do with illegitimacy or original sin. In Dickens' greatest novels, there is a full recognition of the ways in which we incur guilt and lose forever our precious innocence. In *David Copperfield*, the young David begins to perceive Annie Strong through the jealous, suspicious eyes of Mr. Wickfield, without at the time being aware that he is doing so. David becomes, however unwittingly, responsible for his misunderstanding of Annie. He is guilty *and* innocent. He has been unknowingly deceived by an adult. But when he becomes aware, later, of what has happened, he must feel that his miscomprehension of Annie Strong has been a subtle violation of her integrity. This is not melodramatic in the way of Esther's illegitimacy, which tends to obscure the fact that, in *Bleak House*, Dickens is always getting at something more than Victorian sexual mores and their inadequacies.

Esther's dilemma is always both psychological and moral. Her "progress" involves Dickens', if not Esther's, emerging recognition that, sinned against as she may be, Esther is not fully the innocent, the victim. Her attempts to cope with herself may involve her, like David, in the violation of others. She must learn to see herself and her situation as clearly as she can in a world permeated by fog, dust, drizzle, and all that obscures one's vision. It is in this context that the verse from I Corinthians becomes so central to the novel: "For now we see through a glass darkly; but then face to face: now I know in part; but then shall I know even as also I am known." Within this novel we rarely know other than in part; we "know," at best, detached, isolated letters which seem to form no intelligible word. We read newspapers in the midst of a "London particular," without understanding what the words mean. We may not know even our own names, our own selves: for "now we see through a glass darkly." There is no assurance we shall ever see "face to face," to know even as one is, presumably, known by God—if there is a God in *Bleak House*.[5]

Dickens suggests the inadequacy of the ways in which Esther chooses to know herself, and to be known by others, through her relationships with Ada and Caddy. She presides over, and is enchanted by, Richard's courtship of Ada. She is at least indirectly responsible for Caddy's marriage to Prince Turveydrop, for the two have met at Miss Flite's, and it is through Esther that Caddy first encounters the mad old woman. She becomes involved, inevitably, in the sufferings of others, especially in those of Ada through whom she tries to realize what she has denied herself. But these developments exist upon the periphery of Esther's story. It is through Esther's relationships to Jo, the illiterate crossing-sweeper, and to Lady Dedlock that Dickens explores more fully her situation and her response to it. The visit to Boythorn's estate, in the company of Ada, Jarndyce, and Skimpole, leads to the inevitable meeting between Esther and Lady Dedlock, and to a series of events culminating in her exposure to the diseased Jo and in her physical disfigurement.

The meeting occurs in the church near Chesney Wold and is introduced as the service begins, " 'Enter not into judgment with thy servant, O Lord, for in thy sight [shall no man living be justified]' " (xviii). The verse from Psalm 143, the explicit reference to "judgment," returns us to the question of innocence and guilt and to that moment when Esther, however unconsciously, had challenged her godmother and precipitated the fatal stroke. As the priest reads, Esther encounters the eyes of the woman who will prove to be her mother:

> Shall I ever forget the rapid beating at my heart, occasioned by the look I met, as I stood up! Shall I ever forget the manner in which those handsome proud eyes seemed to spring out of their languor, and to hold mine! It was only a moment before I cast mine down—released again, if I may say so—on my book, but I knew the beautiful face quite well, in that short space of time.
>
> And, very strangely, there was something quickened within me, associated with the lonely days at my godmother's; yes, away even to the days when I had stood on tiptoe to dress myself at my little glass, after dressing my doll. And this, although I had never seen this lady's face before in all my life—I was quite sure of it—absolutely certain. (xviii)

What Esther sees, of course, is a version of her own face. She "knows" the beautiful face as Guppy knew the portrait of Lady Dedlock: " 'I'm dashed!' adds Mr. Guppy . . . , 'if I don't think I must have had a dream of that picture, you know!' " (vii). Esther is thrust back into the

past, to her godmother's house, to her doll and to herself on tiptoe
before her "little glass." It is a moment in time when she first sees herself in a mirror and becomes self-conscious. What Esther has seen in
the mirror is not just a reflection of herself; rather, it is a vision of herself deeply rooted in her godmother's conception of her. Her vision of
herself, even the reflection, is mediated by Miss Barbary's perception of
the child. And Esther wills to be something quite different: good, industrious, contented. It is the image of herself by which she tries to
live, in order to make life possible. But it is an image, however "good,"
conditioned by the inescapable shadow of her illegitimacy. Hers is a self
founded upon a twisted definition of innocence and guilt, and as such
it is false.

In Lady Dedlock she sees a reflection of her own face quite different from the face of one set apart by a nameless disgrace (she cannot
know that Lady Dedlock is, in fact, secretly set apart as much as she).
Esther encounters a potentiality quite beyond that she has imagined for
herself. That beautiful face becomes, "in a confused way, like a broken
glass" to Esther in which she sees "scraps of old remembrances." She
thinks, appropriately, of the broken glass. The fragments of her unin-
tegrated past are assembling themselves mysteriously before her. The
impact of Lady Dedlock's appearance is so disorienting that Esther
ceases to hear the reader's voice: instead, she hears "the well-remem-
bered voice of [her] godmother." And she links Lady Dedlock's face to
that of the dead woman whom Esther thinks of, throughout this
sequence, not as her aunt, but as her godmother, as if to deny any real
relationship to her. But the broken glass refers to the present, as well as
to the past: Esther's image of herself has failed her as it has once before
in the dream in which she became "no one."

As she dwells upon the way in which Lady Dedlock has magically
evoked her childhood self "before [her] own eyes," Esther gradually
becomes aware of the gaze of the French maid, Hortense. Dickens
reveals in a stroke that curious triad for which he has already prepared.
Hortense has been introduced as "a very neat She-Wolf imperfectly
tamed," with "something indefinably keen and wan about her anatomy"
(xii). And, through the imagery of the glass, a special relationship between Hortense and Lady Dedlock emerges, a relationship Lady Dedlock tries to deny:

> One night, while having her hair undressed, my Lady loses
> herself in deep thought . . . , until she sees her own brooding
> face in the opposite glass, and a pair of black eyes curiously ob-
> serving her.
> "Be so good as to attend," says my Lady then, addressing the
> reflection of Hortense, "to your business. You can contemplate
> your beauty at another time."

"Pardon! It was your Ladyship's beauty!"
"That," says my Lady, "you needn't contemplate at all." (xii)

The juxtaposition of Lady Dedlock's brooding face and Hortense's black eyes connects the two by contiguity alone. But Lady Dedlock has already disguised herself in her maid's cloak to visit Captain Hawdon's grave. The fusion of the two women is more or less complete. Whatever Lady Dedlock has suppressed by falling into a "freezing mood," as her sister fell into the frozen immobility of paralysis, still exists within her, projected, however melodramatically, in the form of Hortense. The scene anticipates that in *A Tale of Two Cities* when Charles Darnay glances up at the "glass" fixed above the prisoner's box in the Old Bailey: it is like gazing into the ocean which is "one day to give up its dead" (II, ii). The mirror does not simply reflect; it offers a glimpse into the self's depths. What Lady Dedlock sees are those eyes which always lurk within the depths of her habitually languid gaze. She characteristically rebuffs the Provence-bred Hortense and that teeming, fecund world for which Provence traditionally stands in British fiction.

The triangular configuration Dickens has so deftly forged continues to haunt Esther during this visit to Boythorn's and through other episodes in *Bleak House*. For when she, with Ada and Jarndyce, takes refuge from the sudden storm in the keeper's lodge on the edge of Chesney Wold, Esther undergoes a further reconfirmation of all the possibilities which the appearance of Lady Dedlock has already raised. The voice which warns the girls not to sit near the window, "in so exposed a place," is Lady Dedlock's, not Esther's. But Ada, responding not only to the concern in the words, but to a familiar tone, turns to Esther, and the "beating of [Esther's] heart [comes] back again": "I had never heard the voice, as I had never seen the face, but it affected me in the same strange way. Again, in a moment, there arose before my mind innumerable pictures of myself" (xviii). Esther confronts, if not the intuition that this stern and beautiful woman is her mother, at least the sense that they are not so unlike. The "innumerable pictures" of herself which occur in her imagination suggest a world of possibilities as well as the swirl of remembered moments. And to initiate her further into the ambiguous energies and potentialities within herself and others, Esther is left, as the episode ends, with an unforgettable sight: the enraged Hortense, spurned by Lady Dedlock, removes her shoes and walks toward Chesney Wold, "through the wettest of the wet grass"; which, someone speculates, she fancies is blood:

We passed not far from the House, a few minutes afterwards. Peaceful as it had looked when we first saw it, it looked even more so now, with a diamond spray glittering all about it, a light wind blowing, the birds no longer hushed but singing

strongly, everything refreshed by the late rain, and the little
carriage shining at the doorway like a fairy carriage made of
silver. Still, very steadfastly and quietly walking towards it, a
peaceful figure too in the landscape, went Mademoiselle Hortense, shoeless, through the wet grass. (xviii)

Chesney Wold, its enchanted world and the people fortunate enough
to inhabit it become fragile, delicate artifacts totally vulnerable to the
implacable juggernaut moving toward them. Esther has been introduced to forces which have no place in *her* world, or so she thinks.
Soon, she will, however mistakenly, become identified with these forces.
She will have to deal with their implications for her own life.

Hortense's attempt to offer her services to Esther as her "domestic" is, in part, a suggestion that the energies Hortense possesses either
exist in some form within Esther or that they may be conferred upon
her magically through some proximity to the Frenchwoman. But
Esther, true to her version of herself, recoils, especially from the ardor
which Hortense so clearly possesses. Madame Defarge already exists
within Esther's response to the maid: she "seemed to bring visibly before me some woman from the streets of Paris in the reign of terror"
(xxiii). Esther's response to Lady Dedlock remains more ambiguous
and complex: it involves admiration, fear and yearning, a yearning
based on the "fancy . . . that what this lady so curiously was to me, I
was to her—I mean that I disturbed her thoughts as she influenced
mine, though in some different way" (xxiii).

The three women become inextricably joined, in Esther's imagination and in the shape of the novel itself, when Jo and Esther finally
meet at St. Albans. Jo has come from London in search of Jenny, the
other woman in whose clothes Lady Dedlock will finally disguise herself. What happens in this meeting involves more than the inescapable
taint of the disease which emanates from Tom-all-Alone's and the cem-
etery where Nemo is buried. The night is stormy, toward London "a
lurid glare [overhangs] the whole dark waste"; and as she proceeds
toward the brickmakers' cottage, Esther has, "for a moment an un-
definable impression of [herself] as being something different from
what [she] then was" (xxxi). Her impression, her vague sense of her
inauthentic condition, is only confirmed by Jo's apparently delirious
response to her. The boy has already seen both Lady Dedlock,
disguised in her maid's cloak, and later Hortense herself in Tulkinghorn's chambers. He at first mistakes the veiled Esther for the "t'other
lady" he has led to the "berryin ground." Even after Esther raises her
veil and Jenny seeks to assure him that this is *her* lady standing before
them, Jo remains unconvinced: "She looks to me the t'other one. It
ain't the bonnet, nor yet it ain't the gownd, but she looks to me the

t'other one." Jo's doubt, in the face of the assurances of Jenny and Charley, simply cannot be dispelled. At last, he makes the connection which is the most disturbing of all: "Then he hoarsely whispered Charley. 'If she ain't the t'other one, she ain't the forrenner. Is there *three* of 'em then?' Charley looked at me a little frightened. I felt half frightened at myself when the boy glared on me so" (xxxi). The connection between Lady Dedlock, Hortense, and Esther has become inescapable.

Jo's confusion only mirrors Esther's own sense of her being different from what she has, until now, thought herself to be. To be mistaken for a Lady Dedlock or a Hortense is to be seen in some way as like them. It is not a question of how much Esther "knows" at this point in the novel, the extent to which she associates herself, in her own consciousness, with these two women. Dickens has asserted, through plot and language, a relationship. Its full meaning may at best be working within Esther in an inarticulable way. But the moorings of her old self have been cut loose upon this stormy, disorienting night. Esther must begin to live with the possibility that, metaphorically, Jo is right: there are *"three* of 'em then," floating somewhere behind the veil of Esther's public self.

The illness which follows is the natural consequence of the dilemma Esther now faces. The identity of Dame Durden no longer protects her from the complexities into which she has been pushed. She is responsible for Jo without having known him. On one level the responsibility is clearly social: no one can legitimately claim to be innocent of the horrors of Tom-all-Alone's which touch every one. But social guilt is only one element of the illness which follows. As Esther herself remarks, "It may be that if we knew more of such strange afflictions, we might be the better able to alleviate their intensity" (xxxv)—curious words to use in speaking of smallpox, but not at all inappropriate for the spiritual and psychological affliction which is Esther's. The first stage of her travail is marked by blindness. In a novel obsessed with the interpretation of signs, blindness, like the illiteracy of Krook and Jo, is hardly the result of pure contingency.[6] Jo shuffles through the streets of London "in utter darkness as to the meaning, of those mysterious symbols, so abundant over the shops, and at the corners of streets, and on the doors, and in the windows!" (xvi). He is "stone blind and dumb" to the language of the written word. But Esther, too, has been accosted by "mysterious symbols"; she sinks into blindness through her inability, or her unwillingness, to "see": to decipher and give meaning to the signs which threaten her.

Esther's blindness is a prelude to a sense of disorientation and her attempt to deal with everything she has so recently experienced. She has, in the broadest terms, been confronted with the terrible complexities of being human, complexities which transcend the fact of her ille-

gitimacy. Her sexuality and her relatedness to others are involved. In
her delirium, the "stages of [her] life" become confused and mingled
"on the healthy shore," while she is separated from them by "a dark
lake":

> At once a child, an elder girl, and the little woman I had been
> so happy as, I was not only oppressed by cares and difficulties
> adapted to each station, but by the great perplexity of endlessly
> trying to reconcile them. I suppose that few who have not been
> in such a condition can quite understand what I mean, or what
> painful unrest arose from this source. (xxxv)

Esther has lost a sense of unified being, and with it her usual relation to
time.[7] She perceives herself in fragments. Like the pieces of a shattered
glass, each fragment mirrors back to her disparate and incompatible
images of herself. She is in pieces. The fragile self she has created, with
the help of Jarndyce, Ada, and Richard, has momentarily ceased to be,
broken by its contact with the very realities it was designed to evade. If
she accepts the shattering of herself and the need to forge a new identity, Esther risks immersion in the world of sexuality, social injustice,
and victimization inhabited by Lady Dedlock, Hortense, and Jo. This is
both dangerous and frightening. It would also involve an act of disloy-
alty. To cease to be Dame Durden is a betrayal, implicitly, of the community which has sustained that identity through a mutual effort. And
the community of Bleak House is comprised of all those for whom she
most deeply cares. If the re-creation of herself in new terms seems impossible, her present state of disunity offers no viable alternative: it is
non-being.

Esther's impasse is at the center of her "disorder"; it is revealed in
the frustrated yearnings for rebirth: "it seemed one long night . . . I
laboured up colossal staircases, ever striving to reach the top, and ever
turned, as I have seen a worm in a garden path, by some obstruction,
and labouring again." This almost De Quinceian "labour" which does
not fulfill itself in birth leads Esther to that "worse time when, strung
together somewhere in great black space, there was a flaming necklace,
or ring, or starry circle of some kind, of which *I* was one of the beads!
And when my only prayer was to be taken off from the rest, and when
it was such inexplicable agony and misery to be a part of the dreadful
thing" (xxxv). The passage is unique in Dickens' novels. There is no
other place in which Dickens so completely expresses what we would
call both religious and existential despair. Esther's prayer "to be taken
off from the rest" is her denial of herself and the chain of interconnect-
edness which comprises the human condition. She wishes to escape
from the incongruities inherent in her own humanity. There is the in-

justice of her illegitimate birth. There is the inevitable loss of innocence which occurs as one moves from childhood to adulthood. There is the unbearable fact that one's fate is joined, however mysteriously, with the fates of others. Esther is incapable of experiencing, at this point in the novel, the kind of acceptance of herself embodied in this account of a woman, also illegitimate, which appears in *Existence:*

> I remember walking that day under the elevated tracks in a slum area, feeling the thought, "I am an illegitimate child." I recall the sweat pouring forth in my anguish in trying to accept that fact. Then I understood what it must feel like to accept, "I am a Negro in the midst of privileged whites," or "I am blind in the midst of people who see." Later on that night I woke up and it came to me this way, "I accept the fact that I am an illegitimate child." *But* "I am not a child anymore." So it is, "I am illegitimate." That is not so either: "I was born illegitimate." Then what is left? What is left is this, *"I Am."* This *act* of contact and acceptance with "I am," once gotten hold of, gave me (what I think was for me the first time) the experience "Since I Am, I have the right to be." [8]

In the case of this woman, as in Esther's, the fact of illegitimacy is fundamentally metaphorical: it poses the question of every one's "right to be." The woman whose story appears in *Existence* unravels the contradictions in her conception of herself and comes to a moment of affirmation. Esther only wants to escape the contradictions which plague her. When she awakens from *her* long night, she has failed to change significantly her idea of herself. She has been unable to accept the "flaming necklace" or "starry circle" of which she is a part.

Esther seeks, in short, a simplification of the human condition. She accepts what she calls her "altered self" because it seems to offer the security she knew as Dame Durden. The absent mirrors do not go unnoticed. But when Esther speaks to Charley there is a curious ambiguity in her question: " 'Yet, Charley,' said I, looking round, 'I miss something, surely, that I am accustomed to?' " (xxxv). She can live without the "old face" which has marked her resemblance to Lady Dedlock, or so she thinks. Perhaps she can even live without her love for Allan Woodcourt. But to do this she must think of the past, of the "childish prayer of that old birthday, when [she] had aspired to be industrious, contented, and true-hearted, and to do good to some one, and win some love to [herself] if [she] could" (xxv). She repeats the prayer in an effort to fix herself, once again, in a state beyond temptation, a state which in some way will reconcile "the various stages of [her] life" and protect her from the shame of her unknown mother and from the ambiguous power embodied both in Lady Dedlock and Hortense. She acquiesces to the "old conspiracy to make [her] happy."

Esther knows that she has undergone some physical change. But it is only when she arrives at Boythorn's in Lincolnshire that she has the courage, finally, to look into the glass and face her altered self:

> My hair had not been cut off, though it had been in danger more than once. It was long and thick. I let it down, and shook it out, and went up to the glass upon the dressing-table. There was a little muslin curtain drawn across it. I drew it back: and stood for a moment looking through such a veil of my own hair, that I could see nothing else. Then I put my hair aside, and looked at the reflection in the mirror; encouraged by seeing how placidly it looked at me. I was very much changed— O very, very much. At first, my face was so strange to me, that I think I should have put my hands before it and started back, but for the encouragement [of Jarndyce and the others] I have mentioned. (xxvi)

Esther moves through a number of veils, that of the muslin curtain and the veil of her own hair, toward a view of her "self" in the glass, a self which seems to look autonomously back at her. It is a moment of discovery echoing moments in the past, foreshadowing others in the future. It repeats her childhood emergence into self-consciousness when she first saw her face in her "little glass . . . after dressing." It calls up that moment in the church when Esther first sees Lady Dedlock and Hortense. Even poor Jo's surprise and terror at the sight of the veiled, and unveiled, Esther are evoked as Esther sees herself, however darkly, in the glass. All the characters in *Bleak House* are veiled, to some extent, to others and themselves. The muslin curtain and the dark hair through which Esther moves suggest levels of ignorance. The image she sees may be but another veil, another reflection floating upon the surface of the depths which Esther chooses not to plumb. She has not yet seen herself face to face: perhaps she only does so later in the novel when she pulls aside the "long dank hair" which veils the features of her dead mother.

Gradually the face before Esther ceases to be strange: "very soon it became more familiar." Esther pieces herself together by accepting the face from which she originally recoils. She submits to her godmother's notion of her as someone tainted, to Jarndyce's notion of her as the "little housewife." She chooses to diminish herself through this "new" identity, altered, scarred, desexualized. She feels a sense of loss. Her muted, "I had never been a beauty, and had never thought myself one; but I had been very different from this," and her allusion to Allan Woodcourt's flowers reveal, in Esther's perhaps too quiet way, the pro-

test rising within her. But disfigurement, real or imagined, offers a
sanctuary, even if an illusory one, from the agonies of the flaming
necklace. Esther ceases to be a "perfect likeness" of Lady Dedlock, as
her visit to Guppy will prove. No one will be able, apparently, to connect the two of them. When Lady Dedlock acknowledges her and ful-
fills something the girl has "pined for and dreamed of . . . [as] a little
child," Esther feels "a burst of gratitude to the providence of God that
I was so changed as that I never could disgrace her by any trace of likeness; as that nobody could ever now look at me, and look at her [as
Hortense has done], and remotely think of any near tie between us"
(xxxvi). Esther's gratitude is double-edged, to say the least. The tie
binding the two, and seemingly sundered by Esther's illness, reaches
beyond that between mother and daughter. The relinquished likeness
is a relinquished potentiality. Esther will never encounter the situation
which led to her mother's love for Captain Hawdon and her own birth.
She will never be humbled, as Lady Dedlock so gratifyingly is, before
the living embodiment of a past indiscretion.

Esther's "strange affliction" becomes a denial both of her mother
and herself. Her forgiveness of her mother is a terrible rebuke: "I told
her that my heart overflowed with love for her, . . . [that] it was not
for me, then resting for the first time on my mother's bosom, to take
her to account for having given me life; but that my duty was to bless
her and receive her, though the whole world turned from her" (xxxvi).
How deftly the knife is turned in the wound! Esther's words to Lady
Dedlock are full of Victorian rectitude. They are as suspect as the hauteur in Lady Dedlock's denial to Jo's innocent query, " 'You didn't
know him [Nemo], did you?' " (xvi). Dickens has captured the mother,
and the daughter, in situations which expose the radical dishonesty of
their lives. Lady Dedlock denies that she has known the dead law-writer. Esther implicitly denies her mother. Each response is morally and
psychologically untenable. And Esther's sense of worthlessness and fear
reveals how difficult it will be for her to live with the knowledge she now
possesses. Lady Dedlock's letter to Esther undermines completely whatever "right to be" Esther has ever possessed: "I had never, to my own
mother's knowledge, breathed—had been buried—had never been endowed with life—had never borne a name" (xxxvi). Had never *been*.
Esther is once again momentarily nameless, a no one, like Nemo; she
weeps "afresh to think [she is] back in the world, with [her] load of
trouble for others." No wonder that, as she walks near Chesney Wold
and the Ghost's Walk, she imagines her echoing footsteps are those of
the legendary ghost and that she runs, in terror, from herself and "everything."

Esther runs, of course, to Bleak House and to Jarndyce and Ada.
She returns to her former role as Dame Durden and to her curious

relationship with Ada, through whom she seems willing to live. But none of this is ever really satisfactory, for us, for Dickens, even for Esther, who remains far more knowing than even she is willing to admit.

> It matters little now, how much I thought of my living mother who had told me evermore to consider her dead. I could not venture to approach her, or to communicate with her in writing, for my sense of the peril in which her life was passed was only to be equalled by my fears of increasing it. Knowing that my mere existence as a living creature was an unforeseen danger in her way, I could not always conquer that terror of myself which had seized me when I first knew the secret. At no time did I dare to utter her name. I felt as if I did not even dare to hear it. If the conversation anywhere, when I was present, took that direction, as it sometimes naturally did, I tried not to hear—I mentally counted, repeated something that I knew, or went out of the room. I am conscious, now, that I often did these things when there can have been no danger of her being spoken of. (xliii)

In retrospect it may matter little. But *then* it mattered a great deal. Nor is it simply the melodramatic plight of Lady Dedlock which is central. Rather, it is that Esther dares not to utter her mother's name, dares not even to hear it. And if it were possible, she would perhaps choose not even to think it. She resorts to a device which will drive "Lady Dedlock" out of her very consciousness. Perhaps the "something" that she knew which she repeats is Dame Durden, Dame Durden, Dame Durden. She remains in full flight from her mother and herself. To make the flight complete, to consolidate her loss into something permanent and irreversible, for the loss involves, really, a state of mind or being, she accepts John Jarndyce's proposal, knowing that in this act she is being untrue to herself.

Esther commits herself to John Jarndyce not out of love, or passion, but out of gratitude; she is aware that she will "become the dear companion of his remaining life" (xliv). She chooses to acquiesce once more to that "conspiracy" to make her happy which has in it the element of coercion which even Esther can detect. But her decision to marry Jarndyce is, finally, her own doing. She is repeating her mother's fateful, and fatal, decision to marry Sir Leicester Dedlock. Esther will fall into her own version of a "freezing mood," a condition of stasis only apparently beyond the realities of time and change, innocence and guilt. As she reads Jarndyce's letter of proposal, Esther girds herself for the "one thing to do":

Still, I cried very much; not only in the fulness of my heart
after reading the letter, not only in the strangeness of the prospect—for it was strange though I had expected the contents—
but as if something for which there was no name or distinct
idea were indefinitely lost to me. I was very happy, very thank-
ful, very hopeful; but I cried very much. (xliv)

This is quintessential Esther. But it reveals not just the enduring, self-
negating touchstone of goodness, but a woman who is relinquishing
something, however threatening to her, of real value, the opportunity
for passion in her life. Esther's choice leads to the almost ghoulish act
in which she kisses the sleeping Ada and presses Allan Woodcourt's
withered flowers to Ada's lips before she burns them and they turn to
dust: the same kind of "dust" existing within the combusting selves of
so many in the novel. She will sacrifice her own legitimate desire for
self-fulfillment and live vicariously through Ada and Richard. But even
this morbid act of self-sacrifice occurs only after Esther has conducted a
curious dialogue with herself in her "old glass." She talks to her reflected face, even holds up her finger at it, in her determination to re-
establish that "composed look you [the face in the glass] comforted me
with, my dear, when you showed me such a change!" (xliv). She gazes
at a Medusa's head, her own scarred face, and turns herself to stone, as
her mother and her dead aunt have done before her.

Dickens knows very well that this will not do, for a number of
reasons. Apart from that Victorian commitment to the satisfying happy
ending, there is in Dickens' imagination a streak of integrity which
modern readers continue to underestimate or to ignore. It is this integrity and the equally fierce will to overcome the very paradoxes he has
posed which generate the fixated structures in so many of Dickens'
novels, both early and late. Time and again we see a hero or heroine
reenacting the same experience or a slightly transmuted version of it.
This is true of the early *Oliver Twist,* of *David Copperfield,* even of the
last completed novel, *Our Mutual Friend.* The novels begin with a paradox, recurrently involving someone burdened with that confused sense
of innocence and guilt, inextricably combined. The novels proceed to
unravel the very Gordian knot which, by definition, seems impervious
even to the sword of Dickens' imagination. *Oliver Twist* deals obsessively
with the fact that Oliver's birth is inseparably connected with his
mother's death, and that Oliver's genteel aspirations, however legitimate, entail the destruction of Nancy, Sikes, and Fagin who preside
over Oliver's final resurrection into the Brownlow world of unassailable
bourgeois respectability. This almost naïve persistence in grappling
with the unresolvable lies at the center of *David Copperfield* as David returns again and again to the experiences of his childhood, finally to

emerge successful, famous, and married to Agnes. The sea changes which John Harmon chooses to undergo in *Our Mutual Friend* are designed to free him from the temptation posed by his father's will, a temptation to become forever implicated in, and compromised by, the Harmon fortune, built upon the dust mounds. Much of *Our Mutual Friend* deals with Harmon's earning, however dubiously, both Bella Wilfer and his father's money through a series of rebirths modeled on the paradigmatic rebirths of Oliver Twist and David Copperfield.

In *Bleak House* Esther's acceptance of John Jarndyce's proposal is her attempt to deal with the old Dickensian paradox. But her meeting with the returned Allan Woodcourt illustrates how intolerable her situation has become. By now Esther is all too clearly in dialogue, not with herself, but with a "self" conjured up by her own imagination and designed to obliterate the traces of the past. But, however earnestly she may address the Esther in the mirror, the old longings return: "I saw that he was very sorry for me. I was glad to see it. I felt for my old self as the dead may feel if they ever revisit these scenes. I was glad to be tenderly remembered, to be gently pitied, not to be quite forgotten" (xlv). Esther sees, in part, what she wishes to see in Allan Woodcourt's manner; she reads the signs and tokens he presents to confirm the wiseness of her decision and to keep her "old self" down. But that self is not dead: it exists beyond the face she sees in her glass, and even in the eyes of others who are equally mirrors of herself. Like the ghost of the Ghost's Walk, its footsteps can be heard in Esther's consciousness and the consciousness of others. The willed "deadness" which Esther as Dame Durden feels must be confronted and dispelled. If not, it will become a permanent condition: she will be no less a "sleeping beauty" than her mother, Lady Dedlock.

The concluding episodes of the novel represent Dickens' efforts to resolve the impasse, to sever the Gordian knot he has himself so deftly tied. Through Sir Leicester Dedlock's stroke and the pursuit of Lady Dedlock by Esther and Inspector Bucket, Dickens seeks to resolve Esther's situation. Sir Leicester's continued loyalty to his wife, even after he has been felled by the news of her past and reduced to almost total silence, plays off revealingly against Esther's response to her mother. For he accepts and acknowledges his wife, as she is, in the presence of witnesses: " 'in case I should not recover, in case I should lose both my speech and the power of writing, . . . I desire to say, and to call you all to witness . . . that I am on unaltered terms with Lady Dedlock. That I assert no cause whatever of complaint against her. . . . Say this to herself, and to every one' " (lviii). It is a noble gesture, and a sincere one. There is no note of reproach as there has been in Esther's response to her mother. Sir Leicester's compassion reminds us of Esther's failure to accept her mother and herself.

So Esther and Bucket move through the snow into which the stricken Sir Leicester stares, "the giddy whirl of white flakes and icy blots," which suggests the ultimate inscrutability of the world in which these characters find themselves. Her previous illness, an abortive Carlylean "Baphometic Fire-baptism," has not produced a "Spiritual New-birth." The earlier experiences are reenacted: but this time the process of rebirth involves the more traditional baptismal process of immersion. The disorientation through which Esther passed during her "fever-paroxysms" returns. As she rides with Bucket, she feels that she is in a dream, that she is entering the labyrinthine world of streets, bridges, and serpentining river which is as much internal as external. She is losing herself once more, descending into a world in which she may again encounter the ambiguous self she has relinquished or finally succeed in exorcising its presence forever.

The "something wet" which Bucket and another man, "dark and muddy, in long swollen sodden boots and a hat like them" (lvii), inspect proves not to be the body of a drowned Lady Dedlock. But Esther continues to fear, and perhaps to hope, that the tide in its rush toward her will "cast [her] mother at the horses' feet." In her dreamlike state Esther's identification with her mother is now so complete that even the "shadowy female figure" which flits past the carriage is as much herself as Lady Dedlock:

> The river had a fearful look, so overcast and secret, creeping away so fast between the low flat lines of shore: so heavy with indistinct and awful shapes, both of substance and shadow: so deathlike and mysterious. . . . In my memory, the lights upon the bridge are always burning dim; the cutting wind is eddying round the homeless woman whom we pass; the monotonous wheels are whirling on; and the light of the carriage-lamps reflected back, looks palely in upon me—a face, rising out of the dreaded water. (lvii)

But whose face rises out of the water? The entire sequence is constructed upon the logic of dreams. Esther, Lady Dedlock, and the homeless prostitute are one. In this phantasmagoric setting, Esther gazes into the night, the water, or both, and looks into a watery mirror out of which rises not her mother's face, but her own: the face of that unquiet ghost which has not been charmed by the spell Esther has tried so vainly to cast upon it.

Dickens has transported Esther back into the past, to earlier events with which she has not come to terms. She is returned to the brick-maker's cottage and Jo's unnerving query: " 'If she ain't the t'other one,

she ain't the forrenner. Is there *three* of 'em then?' " (xxxi). Verbal parallels to Jo's words occur throughout the events following Tulkinghorn's murder. The arrested George Rouncewell recalls that on the
night of the murder " ' [he] saw a shape so like Miss Summerson's go by
[him] in the dark, that [he] had half a mind to speak to it' " (lii). Esther
shudders at George's words: she thinks at once of Lady Dedlock.
Within the larger structure of the novel, beyond Esther's consciousness,
we see that, metaphorically, all three women—Esther, Lady Dedlock,
and Hortense—are placed at the scene of the crime. George's observation becomes but another sign or token to be understood before the
mysteries of Tulkinghorn's murder and Esther's identity can be fully
resolved. When Esther and Bucket arrive at the brickmaker's cottage,
they learn, in the words of Jenny's husband, that " 'one went right to
Lunnun, and t'other went right from it.' " Once again words are
spoken which echo those of Jo. The former confusion of identities is
reinforced. Esther is back at the moment when she first *must* have perceived, however darkly, the implications of her similarity to Lady Dedlock and Hortense. The old triad reasserts itself once more, as it did
when Esther gazed from the carriage window at the "homeless woman"
in the dark. Esther and Lady Dedlock are fixed into an apparently eternal configuration, of which they are the two constants; only the third
term alters: first Hortense, then the homeless woman of the streets,
now Jenny.

Under the pressure of these most recent events, Esther retraces
more and more closely the course of her earlier illness. She is blind to
the signs at which Bucket so eagerly grasps. She begins to lose her
sense of time and feels, "in a strange way, never to have been free from
the anxiety under which [she] then [labours]" (lvii). But on this occasion
the psychic laboring is designed to bring forth a more legitimate off-
spring. Esther has begun to be able to think of her mother, even if in
death, and to speak of her, even if only in a whisper to Inspector
Bucket. She is moving toward a gesture of loyalty and acceptance like
that Sir Leicester Dedlock has made, in the presence of witnesses.
Esther's moment of what should be authentic rebirth approaches. As it
does, the falling snow continues to melt and find its way into the moving carriage: the wetness penetrates her dress. Esther and Bucket de-
scend further into "a deeper complication" of the "narrowest and worst
streets in London" (lix), moving inexorably toward Nemo's grave and
Lady Dedlock.

The rhythms of Esther's previous suffering have come finally to
dominate Dickens' imaginative conception of the search for Lady Dedlock. Once the parallels between these two critical episodes in Esther's
life become established, Bucket's lecture to the near-maddened Mrs.
Snagsby becomes curiously inevitable: "And Toughey—him as you call

Jo—was mixed up in the same business, and no other; and the law-writer that you know of, was mixed up in the same business, and no other; and your husband, with no more knowledge of it than your great-grandfather, was mixed up (by Mr. Tulkinghorn, deceased, his best customer) in the same business, and no other; and the whole bile-ing up of people was mixed up in the same business, and no other" (lix). Bucket's prosaic litany, with its persistent refrain, "the same business, and no other," takes us, and Esther, back to that "flaming neck-lace, or ring, or starry circle of some kind, of which [she] was one of the beads!" Bucket's matter-of-factness, his wry acceptance of the unthink-able, makes it all too clear that no one can cease to be "a part of the dreadful thing." No process of physical or psychic disfigurement can free an individual, even an Esther, from her participation, "with no more knowledge of it than [her] great-grandfather," in this same busi-ness, and no other. The only viable response to this predicament, though it need not be like Bucket's too easy professional acceptance, is one's immersion into the world of *Bleak House.*

As she approaches the figure of the woman lying before the gate to the burial ground, in which her father's body has been placed, Esther experiences not just the melting, and dissolution, which her mother has undergone since the disclosure of the great secret. Esther melts within herself. She remembers "that the stained house fronts put on human shapes and looked at [her]; that great water-gates seemed to be open-ing and closing in [her] head, or in the air; and that the unreal things were more substantial than the real" (lix). The unreal *is* more substan-tial than the real. The "clogged and bursting gutters and water-spouts" are within: her state of mind, associated with the breaking of the wa-ters, is the real truth of this moment. The fixed and frozen waters of the self break apart, melt: the waters within her flow once more. The tide of the river rushes at her, to deliver the body of her mother at her feet: "I passed on to the gate, and stooped down. I lifted the heavy head, put the long dank hair aside, and turned the face. And it was my mother cold and dead" (lix).

The death of Lady Dedlock is, of course, unsatisfactory in many ways. Esther's inability to understand that it is *not* "Jenny, the mother of the dead child," before the graveyard gate pushes the irony almost too far, though it may accurately reflect Esther's unwillingness to know and to experience the truth fully. The death seems also to reflect too readily the Victorian notion that this is the only satisfactory punish-ment for the sin that Lady Dedlock has committed. But Dickens, through Nemo, Krook, Tulkinghorn, Miss Barbary, and others, has as-serted throughout the novel that certain ways of being constitute a cor-rosive death-in-life which can lead to literal death. Lady Dedlock has lived too long with her secret, with her bored and emptied self, to survive. But what is most disquieting is that Esther comes face to face with her mother only in death; she sees her, in the presence of witnesses, only after her mother is no longer the kind of threat a living Lady Dedlock poses. When Esther pulls aside the veil of hair, as she once pulled aside her own hair before the mirror, to see that the heavy head is *not* Jenny's, the moment seems emptied of its full meaning. Cold and dead, no longer passionate, haughty, and alive, Lady Dedlock offers nothing really dangerous to encounter. And, in dying for her own sins, she seems also to atone for those which have accrued to Esther as an essentially innocent participant in the "dreadful thing" that is the human condition.

The endings of Dickens' novels are rarely satisfactory. Inseparable from that imaginative integrity which I have mentioned there is in Dickens that equally powerful desire to eradicate much that his novels so effectively dramatize. No honest reader can be really comfortable with the concluding pages of *Bleak House.* Esther's marriage to Allan Woodcourt, their retreat to a virtual reproduction of the original Bleak House are, I think, discordant notes in the novel. But there is evidence that Dickens himself is aware of the falseness of the ending and works to emphasize the arbitrariness of it. For Esther's happiness is achieved in the midst of general misery. Richard Carstone dies. Ada becomes the captive of Jarndyce's coercive benevolence. Caddy Jellyby's [*sic*] baby is deaf and dumb, her husband an invalid. Even Mrs. Snagsby's jealousy reminds us that marriage is no final answer to the human capacity for the irrational: there will always be Mrs. Snagsbys convinced of their husbands' infidelities—and there will always be, in fact, unfaithful husbands and unfaithful lovers.

The double narrative itself helps us to retain a complex awareness of things. A final description of Chesney Wold precedes Esther's final words about herself and her felicity:

> Thus Chesney Wold. With so much of itself abandoned to darkness and vacancy; with so little change under the summer shining or the wintry lowering; so sombre and motionless always—no flag flying now by day, no rows of lights sparkling by night; with no family to come and go, no visitors to be the souls of pale cold shapes of rooms, no stir of life about it;—passion and pride, even to the stranger's eyes, have died away from the place in Lincolnshire, and yielded it to dull repose. (lxvi)

It is a place inhabited by invalids with blighted dreams, an asylum for those who cannot deal with the new hell that Mr. Rouncewell, the ironmaster, is now creating to replace the hell of the dying aristocracy. "Thus Chesney Wold." Thus Bleak House in Yorkshire. Perhaps Allan

Woodcourt and Esther, surrounded by the blighted lives of their friends, are no less refugees from an alien world than are Volumnia, Mrs. Rouncewell, George, and Sir Leicester.

Bleak House ends, as it begins, in ambiguity. Esther seems to have gained the "right to be." She observes, "the people even praise Me as the doctor's wife. The people even like Me as I go about, and make so much of me that I am quite abashed" (lxvii). Esther seems at last to possess an identity, even if it is primarily that of "the doctor's wife." And, yet, this gentle affirmation is not the conclusion of Esther's narrative. Rather, Esther finds herself before her "glass," puzzling over the image that is reflected there:

> "My dear Dame Durden," said Allan, drawing my arm through his, "do you ever look in the glass?"
> "You know I do; you see me do it."
> "And don't you know that you are prettier than you ever were?"
> I did not know that. I am not certain that I know it now. (lxvii)

This is not simply Esther at her self-abasing worst. There is no reason to assume that the face she sees "now" in her glass is any more herself than the altered face which met her eyes after her illness. She lives in a relationship to that image of herself which she perceives in her glass, in her imagination, in the eyes of others. But that the image is truly herself can never be known. Even the words of others cannot be fully trusted. Allan Woodcourt has never known Esther completely. She has been quite forthright when she tells him, however quietly, that during and following her illness she has had "many selfish thoughts." Woodcourt's response resonates throughout the final exchange of the novel: " 'You do not know what all around you see in Esther Summerson' " (lxi). But what others choose to see in Esther may be no more than their own conception of her. Ultimately, neither Woodcourt nor others can affirm the absolute validity of that face they see. Esther, after all, has found herself at the conclusion of her progress in but another conspiracy to make her, and others, happy. To be known as Dame Durden is not, finally, to be Dame Durden. This version of Esther may not be consonant with what she truly is. We are left, with Esther, not seeing face to face, but looking through a glass darkly, seeking the forever elusive self floating within the mirror's depths beyond the reflection on its surface. The veil between the self and self-knowledge is never fully raised.

"It is too often forgotten that man is impossible without imagination, without the capacity to invent for himself a conception of life, to

'ideate' the character his is going to be. Whether he be original or a pla-
giarist, man is the novelist of himself." [9] There is no end, no period, to
Bleak House or to the novel which is Esther's unfolding self: there is a
dash, a hiatus, and no more. We encounter another mystery. Esther
remains as enigmatic as the Roman figure of Allegory floating upon the
ceiling of Tulkinghorn's chambers, a silent witness whose pointing
hand is subject to the arbitrary suppositions of the "excited imagination," and to endless interpretation.

Harvey Peter Sucksmith

SIR LEICESTER DEDLOCK, WAT TYLER, AND THE CHARTISTS

The Role of the Ironmaster in Bleak House

WHEN DICKENS introduces Sir Leicester Dedlock into *Bleak House,* he deflates the Baronet's reactionary social and political attitude in a characteristic—some might say, all too characteristic—manner.

> Sir Leicester has no objection to an interminable Chancery suit. It is a slow, expensive, British, constitutional kind of thing. To be sure, he has not a vital interest in the suit in question, her part in which was the only property my Lady brought him; and he has a shadowy impression that for his name—the name of Dedlock—to be in a cause, and not in the title of that cause, is a most ridiculous accident. But he regards the Court of Chancery, even if it should involve an occasional delay of justice and a trifling amount of confusion, as a something, devised in conjunction with a variety of other somethings, by the perfection of human wisdom, for the eternal settlement (humanly speaking) of everything. And he is upon the whole of a fixed opinion, that to give the sanction of his countenance to any complaints respecting it, would be to encourage some person in the lower classes to rise up somewhere—like Wat Tyler.[1]

Entering partly into Sir Leicester's mode of thinking, the omniscient narrator ironically undermines the Baronet's position. The final suggestion that Sir Leicester's attitude is identical with that of a medieval aristocrat toward the Peasants' Revolt of 1381 completes the process of deflation with a comparison calculated to produce bathos. At first sight, the reference to Wat Tyler may seem to betray Dickens' most extravagant method of caricature, a method that has led critics of a conservative political persuasion during his own lifetime [2] and since [3] to accuse him of oversimplification and exaggeration and critics concerned ostensibly with aesthetics rather than politics to charge him with gross and farfetched comic ideas and effects.[4]

[113

Whether Dickens is guilty of gross caricature on other occasions, in this instance we must surely consider him less so, if at all, when we take into account two relevant facts. The first is Dickens' concept of Wat Tyler, particularly while he was writing *Bleak House,* together with the concept of the famous peasant leader popular at the time. The second fact is an incident, linking Wat Tyler's name with the Chartist troubles of 1848, which occurred three years before Dickens began to write *Bleak House.* Furthermore, an enquiry into these two relevant facts throws some light on the significance of Mr. Rouncewell and the affair between Watt and Rosa in the scheme of *Bleak House* and helps to settle a recent controversy about the Ironmaster.

At least as early as 1840, Dickens reveals a highly partisan view of Wat Tyler:

> I object on principle to making Wat such a thorough-paced villain, because a rebel on such grounds has a certain claim to one's sympathy, and I feel that if I had lived in his time, I should have been very likely to have knocked out the Collector's brains myself,—or at all events to have looked upon the man who did so, as a demi-God. Fathers may naturally object to having gross indecencies practised upon their daughters even by government servants; and bystanders can scarcely shew their manhood better than by resenting such things when they are done before their eyes.
>
> Therefore, if Wat Tyler and his followers when their passions were once let loose, had burnt down the City and got drunk with blood, I should still entertain some respect for their memory.[5]

This extract from a letter giving advice to an apprentice writer, bent on making Wat Tyler the villain of his piece, is interesting for a number of reasons. It reveals Dickens' strong affective reaction to an act of sexual exploitation in a context of social injustice and rebellion, which as we shall see is not unconnected with *Bleak House.* Instant death as a punishment for indecent assault may seem totally out of proportion, even mentally unbalanced, to a twentieth-century mind. Yet Dickens writes confidently, as if he could expect the approval of all decent men, and, having to calculate the reaction of Victorians so extensively as he did, who will venture to say he was very far wrong in his estimate? [6] Above all, however, the letter to Overs reveals how closely Dickens could identify himself with revolutionary violence and how far he was prepared to go, at least privately and under certain circumstances, in approving and justifying such violence. The passage is all the more striking in that it was written only a year after the most violent act the "physical force" Chartists ever perpetrated: several thousand armed miners attempted

to storm Newport Jail on 3 November 1839. True, Dickens seems to
have taken up a very different public attitude toward revolutionary violence during the same period. Both in his description of a Chartist
demonstration in *The Old Curiosity Shop* and of the Gordon Riots in *Barnaby Rudge,* Dickens seems to express the Victorian middle-class anxiety
about revolutionary mob violence, though he also clearly savors the accompanying excitement as he does later in writing about the French
Revolution in *A Tale of Two Cities.* No doubt Dickens expresses the ambivalence and contradictory attitudes many men experience with
regard to rebellion and violence, a point to which we must return later.
Meanwhile, in view of the attention the attitudes in these three novels
have quite properly attracted and the publicity his more reactionary
opinions have recently received, it is perhaps worth noting how openly
and uncompromisingly he expresses his approval of Wat Tyler.

For, although Dickens, like many men, did become rather more
conservative in some ways as he grew older,[7] his view of Wat Tyler does
not seem to have changed in the least. Not, at any rate, by 1852, when
he was still at work on *Bleak House,* the first number of which, containing Chapter ii and the earliest reference to Sir Leicester Dedlock and
Wat Tyler, appeared in March. In June, the same year, Dickens published his account of the Peasants' Revolt of 1381 in Chapter xvii of the
serialized version of *A Child's History of England.*[8] Dickens begins this account with a review of the causes of the revolt highly sympathetic to the
rebels:

> A certain tax, called the Poll-tax, which had originated in the
> last reign, was ordered to be levied on the people. This was a
> tax on every person in the kingdom, male and female, above
> the age of fourteen. . . .
> I have no need to repeat that the common people of England
> had long been suffering under great oppression. They were
> still the mere slaves of the lords of the land on which they lived,
> and were on most occasions harshly and unjustly treated. But,
> they had begun by this time to think very seriously of not bear-
> ing quite so much.

In going on to describe how Wat Tyler became involved in the rebellion, Dickens gives substantially the same account and records the same
indignant reaction to the indecent assault on Wat's daughter as he had
done in the letter to Overs, twelve years earlier.

> The people of Essex rose against the Poll-tax, and being
> severely handled by the government officers, killed some of
> them. At this very time one of the tax-collectors, going his
> rounds from house to house, at Dartford in Kent, came to the

cottage of one WAT, a tiler by trade, and claimed the tax upon
his daughter. Her mother, who was at home, declared that she
was under the age of fourteen; upon that, the collector (as
other collectors had already done in different parts of England) behaved in a savage way, and brutally insulted Wat Tyler's daughter. The daughter screamed, the mother screamed.
Wat the Tiler, who was at work not very far off, ran to the spot,
and did what any honest father under such provocation might
have done—struck the collector dead at a blow.

Instantly the people of that town uprose as one man. They
made Wat Tyler their leader; they joined with the people of
Essex, who were in arms under a priest called JACK STRAW.

It is implied pretty plainly here that the tax collector tried to determine
whether Wat's daughter was likely to be fourteen or not by the simple
expedient of discovering whether she had pubic hair, either by lifting
her skirts or putting his hand under them. And it may seem odd that in
a history designed for children, possibly for family reading aloud,
Dickens should draw attention to this point, particularly in view of all
that has been written about sexual reticence during the Victorian
period and especially in the middle-class family circle; [9] it is perhaps
worth noting that some popular accounts of the episode in our time
omit the incident of the indecent assault.[10] We are, of course, just
beginning to appreciate the skillful way that Dickens and other Victorian writers were able to write for two general classes of readers at the
same time by conveying sexual information in a discreet rather than
evasive manner.[11] It should be borne in mind, particularly in view of
what will be said later about the Ironmaster, Watt, and Rosa, that the
sexual exploitation of social inferiors, especially female employees and
particularly domestic servants, was a serious and sensitive problem during the Victorian period.[12] In an age dominated by middle-class mores,
social sensitivity about female chastity [13] no doubt encouraged a horrified view of sexual exploitation as the final degradation of servitude
and social injustice. Certainly, we might recall that Dickens was de-
scended from domestic servants on his father's side and likely to be as
sensitive as most on that account.[14]

When Dickens comes to describe the violent course of the Peasants'
Revolt, he is at great pains to excuse the rebels at every possible point:

It is said that they wanted to abolish all property, and to de-
clare all men equal. I do not think this very likely; because they
stopped the travellers on the roads and made them swear to be
true to King Richard and the people. Nor were they at all
disposed to injure those who had done them no harm, merely
because they were of high station; for, the King's mother, who

had to pass through their camp at Blackheath, on her way to her young son, lying for safety in the Tower of London, had merely to kiss a few dirty-faced rough-bearded men who were noisily fond of royalty, and so got away in perfect safety. . . . They broke open the prisons; they burned the papers in Lambeth Palace; they destroyed the DUKE OF LANCASTER'S Palace, the Savoy, in the Strand, said to be the most beautiful and splendid in England; they set fire to the books and documents in the Temple; and made a great riot. Many of these outrages were committed in drunkenness; since those citizens, who had well-filled cellars, were only too glad to throw them open to save the rest of their property; but even the drunken rioters were very careful to steal nothing. They were so angry with one man, who was seen to take a silver cup at the Savoy Palace, and put it in his breast, that they drowned him in the river, cup and all.

Again, Dickens stresses the justness of the demands the rebels made to the king and with this contrasts Richard II's deceitfulness: "Heaven knows, there was nothing very unreasonable in these proposals! The young King deceitfully pretended to think so, and kept thirty clerks up, all night, writing out a charter accordingly." And Dickens concludes by comparing the character and conduct of the king and his followers unfavorably with Wat Tyler's character and behavior.

Some declared afterwards that as Wat said this, he laid his hand on the King's bridle. Others declared that he was seen to play with his own dagger. I think, myself, that he just spoke to the King like a rough, angry man as he was, and did nothing more. At any rate he was expecting no attack, and preparing for no resistance, when Walworth the Mayor did the not very valiant deed of drawing a short sword and stabbing him in the throat. He dropped from his horse, and one of the King's people speedily finished him. So fell Wat Tyler. Fawners and flatterers made a mighty triumph of it, and set up a cry which will occasionally find an echo to this day. But Wat was a hard-working man, who had suffered much, and had been foully outraged; and it is probable that he was a man of a much higher nature and a much braver spirit than any of the parasites who exulted then, or have exulted since, over his defeat. . . . The King's falsehood in this business makes such a pitiful figure that I think Wat Tyler appears in history as beyond comparison the truer and more respectable man of the two.

However inadequate Dickens' view of Wat Tyler and the Peasants' Revolt may seem to modern historians, it does, in essence, represent the popular Victorian radical view.[15] This can be seen in Dickens'

source, Thomas Keightley's *The History of England.*[16] Though Keightley
is more restrained and does not condone the violence of the rebels, he
is sympathetic to their social aspirations: "The equal and beneficent
spirit which the Gospel breathes had imperceptibly penetrated all
ranks. . . . The extent of commerce and the consequent wealth of the
inhabitants of towns, and their importance in the eyes of monarch and
nobles, had given a kind of elevation to all parts of the commonalty;
and even the rude serfs of the country felt their natural rights, and
panted beneath the oppression of their lords after a state of freedom
for which they were not perhaps yet fully qualified." Similarly, Keightley presents the incident involving Wat Tyler's daughter as an outrage
which led directly to the rising of the men of Kent with Wat at their
head:

> The collection of the poll-tax was first resisted in Essex, where
> the people rose under the guidance of a priest, who assumed
> the name of Jack Straw. At Dartford in Kent one of the collec-
> tors demanded the tax for a young girl, the daughter of a tiler.
> Her mother asserting that she was under fifteen, the brutal
> collector laid hold of the girl and was proceeding to give a very
> indecent proof of the truth of this assertion, when her father
> came in from his work, and raising the implement which he
> happened to have in his hand struck the collector dead at a
> blow. His neighbours applauded and vowed to stand by him,
> and the surrounding villages soon joined in the common cause.
> The whole of Kent speedily rose. At Maidstone the people
> forced the archbishop's prison and liberated a priest named
> John Ball, who was confined in it for preaching against the
> wealth and corruption of the church. Wat the Tyler was now
> their acknowledged leader; they were joined by the Essex in-
> surgents under Jack Straw.

Furthermore, Keightley, on the whole, shares Dickens' low opinion of
Richard II and his followers: "The king . . . in compliance with the
desires of these lords,—whose conduct justifies the severe remarks of a
modern historian that 'the masters of slaves on such occasions seem
anxious to prove that they are not a race superior in any moral quality
to the meanest of their bondmen,' issued (July 2) a proclamation revok-
ing all the charters he had granted." That Dickens was confidently
putting forward a popular view of Wat Tyler can also be gathered from
its appearance in his own journal, which enjoyed a large circulation,
from his general and reliable sensitiveness to what his public would
approve, and from a remark to Overs which shows disapproval of relating historical incidents which would, he believed, offend the public:
"Beware of writing things for the eyes of everybody, which you would

feel the smallest delicacy in *saying* anywhere. Mrs. Scutfidge may have stripped in public—I have no doubt she did—but I should be sorry to have to tell young ladies so in the nineteenth Century, for all that." [17]

One question that suggests itself at this point is why Dickens chose to refer to Wat Tyler in *Bleak House* rather than another English peasant leader of the Middle Ages. True, Wat Tyler was famous but Jack Cade, who headed the rebellion of 1450 which closely followed the pattern of events in 1381, was equally celebrated. Cade was perhaps even better known during the nineteenth century owing to his appearance in Shakespeare's *Henry VI, Part 2*. Since, however, the image of a peasant leader who had endured personal indignity from a social superior, who had natural justice on his side, and was an honest and hard-working plebeian, suited Dickens' purpose admirably in *Bleak House,* as we shall see, Dickens would inevitably prefer Wat Tyler to Jack Cade. About the latter, he wrote in a further installment of *A Child's History of England* published in September 1852: "Jack, in imitation of Wat Tyler, though he was a very different and inferior sort of man, addressed the Kentish men upon their wrongs, occasioned by the bad government of England, among so many battledores and such a poor shuttlecock; and they rose up to the number of twenty thousand." [18]

Yet there is a further factor which may have influenced Dickens' choice of Wat Tyler. This was a sensational incident which was displayed prominently in the *Times,* a newspaper Dickens read regularly. Describing the riotous Chartist disturbances that took place in the West Riding during May 1848, including illegal drilling under black banners at Wilsden, the *Times* reported:

> On Monday morning the Bradford magistrates issued the following caution [i.e. against illegal drilling]. . . .
> Simultaneously with the issuing of this notice a posse of special constables were called out for the purpose of apprehending two of the most violent and dangerous of the Chartist leaders, namely David Lightowler (one of the representatives of the National Convention and Assembly) and Isaac Jefferson, *alias* "Wat Tyler," the reputed principal Chartist pike maker of the district, a rabid speaker and a man of ferocious aspect and Herculean strength, who had openly boasted of the amount of cold steel he would give to any man who attempted his arrest. About 40 special constables started on this awkward mission, the men they were directed to capture living in the strongholds of Chartism in Bradford, namely, Manchester-road and the small streets leading into it. The specials arrived at Adelaide-street, Manchester-road, about 7 o'clock in the morning, at which time Lightowler and "Wat Tyler" were at home; but by the advice of their friends, when the constables arrived at the

front door of their houses, they themselves escaped out of the
back. In a few minutes, and before they could satisfy themselves that the two fellows they were in search of had escaped,
the special constables found themselves surrounded by more
than 1,000 men, women, and children, who pounced upon
them from every avenue, and completely hemmed them in the
narrow street.

After describing the total rout of the special constables, the *Times* continues:

During the principal part of the day the local magistracy,
with the Earl of Harewood, the Lord-Lieutenant of the West
Riding, and General Thorne, the commandant of the district,
sat in council at the Court-house, and a large accession of military arrived in the town. . . .
    At 4 o'clock the whole of the police force, headed by Super-
intendent Brigg, marched from the Court-house; they were
followed by 1,000 special constables, the mayor and magistrates, 200 infantry with fixed bayonets, and two troops of
dragoons. This imposing force proceeded to Manchester-road,
their object being to capture all the Chartist leaders residing
there, and to search for arms.

It took this imposing force all their time to subdue the Chartists.

The forces then proceeded down Adelaide Street and all the
other streets and alleys in that populous neighbourhood known
as the rendezvous of the Chartists, again visiting the houses of
"Wat Tyler" and Lightowler, neither of whom, however, was at
home; and the search for arms in their dwellings was also un-
successful. In one house a pike or spear, mounted upon an
eight-foot shaft, was found, and in others several pike shafts
and pike heads, evidently recently separated, were discovered.
Bullet moulds, quite warm, as if just used, lead models of pike
heads, apparently to be used in casting pikes, were taken from
other houses.[19]

There was no loss of life, though the *Times* in a leading article was
clearly impressed by the resistance put up by the Chartists,[20] and the
affair had a typically English sequel. In September 1848, under the
general heading, "FURTHER CHARTIST COMMITTALS," the *Times*
reported:

On Thursday last Isaac Jefferson, a blacksmith, residing in the
borough of Bradford, in the West Riding of the county of

York, who was known by the title of "Wat Tyler, the pike-maker," and who had for some time been "wanted" by the authorities for unlawful practices in connexion with the Chartist tumults in that borough, was taken before the magistrates of that place charged with illegal drilling to the use of arms. The prisoner had been apprehended by three of the West Riding police-constables, on Tuesday night, at a lonely place called Swilling, on the borders of the parishes of Halifax and Bradford. Evidence having been heard against him, the magistrates committed him for trial at the next assizes at York, on a charge of being unlawfully drilled at Drizlington in May last. It is said that indictments for rioting will also be preferred against him.[21]

Yet, when the case came on in December, it ended without a bang and scarcely a whimper. After a legal interchange about certain technicalities, Jefferson and the other prisoners were charged with misdemeanor. Jefferson's case, as the *Times* reported it, was typical of the rest:

> Isaac Jefferson, aged 36, was indicted for drilling and being drilled and trained to the practice of military exercise, movements, and evolutions, at Drizlington, in the West Riding, on the 28th of May. . . .
>
> It appeared from the evidence of Joseph Thomson, that on the 28th of May, which was on a Sunday, the prisoner and a crowd of 40 or 50 persons were being drilled at Drizlington. The men were standing two deep, and at the word of command they "fell in," "right-about faced," and "marched." This evidence was supported by that of other witnesses, who saw the same drilling.
>
> Mr. BLANCHARD having addressed the jury for the defence,
>
> His LORDSHIP [Mr. Justice MAULE] summed up, and the jury found the prisoner *Guilty.* . . .
>
> His LORDSHIP then proceeded to pass sentence on the prisoners. He told them they might have erred from ignorance of the law; that might have availed them as an excuse a good deal, had the object of their drilling been innocent. But at that time there was a spirit of insubordination throughout the country approaching to rebellion, fomented by a number of foolish and wicked people. Had the objects they contemplated been carried out, this country would not be fit to live in. It would be better to live under an absolute despotism with peace and protection for property. His Lordship then sentenced the prisoner Hunt to be imprisoned 8 months, Jefferson 4 months, Angus 10 months, Frith 11 months, and Lightowler 9 months.[22]

There is something amusing, an impression of anticlimax not without its ironic point, in the way this "Wat Tyler" of the mid-nineteenth century shrinks in the *Times* reports from a bogyman of the middle classes to the size and shape of a human being. Certainly, the point, together with the bathos and irony, would not have been lost on Dickens. Nor what is highly amusing, too, in the ironic contrast between the reactionary nonsense talked by the judge, presumably quite prepared to sanction his country delivered over to an absolute despotism provided it safeguarded the rights of property, his paranoic terror of the lower classes who were, after all, only aiming at parliamentary representation and reforms conceded in principle by 1832, and yet his curious desire to be fair to the human beings actually before him and what does seem his surprising leniency in practice.[23] Is there a shade of Sir Leicester Dedlock here? If the resemblance is not intentional, it still helps to confirm that Dickens' portrayal of the Dedlock attitude is no wild caricature.

Nevertheless, it is important to stress that Dickens seems to have read the *Times* not only regularly but also most carefully and with a particular eye for possible source material. Indeed, while writing *Bleak House,* he appears to have used passages from the *Times*[24] in a manner comparable with Shakespeare's use of North's Plutarch. Furthermore, it may just be relevant that Dickens was in the North of England for a short time during June 1848, when he visited Manchester and Liverpool, both centers of areas which witnessed Chartist disturbances during May and certain to be humming with the sensational news of Chartist doings in the North.[25] On the whole, it seems unlikely that he would have missed the titbit about Wat Tyler and, if he did read or hear about it, hardly likely he would have forgotten it.[26] The Dickensian humor in the incident seems quite unintentional, certainly as it appears in the *Times* reports, though Cole and Postgate, possibly following the brief account in Gammage's contemporary history of Chartism, which does not identify "Wat Tyler" as Isaac Jefferson, a real person, have apparently jumped to the conclusion that the episode was a hoax perpetrated on a gullible magistrate: "The warrant issued by an innocent magistrate for 'Wat Tyler' could not be executed."[27] All the same, unintentional or not, the joke is there at the expense of the reactionary upper classes seeking to subdue what they regarded as a dangerous uprising of the lower orders, though it was, in fact, despite wild talk and gestures, simply a violent but bloodless demonstration in favor of parliamentary reform, and it is the same joke that Dickens uses at Sir Leicester's expense. Unlike many of his contemporaries, Dickens regarded the Middle Ages with aversion.[28] The implication that the upper-class attitude to the lower orders is positively medieval in its worst sense clearly aligns Dickens' humorous sympathy with the Chartists as we can see from the text of *Bleak House* in which Sir Leicester, Wat Tyler, and Chartist demonstrations are almost invariably presented in close association. If he did not draw on this historical episode three years later while writing *Bleak House,* it does seem a fairly remarkable coincidence. But, if he did not, the coincidence demonstrates an even more remarkable climate of radical feeling in which the humor of a great artist should imitate the comic life of history so exactly.

— 2 —

As we might expect, whenever Dickens refers to Wat Tyler in *Bleak House* after Chapter ii, he continues to do so in connection with Sir Leicester Dedlock and the attitudes he represents, that is, Wat Tyler is presented, with satirical irony, as the Dedlock concept of the social threat against its position. Thus, Wat Tyler is linked by a characteristically bold and brilliant stroke of valid humorous imagination both with the class of inventors and industrial capitalists, represented by the Ironmaster, and with the Chartist workers:

> Her [Mrs. Rouncewell's] second son would have been provided for at Chesney Wold, and would have been made steward in due season; but he took, when he was a schoolboy, to constructing steam-engines out of saucepans, and setting birds to draw their own water, with the least possible amount of labour; so assisting them with artful contrivance of hydraulic pressure, that a thirsty canary had only, in a literal sense, to put his shoulder to the wheel, and the job was done. This propensity gave Mrs. Rouncewell great uneasiness. She felt it with a mother's anguish, to be a move in the Wat Tyler direction: well knowing that Sir Leicester had that general impression of an aptitude for any art to which smoke and a tall chimney might be considered essential. But the doomed young rebel (otherwise a mild youth, and very persevering), showing no sign of grace as he got older; but, on the contrary, constructing a model of a power-loom, she was fain, with many tears, to mention his backslidings to the baronet. "Mrs. Rouncewell," said Sir Leicester, "I can never consent to argue, as you know, with any one on any subject. You had better get rid of your boy; you had better get him into some Works. The iron country farther north is, I suppose, the congenial direction for a boy of those tendencies." Farther north he went, and farther north he grew up; and if Sir Leicester Dedlock ever saw him, when he came to Chesney Wold to visit his mother, or ever thought of him afterwards, it is certain that he only regarded him as one of a body of some odd thousand conspirators, swarthy and grim, who were in the habit of turning out by torchlight, two or three nights in the week, for unlawful purposes. (84)

The deliberate fusing of inventors, industrialists, Chartist workers at
torchlight demonstrations, and the Wat Tyler image is not an instance
of *gross* caricature on Dickens' part. The Dedlock protest is that of the
Tory landed aristocracy and interest against all the social and political
forces unleashed by the Industrial Revolution. Even intelligent Victorians with widely differing social and political beliefs, such as Augustus
Pugin, Disraeli, Carlyle, and later the socialist William Morris, saw the
Industrial Revolution as threatening and destroying social values essentially medieval. Dickens' satire against medieval things and their de-
fenders and devotees is, in the context of his time, no mere punch into
empty air.

Moreover, far from oversimplifying the social situation, Dickens'
satire takes accurate note of its complexity. Thus, we know from social
historians and biographers that the industrial capitalists of the eighteenth and early nineteenth centuries came very largely from either the
yeoman class [29] or from artisans, often inventors, like James Watt,
George Stephenson, Samuel Crompton, James Hargreaves, Richard
Arkwright, and John Brown.[30] The Lancashire proverb, "From clogs to
clogs in three generations," certainly bears this out. Dickens' satire on
the self-made industrialist, Bounderby, in *Hard Times* only plays ironically on what was unfortunately a familiar, though not a universal,
truth.[31] Indeed, Dickens accurately describes the progress of the working-class artisan, with a talent for invention, both in Daniel Doyce's case
in *Little Dorrit* (188–89) and that of the Ironmaster in *Bleak House:* " 'I
have been,' proceeds the visitor [Mr. Rouncewell], in a modest clear
way, 'an apprentice, and a workman, I have lived on workman's wages,
years and years, and beyond a certain point have had to educate myself. My wife was a foreman's daughter, and plainly brought up' "
(396). Again, we can see that Dickens is by no means indulging in *gross*
caricature when Sir Leicester Dedlock associates Wat the Tiler, an artisan leader of peasants, who threatened medieval privilege, with the
Ironmaster of working-class origin, who has risen into the middle class
to become an organizer of labor and threaten the relics of that medieval privilege.

> "Now, my son [i.e. Rouncewell's son, Watt] is a very young
> man, and Rosa is a very young woman. As I made my way, so
> my son must make his; and his being married at present is out
> of the question. But supposing I gave my consent to his engag-
> ing himself to this pretty girl, if this pretty girl will engage her-
> self to him, I think it a piece of candour to say at once—I am
> sure, Sir Leicester and Lady Dedlock, you will understand and
> excuse me—I should make it a condition that she did not re-
> main at Chesney Wold. Therefore, before communicating fur-
> ther with my son, I take the liberty of saying that if her removal

would be in any way inconvenient or objectionable, I will hold the matter over with him for any reasonable time, and leave it precisely where it is."

Not remain at Chesney Wold! Make it a condition! All Sir Leicester's old misgivings relative to Wat Tyler, and the people in the iron districts who do nothing but turn out by torchlight, come in a shower upon his head. (394–95)

If we still think it strange that Sir Leicester should identify the Ironmaster with Chartist demonstrators, we must remember that, although the Chartists failed because they enjoyed little middle-class support,[32] the Reform Bill of 1832 did not finally establish a Britain in which the middle classes immediately assumed paramountcy over the landed aristocracy nor by 1846 when Free Trade won its victory over the Corn Laws is this wholly true.[33] On the contrary, in mid-Victorian Britain, the old aristocracy and upper levels of the middle class, as W. L. Burn has shown,[34] continued to exercise enormous power and influence, hence the aptness and topicality of Dickens' attack on Sir Leicester. Neither did the Reform Bill of 1832 mean that the struggle between capital and labor was immediately substituted for the struggle between the manufacturers and the relics of feudal aristocracy. On the contrary, although the extension of parliamentary representation in areas where they were strong and its reduction in areas where they were weak meant that the manufacturers won more power in Parliament through their influence on electors, it was at first a tactical advance in their struggle against the landed interest rather than total victory.[35] Moreover, at the end of the hungry forties during a recession in the Iron Trade, the Ironmasters and their workmen remained on good terms. On the other hand, the continued parliamentary struggle between the radical manufacturers and the Tory landed aristocracy for political power is carefully reflected in *Bleak House* in the clash between the electioneering interests of Sir Leicester and the Ironmaster. There can be little doubt, here, to which side Dickens directs our sympathy for, while Sir Leicester is shown involved in bribery and wild reactionary abuse and recriminations, the Ironmaster and his son, Watt, are shown throughout in a calm, intelligent, and rational light all the more impressive since our view of them is conveyed through the eyes of Tulkinghorn: "He is a very good speaker. Plain and emphatic. He made a damaging effect, and has great influence. In the business part of the proceedings he carried all before him . . . And he was much assisted . . . by his son" (566–70). If it is contended that Dickens gives an unfair representative picture of the manufacturing and the aristocratic contenders in a contemporary parliamentary election, then that very unfairness would only demonstrate further where Dickens' sympathies lie. Sir Leicester had already commended the propriety of Rouncewell in not standing for Parliament himself, but his reaction on learning that Rouncewell and his son have intervened in the election against Sir Leicester's party is that "the floodgates of society are burst open, and the waters have—a—obliterated the landmarks of the framework of the cohesion by which things are held together!" (570–71). He goes on to suggest that Lady Dedlock keep her maid, Rosa, out of Watt's clutches: " 'You should exert your influence to keep her from these dangerous hands. You might show her what violence would be done, in such association, to her duties and principles; and you might preserve her for a better fate. You might point out to her that she probably would, in good time, find a husband at Chesney Wold by whom she would not be—' Sir Leicester adds, after a moment's consideration, 'dragged from the altars of her forefathers' " (571). And when Tulkinghorn hints that a man like Rouncewell might not wish to have a daughter associated with a landed aristocrat whose wife had had an illegitimate child, "Sir Leicester generally refers back in his mind to Wat Tyler, and arranges a sequence of events on a plan of his own" (573).

We saw earlier how Dickens regarded a sexual indignity inflicted on one's daughter as the ultimate indignity of medieval servitude, completely justifying Wat Tyler's homicidal attack on an officer of the Crown upon which he became leader of the Peasants' Revolt of 1381. Now, it does, of course, seem a very far cry from the brutal and offensive tax collector of Wat's time to the gentlemanly baronet whom Dickens constantly concedes has much chivalry in his conduct, yet in *Bleak House* the dramatic clash between Sir Leicester and the Ironmaster centers very largely on the love affair between Watt Rouncewell and Lady Dedlock's maid, Rosa, with the Dedlocks abrogating to themselves the almost feudal right to dictate the sex choice of the young woman, treating her as almost a social appendage of their own, a mere chattel, while the Ironmaster regards her throughout as a prospective daughter-in-law who must be helped in adjusting herself to a human as well as a social relationship and is much concerned over what he regards as the degradation of his son's future wife in remaining in domestic service. We can see that both the episode in Dickens' account of the indecent assault on Wat Tyler's daughter and that involving Sir Leicester, the Ironmaster, Watt, and Rosa, represent forms, however different, of sexual indignity, even outrage, by social superiors on inferiors against which family honor and human dignity revolt. Moreover, the sense of outrage, though subtle in *Bleak House,* is all the keener in that the Ironmaster, who wishes to withdraw Rosa from Chesney Wold in order to have her educated further as more befitting his son's wife, meets Sir Leicester's arrogant superiority with calm and polite attempts to explain the rationale of his own position and, even when Sir Leicester rudely refuses to come to any compromise arrangement or to discuss the matter any further, the Ironmaster says he will "very seriously recommend my son to conquer his present inclinations" (394–98). Nor is Mr. Rouncewell simply playing a social game for we are later shown Rosa in the happy bosom of the Ironmaster's family, treated on an equal footing with Watt's sisters (847–48). It might be going too far to assert that the story of Wat Tyler suggested the clash between Sir Leicester and the Ironmaster over the affair between Watt and Rosa, yet the parallel is close enough, in some ways, to be extremely interesting and directs our attention to a disturbing factor in the social conflict of *Bleak House* which Dickens, owing to the conventions of his time, does not dwell on and which we have been apt to ignore.

Trevor Blount has recently argued that we are intended to take a highly critical view of the Ironmaster in *Bleak House,* and, despite one or two good qualities, to see him as a hard and ruthless industrialist, no better as a social alternative than Sir Leicester Dedlock and what he stands for. Seriously enough, David Craig has hailed Mr. Blount's view as a definitive reading of the novel. Miss Anne G. M. Smith has retorted persuasively, in my view, to Mr. Blount's argument. Even more recently, Professor K. J. Fielding has criticized what he believes to be Mrs. Q. D. Leavis' misreading of Dickens' attitude to the Rouncewells as contrary to all our experience of the text and I must concur in his judgment.[36] Yet even more might be added to what both Miss Smith and Professor Fielding have said. It has become unfashionable in some quarters to argue for a critical reading of a text in the context of the historical background and the author's known beliefs, and no doubt such an approach has its dangers when it ignores such of the text as does not fit in with its thesis. Yet, when we are faced with such unlikely interpretations and distorted readings of a plain and unequivocal text from distinguished critics, we are forced to the conclusion that criticism may not yet be in a position to do without external evidence, without scholarship, and we may be reminded of Northrop Frye's warning that evaluative criticism is frequently a rationalization of social, political, religious, intellectual, and moral prejudice.[37]

In the first place, then, Mr. Blount refers in a footnote to the external evidence that Dickens was expressing a high opinion of Ironmasters in April 1852, only to dismiss it. Yet, it does seem incredible that the same man who was recommending to Miss Coutts certain "large ironmasters—of whom there are some notable cases—who have proceeded on the self-supporting principle, and have done wonders with their workpeople"[38] should three or four months[39] later be carefully selecting an Ironmaster as his instance of the hard and ruthless practitioner of laissez-faire in *Bleak House.* True, the study of Dickens'

mode of thinking in his letters, journalism, and fiction, which have
been so widely and extensively compared of late, does reveal some dis-
crepancies, some ambivalences, some changes in attitude, yet none so
immediate, wild, inexplicable, and unlikely as this. Moreover, as Professors John Butt and Kathleen Tillotson have pointed out, during the
previous year, the *Times,* which Dickens took into considerable account
while writing *Bleak House,* had reported on 29 March 1851: "The ironmasters of South Staffordshire are, and ever have been, particularly
anxious not to curtail the employment or reduce the remuneration of
their men; to such an extent has this considerate feeling been exhibited
that many works have been carried on which, if profit only had entered
into the masters' minds would have been closed, for the purpose of giving employment and support to the neighbouring population." [40]

Nevertheless, Mr. Blount correctly argues that it is what Dickens
says in *Bleak House* that finally matters. And, in *Bleak House,* I cannot
find a single unequivocal word or statement that supports Mr. Blount's
view of the Ironmaster as a hard and ruthless practitioner of laissez-
faire, an epitome of the new acquisitiveness, a man as much in the way
of the ultimate well-being of his country as Sir Leicester Dedlock. The
plain fact is that we are hardly shown the Ironmaster in his business
relationships at all, only in his personal relationships which are marked
by extreme kindness, warm affection, and constant consideration for
others, and once in his political conduct which is distinguished by personal restraint and plain and effective speaking on the appropriate occasion. Certainly, the workman George meets on his way to the Ironmaster's does not comment adversely on Mr. Rouncewell but seems
genuinely keen to point out his factory and admire his preeminence
rather than otherwise (845). Mr. Blount would have us infer the business attitude from certain material which he interprets symbolically and
then connects rather tenuously, in my view, with other symbolism in
the novel. Thus, he compares the articles of iron lying about in the factory with the junk in Krook's shop, but the latter is refuse presented as
a dubiously useful accumulation of waste while the former is depicted
either as the finished products or the raw material of a vital industry,
for Dickens concludes his description: "distant furnaces of it glowing
and bubbling in its youth; bright fireworks of it showering about,
under the blows of the steam hammer" (846). If this connects with anything in the novel, it is with the earlier creativity of Mr. Rouncewell as a
boy and youth, and creativity is invariably the certain stamp of approval which Dickens sets on a character or an activity.

It is to Dickens' credit, a mark of the shrewd perceptiveness and
the sane complexity of his genius, which has all too often escaped notice, that he distinguishes fairly consistently between the acquisitive side
of capitalism usually associated with the commercial aspect and the

productive side normally allied with industry. This distinction is particularly well exemplified in the business relationship of Arthur Clennam and Daniel Doyce in *Little Dorrit* when Clennam's financial speculation leads to disaster and the business is put on a sound footing again through Doyce who handles the industrial, inventive, and productive side of the firm. True, Dickens in *Hard Times* does criticize the influence of utilitarian philosophy and political economy on the direction of industrial capitalism which he sees as making for rigidity, restrictiveness, sterility, dehumanization, and the worship of the mechanical means in place of creative ends, but I cannot see that even this criticism amounts to a total rejection of industry. Bounderby remains a comic monster throughout the novel while we are simply never allowed to see the productive principle at work in the factories of Coketown; no doubt we owe this presentation to a necessary satirical selectiveness on Dickens' part, encouraged by the narrow compass in which he was working and about which he frequently complained. Nor can I see that Bounderby is presented in *Hard Times* exclusively or centrally as the epitome of acquisitiveness, though he does drive his workers hard and unfeelingly and though acquisitiveness can sometimes be glimpsed or inferred as a principle at work in the world of *Hard Times,* notably in the gospel of work according to Coketown and in the industrial difficulties between employer and employed. Even more, acquisitiveness is not a central issue in *Bleak House* as it is in *Our Mutual Friend* in which, significantly, commercialism is present but industrial capitalism totally absent. In *Bleak House,* acquisitiveness is a side issue, represented by the Smallweeds and not by the Ironmaster to whom the Smallweeds are never related though so much else in the novel is related, thoroughly and significantly.

Mr. Blount goes on to argue that the "Steel" and "Iron" of Chapter lxiii are intended as an antithesis of the noble and the ignoble. Yet not one word in the chapter supports this view. If anything, the Ironmaster comes out of this chapter in a more favorable light than George, the prodigal son and brother; the difference between the resentful brother in the Bible parable and the Ironmaster is very marked. Mr. Rouncewell even tries to persuade George not to forego his inheritance from his mother in favor of the Ironmaster and his children, hardly the sign of an acquisitive man, and offers George a place. In referring to "Steel" and "Iron," surely Dickens is simply identifying the professions of the two brothers, soldier and ironmaster, in a witty way which also expresses their relationship. Certainly, if Mr. Blount is correct, George is guilty of self-advertisement, however unwittingly, when he calls himself "Steel" on approaching his brother, a wrong note I cannot believe Dickens would have sounded in view of the impression of modesty and self-effacement he clearly wishes throughout the novel to asso-

ciate with George. In the absence of the rest of Mr. Blount's case, his
tenuous link between the dirt of industrialism and other dirt in *Bleak
House* does not hold up; Dickens, like the rest of us, could distinguish
between honest productive dirt and the evil and unnecessary sorts.

That the Ironmaster, in fact, points toward Daniel Doyce of *Little
Dorrit* rather than Bounderby of *Hard Times,* is suggested not only by
the serious rather than comic treatment of the character and, however
slightly, by Rouncewell's inventiveness as a boy but also by his son's
Christian name, Watt. In a brief note, Anne Smith properly suggests a
link with James Watt, inventor of the steam engine, supported by the
reference to the Ironmaster's "constructing steam-engines out of sauce-
pans" as a boy, but she finds the link with Wat Tyler only amusing.[41] I
think the link with Wat Tyler goes much further than she suggests, for
there is also an association with Chartism, the closest mid-Victorian
equivalent of the Peasants' Revolt of 1381.

In so far as *Bleak House* is concerned with the "Condition of England" question, Sir Leicester, for all his saving graces, is at the center
of social and political deadlock.[42] Positive social energy must necessarily
manifest itself, therefore, as a kind of rebellion against an excessively
static status quo, either in the destructive forms of Chartism [43] or
through the constructive experiment of a modern industrial society
freed not from responsibility and humanity but from the restrictiveness
of the aristocratic view of class, social mobility, and progress, a rigid
and perpetual dividedness. Sir Leicester tells Rouncewell that Rosa is
free either to leave his service or to stay as a maid, but the village school
is good enough for her. On the other hand, although Rouncewell believes Rosa is in a lower class than his son, he does not oppose their
marriage, neither personally nor as a general principle, and he wants
her to have the best education he can provide, for social reasons it is
true but within the most intimate and, potentially, the most creative of
human relationships.

> "All this is so frequent, Lady Dedlock, where I live, and among
> the class to which I belong, that what would be generally called
> unequal marriages are not of such rare occurence with us as
> elsewhere. A son will sometimes make it known to his father
> that he has fallen in love, say, with a young woman in the fac-
> tory. The father, who once worked in a factory himself, will be
> a little disappointed at first, very possibly. It may be that he had
> other views for his son. However, the chances are, that having
> ascertained the young woman to be of unblemished character,
> he will say to his son, 'I must be quite sure you are in earnest
> here. This is a serious matter for both of you. Therefore I shall
> have this girl educated for two years'—or it may be—'I shall
> place this girl at the same school with your sisters for such a

time, during which you will give me your word and honour to
see her only so often. If, at the expiration of that time, when
she has so far profited by her advantages as that you may be
upon a fair equality, you are both in the same mind, I will do
my part to make you happy.' I know of several cases such as I
describe, my Lady, and I think they indicate to me my own
course now." (396–97)

This is a new kind of social responsibility from the noblesse oblige and
old-world chivalry of the Dedlocks, which demands a stifling deference
as its eternal due, which calls for an acceptance instead of a carefully
nurtured social mobility which brings classes together, improves the
quality and happiness of their lives, and which does not shirk even the
ultimate test of its sincerity, the final intimacy of human communion.
The point Dickens makes again through the relationship of Eugene
Wrayburn and Lizzie Hexam in *Our Mutual Friend*. But, in *Bleak House*,
it underscores what the novel is, above all, concerned with. The union
of Watt and Rosa does not, as Mr. Blount believes, represent a compromise between the unacceptable, extreme, and alternative ways of
life offered by Sir Leicester and the Ironmaster; we need only try to
construct an analogous comparison with the compromise worked out in
Wuthering Heights to see how inadequate Mr. Blount's view is. Far from
opposing the union of his son and Rosa, Rouncewell throughout actively furthers it, not as an alternative to his way of life but as a living
extension of it. The Ironmaster is prepared to enter into communion
with someone from a lower class not to patronize that person, like Mrs.
Pardiggle, nor to make use of her for his own superior ends, like Sir
Leicester Dedlock, nor to exploit the loyalty which Lady Dedlock is on
the verge of exploiting in Rosa, but to serve a human being's true
needs and ends in a modern society. This is what *Bleak House* is all
about. It is a less dramatic, yet even more profound, instance of the
social concern Esther Summerson demonstrates for Charley and Allan
Woodcourt for Jo. It is Dickens' human interpretation of the democratic answer to the "Condition of England" question. It reveals that
what Dickens believed was best in the democratic tendency sprang
from a genuine uncondescending love of our fellows, a desire to raise
them up to whatever was better in our way of life through our embrace. Yet there is as much practical responsibility as there is idealism
in the Ironmaster's conduct and if Dickens presents his words and actions without sentimentality we have no reason to complain, nor to ignore or misinterpret them.[44]

Gordon D. Hirsch

THE MYSTERIES IN *BLEAK HOUSE*

A Psychoanalytic Study

THE READER'S initial response to *Bleak House* usually consists of some confusion and bewilderment, as well as a desire to organize the complex and seemingly disorganized world of the novel. He tries to make sense of the mysterious and apparently unrelated events of the book, since in reading it he frequently feels himself to be present at scenes where he knows something important is happening, though he doesn't know exactly what it is. Usually only after the second reading of the novel does he begin to estimate the number of times Esther has passed outside her father's door above Krook's shop; to understand that Grandfather Smallweed has made loans to Captain Hawdon and Richard Carstone as well as to George Rouncewell; to grasp the significance of such scenes as Bucket's interrogation of Jo in the presence of an open-mouthed Snagsby, whose lack of comprehension provides a focus for the reader's own confusion. Seemingly insignificant events, such as Lady Dedlock's response upon recognizing Hawdon's handwriting, set off whole chains of puzzling actions that are not completed until the novel's end. *Bleak House* may even be said to be concerned primarily with mystery, curiosity, and investigation—with making connections and finding links.[1] Dickens himself strikes this keynote: "What connection can there have been between many people in the innumerable histories of the world, who, from opposite sides of great gulfs, have, nevertheless, been very curiously brought together!" (xvi).[2]

Not only does the reader find himself confronted by a fragmented world of which he must try to make sense, but he soon discovers that the characters in the novel share his need to penetrate to the heart of the book's mysteries. The central characters—such as Esther, Richard, Tulkinghorn, and Bucket—are all obsessed with the mysteries of the past. They are engaged either in tracking down the mysterious circumstances surrounding Esther Summerson's birth and her parents' sexual "crime," or they are probing into the history of disputed family legacies—a pursuit which proves upon inspection to be another variant of research into "parental" mysteries.

[132

The ultimate equivalence of these seemingly different mysteries and the reason for their central place in the novel can be explained by reference to Freudian psychoanalytic theory, which suggests that the prototype for all curiosity and investigation of mysteries is the infantile sexual research that occurs at the Oedipal phase of development. The mysteries of *Bleak House* are connected at root with the child's curiosity about parental sexuality and his struggle to manage his own complex and ambivalent feelings about that sexuality. Psychoanalytic theory holds that the child is intensely curious about the sexuality of his parents, while at the same time he is disappointed, angry, and hostile because of his exclusion from that sexual partnership. He wishes to replace one of his parents in the relationship with the other, but at the same time he feels guilty and anxious about his aggressive curiosity, his hostility, and his desire. The child's ambivalent fascination with sexual mysteries is, then, simply one specific aspect of his ambivalent response to the entire Oedipal dilemma.

In a famous essay about Leonardo da Vinci, Freud explores this link between adult curiosity and the infant's discovery of his own and his parents' sexuality, and Freud outlines there the transmutations of infantile curiosity that can occur as the child passes out of his Oedipal phase.[3] According to Freud, "When the period of infantile sexual researches has been terminated by a wave of energetic sexual repression, the instinct for research has three distinct possible vicissitudes open to it owing to its fairly early connection with sexual interests." One possible outcome is that curiosity and thought may become inhibited; such severe repression may bring on a neurotic illness. Alternatively, the repressed curiosity may return so strongly that brooding, interminable, and sexually tinged researches—in other words, forms of neurotic compulsive thinking—are the consequence. The third outcome is more favorable and, Freud suggests, may be seen in the case of Leonardo: the originally sexualized energy (libido) is entirely sublimated in the service of intellectual interests, which seek specifically to avoid sexual subjects of investigation. In other words, infantile sexual curiosity, confronted by the repression which is inevitable late in the Oedipal phase, may undergo any of three transformations: the drive to investigate may be inhibited (at a cost, however, to the entire psychic organization); it may be partially converted and expressed through a neurotic compromise formation, such as an obsession; or it may be fully expressed in a sublimated, acceptable, "desexualized" way.

Our understanding of *Bleak House* can be increased by examining it as an unwitting parable about these three vicissitudes of infantile sexual curiosity, and our responses to the central characters can be clarified when they are located along this spectrum of "filial" responses to parental sexual mysteries. Esther Summerson's character

seems formed by the effects of a severe repression resulting in a specific kind of inhibition; Richard Carstone and Tulkinghorn seem to
manifest varieties of self-destructive obsessional thought; while Inspector Bucket manages to sublimate his researches successfully in a socially
adaptive manner. The psychology of each of these characters must be
seen in relation to that of the others, for each represents only one portion of a range of responses to parental mystery and authority which
extends from docility to rage. It is this range of responses which provides an underlying psychological coherence to *Bleak House,* despite the
novel's multitudinous number of characters, two narrative foci, and a
complex plot; and it is this psychological coherence which the present
essay will examine.

Esther Summerson, long a problem for critics, seems to pose the
most serious obstacle to any claim for unity of theme and structure in
Bleak House. I shall begin with a discussion of her psychology as Dickens
presents it, neither to defend her personality nor to justify her position
as the novel's heroine, but in order to place her in a clearer relation to
the other central characters and to the principal psychological dilemma
explored by the novel. I shall focus on the way in which Esther defines
in *Bleak House* one extreme pole of the spectrum of alternative psychological responses to the existence of mystery and the temptation of curiosity.

— *I* —

In recent years literary critics have shown an increasing tendency
to regard *Bleak House* as if it were two discrete novels, one consisting of
Esther Summerson's narrative, and the second that of the omnicient
narrator. The common view of the relative merits of these two parts is
Sylvère Monod's: "The third-person part of *Bleak House* would . . .
have made a very fine novel, remarkably economical in method, if
there had not been, interspersed with it, the first-person narrative supposedly written by Esther Summerson." [4] Monod criticizes Esther more
for her self-praise and sentimentality than for her mere goodness:
"Esther is meant to be perfect, and her perfection is recognized by everyone about her; but as she is telling the tale herself, she cannot ad-
vertise her virtues and must always appear to be naïvely surprised by
the golden opinions she wins from all sorts of people." [5] Confronted by
Esther's pronounced deference and humility, the modern critic sus-
pects a layer of pride hidden beneath the surface, but any such assertive or self-confident response to her life and her problems is most alien
to Esther's personality as Dickens portrays it. Perhaps the most apt
word to describe Esther's psychology would be "inhibited," the word
which Freud uses to describe his paradigm for the first vicissitude of

curiosity. All of Esther's curiosity, active strivings, and self-confidence seem somehow constricted and stifled.

At the heart of Esther's psychology is the deep-seated feeling that she is not loved and that she is not even worthy of anyone's love. She is brought up by her "always grave and strict" aunt as an "unfortunate girl, orphaned and degraded," and her aunt makes her feel unloved, unworthy of love, and unloving:

> I felt so poor, so trifling, and so far off; that I never could be unrestrained with her—no, could never even love her as I wished. It made me very sorry to consider how good she was, and how unworthy of her I was. . . . I never loved my [aunt] as I ought to have loved her, and as I felt I must have loved her if I had been a better girl. (iii)

As a consequence, Esther is "timid and retiring," her doll is her "solitary friend," and she accepts as her goal her aunt's injunction of "submission, self-denial, and diligent work": Esther would "do some good to some one, and win some love if I could" (iii).

These preoccupations of Esther's childhood might call for less attention if they were set aside after the early chapters, but they persist as her central concerns throughout the novel, reappearing most conspicuously after illness has altered her appearance. She is doubtful, for example, whether she ought to keep Allan Woodcourt's flowers after her change, because they had been sent "to one so different" (xxxvi), and she is painfully responsive to the opinions even of relative strangers, as when a child comments, " 'Mother, why is the lady not a pretty lady now, like she used to be?' But when I found the child not less fond of me, and drew its soft hand over my face with a kind of pitying protection in its touch, that soon set me up again" (xxxvi). Esther fears the effect her facial alteration might have on Ada Clare and is genuinely surprised to find in "my angel girl . . . the old dear look, all love, all fondness, all affection. Nothing else in it—no, nothing, nothing!" (xxxvi). John Jarndyce, too, comes under anxious scrutiny:

> But he did not hint to me, that when I had been better-looking, he had had this same proceeding [i.e. proposing marriage] in his thoughts, and had refrained from it. That when my old face was gone from me, and I had no attractions, he could love me just as well as in my fairer days. . . . That his generosity rose above my disfigurement. . . . But *I* knew it, I knew it well now. (xliv)

Esther consistently interprets the love she receives as "generosity" or mere pity, and this is as true of her interpretation of Allan Woodcourt's feelings as John Jarndyce's. Esther avoids Allan upon his return to England after her illness, though she is pleased by his commiseration at their accidental meeting: "I saw that he was very sorry for me. I was glad to see it. . . . I was glad to be tenderly remembered, to be gently pitied, not to be quite forgotten" (xlv). When Allan declares his love for her, Esther discovers to her surprise that "what I had thought was pity and compassion, was devoted, generous, faithful love" (lxi), but she continues to speak of "winning love," just as she did at the start of the novel:

> "Heaven knows, beloved of my life," said [Woodcourt], "that my praise is not a lover's praise, but the truth. You do not know what all around you see in Esther Summerson, how many hearts she touches and awakens, what sacred admiration and what love she wins."
> "O, Mr. Woodcourt," cried I, "it is a great thing to win love, it is a great thing to win love! I am proud of it, and honored by it; and the hearing of it causes me to shed these tears of mingled joy and sorrow—joy, that I have won it, sorrow that I have not deserved it better." (lxi)

The novel ends, in fact, with Esther worrying once again about her "old looks—such as they were" (lxvii), still unconvinced that she is as lovable as she seems to be, still disbelieving that she has really "won" or earned love.

Obviously, Esther's sense of inferiority and her anxieties about whether she is lovable or worthy of love extend far beyond the realities of her situation. One can be sympathetic to her plight after disease has altered her complexion, yet still recognize that in fact the only adverse reactions to her change are Guppy's withdrawal of his marriage proposal—though he will wish to reinstate this before the novel closes—and Mr. Turveydrop's ceasing "to be particular in his attentions, since I had been so altered" (l). Esther's sensitivity about her appearance is to be regarded, then, not as a completely justifiable response to the realities of her new situation, but as a late development of a more generalized lifelong pathology.

What are the origins of Esther's morbid sensitivity about her looks and of her desperate need to win love? Her Calvinist aunt warns Esther early in life that she must "pray daily that the sins of others be not visited upon your head, according to what is written" and that she must try "as hard as ever I could, to repair the fault I had been born with (of which I confessedly felt guilty yet innocent)" (iii). The offense Esther must expiate is her illegitimate birth to Lady Dedlock and Captain Hawdon, of which she obviously cannot be truly guilty. Yet Esther continues to suffer from her personal sense of guilt, even though Dickens mocks and condemns the stern Calvinism from which it is derived.

Aunt Barbary and her "distorted religion" (xvi) are ridiculed mercilessly by the author—for example, the immediate cause of the aunt's demise is her horrified response to a reference to Christ's mercy toward the woman taken in adultery—but a sense of sin and guilt hangs over Esther long after Miss Barbary's version of religion has been thoroughly discredited by the author.

Esther often wonders about the identity of her parents, at times supposing John Jarndyce to be her father, but more frequently simply believing herself an abandoned orphan. Lady Dedlock, Esther's mother, considers Esther to be her "injured" child when she discovers her identity (xxxvi), but Dickens clears Lady Dedlock of any imputation of having deserted her daughter by having her believe that Esther died shortly after birth. In this manner the mother can be absolved, at least on the most serious count—"I had not been abandoned by my mother" (xxxvi)—and the blame can be fixed instead on the aunt who spirited Esther away, functioning like the wicked stepmother in fairy tales as a surrogate for the real mother. With the unexpected revelation of the identity of her mother, Esther, too, suddenly feels free from blame for the sins of her parents: "If the sins of the fathers were sometimes visited upon the children, the phrase did not mean what I had in the morning feared it meant. I knew I was innocent of my birth as a queen of hers; and that before my Heavenly Father I should not be punished for birth, nor a queen rewarded for it" (xxxvi).

The rest of the novel suggests, however, that the individual's feelings of guilt and responsibility, even for his parents' sexual vagaries, are not so easily put aside. In fiction the persistence of such feelings—even in the face of their explicit rejection by the character concerned—is commonly betrayed by his continued vulnerability to the reproaches of his society. No character in the novel suggests that Esther would be disgraced by the public revelation of Lady Dedlock's affair with Hawdon, but Rosa, Lady Dedlock's servant, whom she treats almost like a daughter, does play a significant role in Tulkinghorn's threats against Sir Leicester's wife. If Lady Dedlock's liaison were revealed, the lawyer implies, Mr. Rouncewell might indignantly take Rosa away from the disgrace of connection with the Dedlock household (xl); and when Tulkinghorn learns that Lady Dedlock herself has sent Rosa away, he accuses her of attempting to separate Rosa "as much as possible from . . . any reproach and exposure that impend over yourself" (xlviii), as a result of which he declares that the understanding whereby he was to have kept silent is at an end. Rosa is, then, highly vulnerable to public disgrace, and this fact suggests that Esther, once acknowledged as Lady Dedlock's illegitimate daughter, would not easily escape from the social consequences of the sin of her parents, regardless of how innocent she may feel herself to be.

On a more personal level, as well, Esther can hardly be said finally to surmount the psychological consequences of the overriding sense of sin and guilt with which she has been raised. She continues to live under the curse of her illegitimacy in several ways, including one which Taylor Stoehr notes: symbolically Esther's illness and disfigurement seem to be a consequence of her mother's sin.[6] I find support for this hypothesis in Esther's temporary blindness, a common dream equivalent to castration, which in fantasy is the appropriate penalty for a sexual transgression. Further, Esther's facial disfiguration is similar to that of Monks, the villain in *Oliver Twist,* "in whom all evil passions, vice, and profligacy festered till they found vent in a hideous disease which has made [his] face an index even to [his] mind" (xlix). Monks' disease is plainly venereal, and, if identical symptomatology here implies an analogous etiology, Esther's illness may be an effective symbolic visitation upon her of the sexual transgression of her parents. One pox, in other words, may stand for the other. Certainly Esther's facial scars mesh all too well with those psychic wounds inflicted by the circumstances of her birth from which she has suffered all her life: her scars renew and reinforce her earlier sense of personal inadequacy. They are only the recent physical manifestation of her characteristic psychopathology.

This takes us quite a bit further in understanding Esther than most critics are able to go, but to understand her fully and to appreciate her place and function in the novel as a whole, we must turn from an analysis of Esther's character to a statement about the larger fantasy which the novel embodies and in which Esther plays only a limited role. After all, so many guilty responses are manifested in Esther without any suggestion of the existence of active strivings on her part that it may be necessary to hypothesize the existence of certain wishes and desires which conspicuously do *not* find expression in her character, but which may be located elsewhere in the novel. One must observe that of all the characters in the novel, Esther is undoubtedly most affected by the mystery surrounding her birth, and yet she is probably the least interested in taking action to establish the identity of her parents. She is in fact quite remarkable for her apparently total lack of active desires, for her extreme passivity and deference, for bearing the scars usually associated with the punishment of transgressions without having committed any. In her introjected sense of depravity, in her feelings of inferiority, in her supposed inability to win love, and in her adoption of her aunt's harsh prescription of "submission, self-denial, and diligent work" (iii), Esther exhibits all of the consequences, but expresses none of the wishes psychoanalysis has taught us to expect in every child's fantasies.

And here we come to a crux about Esther's sexual identity: it is too restrictive to see her exclusively as a woman. Rather, she is a child of indeterminate sex, as perhaps even the sexual ambiguity of her surname,

Summer-son, implies. From a psychoanalytic perspective, she may usefully be regarded as less daughterly than filial, less of a heroine than a sexually undifferentiated hero; for she represents only one of a number of alternative filial roles depicted in the novel. Finally, she is a woman because Dickens defines her as passive and submissive and because he chooses to deny in her the presence of those highly charged wishes and fears which are manifest in other, more active "filial" characters in the novel, like Richard or Tulkinghorn, even though Esther seems at times to suffer passively for the desire and hostility which others act out.[7] As the hero with inhibitions, she represents one version of the composite central figure. This explains why Esther continues to feel responsible for and guilty about her illegitimacy, even though it seems perfectly obvious to her conscious mind that she cannot realistically be held accountable for the circumstances of her birth.

Though Esther is troubled by recurring manifestations of past guilt and unworthiness, she survives her ordeals to achieve a small triumph in the domestic sphere at the end of the novel, while Richard, Tulkinghorn, and others learn to their cost the dangers of active attempts at self-assertion or rebellion against "parental" authority. To be an active, hostile "son" is to risk death, but to accept a passive, suffering, feminine identification is presented in this novel as a viable alternative.

To this many readers of Dickens object. Esther's passivity disturbs because she represents a symbolic solution to the psychological issue posed by the novel which, despite Dickens' own preferences, proves unsatisfying. Like many of Dickens' protagonists—male and female alike—Esther is intended by the author to be admired in the wisdom of her resignation: the Dickensian hero characteristically wins both his fortune and a mate through passive waiting and frequently with the aid of a beneficent father figure. Yet the sensitive reader of *Bleak House* comes to suspect that Dickens' proposed solution—that one can achieve happiness through the repression of instinct—is a violation of psychological verisimilitude. The reader grasps intuitively that the inhibition of desire generally takes its toll on the psyche; and he judges that Dickens has finessed or denied the conflict rather than worked it through in Esther's character. Her unacceptability for the modern reader (and for Dickens' contemporaries too—John Forster was singularly unimpressed by Esther) may have less to do with her sentimental portrayal as an ideal of Victorian womanhood than with the particular filial role she adopts and which Dickens seems finally to advocate. Dickens' apparent approval of Esther's choice seems to jar with his intuitive awareness for most of the novel that the consequence of choosing passive renunciation, repression, and inhibition as a mode of avoiding conflict is likely to be neurotic symptomatology. Certainly the reader

senses that active strivings are suppressed only at a cost to the psyche
and that the price that Esther has paid may be read plainly in her face
and in her desperately felt need to "win" love.[8]

— 2 —

If Esther Summerson is remarkable for her inhibition and passivity, the Chancery litigants in *Bleak House* are distinguished by their
obsessional thinking, compulsiveness, and, in some cases, barely suppressed rage. Though not inhibited like Esther, the litigants' more active curiosity still finds expression only in neurosis. Their pursuits conform with Freud's description of the second possible transformation of
the energy associated with sexual curiosity in the child: their researches
are interminable, hopeless, and ultimately self-destructive. If Esther's
mode is the repression of active curiosity, desire, and hostility, the
Chancery litigants exist to indulge their obsessions, nourish their suspi-
cions, and helplessly proclaim their rage.

Critics are quite in agreement about the emotion which is preemi-
nent in Dickens' depiction of Chancery and related social institutions:
Edgar Johnson notes the "indignation" in the novel, and Morton Dauwen Zabel emphasizes its "anger." [9] No critic has attempted, however,
to tie these dominant emotions in the Chancery portions of the novel to
Esther's feelings about her sinful parents; this is understandable, since
Esther's character seems so divorced from any resentment or rage. Although she reports her feelings in a manner which conveys at most a
sense of inferiority, a touch of guilt or anxiety, and nothing more, a
shrewd psychologist might expect to find in such a person traces of
anger, aggression, indignation, and hostility, too. *Bleak House* is one
novel, not two separate works; and if the lessons of psychoanalytic
research are heeded, this implies that it embodies in its two narratives
fantasies which are essentially related rather than utterly dissimilar.[10] It
behooves us, in other words, not to forget Esther altogether in our consideration of the Chancery litigants, however different they may appear to be and however much some critics might be tempted to snip
Esther and her narrative out of *Bleak House,* to exclude them as something alien to the novel's subject.

The court of Chancery in *Bleak House* is primarily a court of equity
for disputed wills, but as superintendent over and protector of the affairs of litigants unable to plead in their own behalf—especially widows,
orphans, and madmen—it also possesses some obviously paternal functions.[11] When the wards in Jarndyce first appear before the court,
Dickens notes, "the Lord Chancellor, at his best, appeared so poor a
substitute for the love and pride of parents" (iii); and, on the deepest
psychic level, it is no accident that if Miss Flite's fanciful speculation
were true—if the mysterious veiled lady (actually Lady Dedlock) were

the Lord Chancellor's wife—then the Lord Chancellor would literally be Esther's father (xxxv).

The paternal aspect of Chancery and the tremendous anger felt toward it by its "children," the litigants, are exemplified by the case of Gridley, the man from Shropshire. Gridley's litigation, like all the suits which come before Chancery in the course of *Bleak House,* concerns a dispute within a family over a will. Gridley is dragged to law over the question of whether his (presumably younger) brother received payment of his rightful share of their father's estate; but the suit ultimately delves into such psychologically significant peripheral issues as "whether I was my father's son—about which, there was no dispute at all with any mortal creature" (xv). Enmeshed in litigation, Gridley begins to fight back at the legal system; he becomes violent and must be imprisoned for contempt of court and threatening a solicitor (xv). Gridley goes frequently to George Rouncewell's shooting gallery, where "he was in that condition of resentment and violence, that he would come and pay for fifty shots, and fire away till he was red hot" (xxiv). Gridley is about to be arrested by Bucket on a warrant from Tulking-horn, who considers the man from Shropshire to be "a threatening, murderous, dangerous fellow" (xxvii), when poor Gridley dies "worn out," presumably of a broken heart (xxiv).

In his lifetime, Gridley has a clear, stark sense of the alternatives open to him: "I must have this vent under my sense of injury, or nothing could hold my wits together. . . . If I took my wrongs in any other way, I should be driven mad! It is only by resenting them, and by revenging them in my mind, and by angrily demanding the justice I never get, that I am able to keep my wits together" (xv). It is significant that Gridley is always speaking of his wrongs and his sense of the injuries done to him, for he feels abused and betrayed by the law, in whose justice he had trusted, as a child puts his trust in his parents. His sense of the irreversibility of entanglement in Chancery and the inevitability of its end is also important: "I can't undo the past, and the past drives me here," he says, sounding rather like Esther (xv). But, although the shortcomings of parents and authority figures are to be found everywhere in *Bleak House,* Gridley's anger and hostility are so different from any feeling Esther can muster or even comprehend that she observes: "His passion was fearful. I could not have believed in such rage without seeing it" (xv).

As Gridley perceives, madness is the alternative to his rage at Chancery, and quite mad Miss Flite is. The origins of her suit are not detailed, but its effects are.

> "I and my sister worked at tambour work. Our father and our brother had a builder's business. We all lived together. Ve-ry respectably, my dear! First, our father was drawn—slowly.

Home was drawn with him. In a few years, he was a fierce, sour, angry, bankrupt, without a kind word or a kind look for any one. He had been so different, Fitz-Jarndyce. He was drawn to a debtors' prison. There he died. Then our brother was drawn—swiftly—to drunkenness. And rags. And death. Then my sister was drawn. Hush! Never ask to what! Then I was ill, and in misery; and heard, as I had often heard before, that this was all the work of Chancery. When I got better, I went to look at the Monster. And then I found out how it was, and I was drawn to stay there." (xxxv)

Miss Flite's father, of course, suffers the debtors' prison that was the fate of Dickens' own father, but her sister's prostitution and her own obsession with looking at "the Monster" seem to lend to Miss Flite's account a lurid quality. The consequence of her participation in Chancery matters—even only to the point of looking—is madness, which, like Esther's disfigurement and temporary blindness, is a common dream-symbol for castration. Again one finds all the degenerative and incapacitating consequences one might expect to accompany a child's guilty wish connected here with an obsessive looking at the activities of Chancery. Viewed psychoanalytically, such scoptophilia usually derives from the child's need compulsively to repeat his observation of or speculations about parental sexuality—his "primal scene" memory or fantasy.[12]

The names of Miss Flite's collection of caged birds make the same point about the threat Chancery poses by virtue of its power to attract and transfix an impressionable mind. The birds are called "Hope, Joy, Youth, Peace, Rest, Life, Dust, Ashes, Waste, Want, Ruin, Despair, Madness, Death, Cunning, Folly, Words, Wigs, Rags, Sheepskin, Plunder, Precedent, Jargon, Gammon, and Spinach" (xiv). One Dickens critic, A. O. J. Cockshut, exclaims that this "has some claim to be the best list in literature," and while I am in accord with his assessment, I believe the list does cry out for explication.[13] In fact the list represents a clever progression through three juxtaposed clusters of associated words: "'Hope' through 'Life' will turn into the items 'Dust' through 'Death' as a result of involvement in a Chancery lawsuit, alluded to in the list by the words 'Cunning' through 'Spinach.'"[14] The blighting aspects of the law, in other words, are stressed in Miss Flite's list: the qualities of an innocent infancy, a youthful Eden, are seen as reduced to forms of death and madness. As Miss Flite repeatedly notes, she was once possessed of youth, hope, and beauty like Esther's (iii), but these have decayed and fallen away, destroyed by Chancery, and they have been replaced by madness. Chancery incapacitates and injures youth just as surely as the conviction of one's utter sinfulness does. The parallels between Miss Flite's loss of sanity and Esther's blighted life, between the evil effects of Chancery and Esther's parents' sin, are significant.

The suits of Miss Flite and Gridley, though perhaps each in its own way a "model of Chancery practice," are of course dwarfed by the main litigation in *Bleak House*, Jarndyce and Jarndyce; and the fullest study of the consequences of active involvement in a Chancery lawsuit is to be found in the life of Richard Carstone. Miss Flite and Gridley are seen essentially only as victims of their obsessions with Chancery, even though there are references to other, happier times in both their lives; but in Richard the reader is shown the full progress and various stages of the disease. Richard first appears in *Bleak House* as ingenuous, laughing, and lighthearted (ii), or as cheerful and good-natured (v), but before long Esther perceives a "carelessness" and a "wild restlessness" in his character (ix). Chancery picks up these tendencies already present in Richard's makeup and gradually promotes them to full-fledged neurotic symptoms.

The most obvious of these symptoms is Richard's "indecision of character," which is manifested particularly in his inability to choose a profession for himself. The origin of this problem is laid in part to his education, but more particularly to Chancery, "that incomprehensible heap of uncertainty and procrastination on which he has been thrown from his birth":

> [Chancery] has engendered or confirmed in him a habit of putting off—and trusting to this, that, and the other chance, without knowing what chance—and dismissing everything as unsettled, uncertain, and confused. The character of much older and steadier people may be even changed by the circumstances surrounding them. It would be too much to expect that a boy's, in its formation, should be the subject of such influences, and escape them. (xiii)

Richard lacks "habits of application and concentration," and his energy is of a "fitful," impatient kind (xvii). He vacillates about whether to become a sailor, a surgeon, a lawyer, a physician, or a military officer—trying one role after another and then putting each aside with the explanation that he must leave everything incomplete because he "was born into this unfinished contention with all its chances and changes, and it began to unsettle me before I quite knew the difference between a suit at law and a suit of clothes" (xxiii). Thus Chancery warps the character of its victim from infancy, and it preoccupies him and leaves him constitutionally incapable of reaching decisions on the important problems of real life. It becomes an obsession, taking over the entire psyche and exacting "dragging years of procrastination and anxiety, and . . . indifference to other aims" (xxxvii). Richard finally emerges as the victim of a full-scale obsessional neurosis, which is the second possible vicissitude of infantile curiosity described by Freud in the Leonardo essay.

It is a rather curious footnote to this discussion of Richard's growing obsession with Chancery and his inability really to choose a profession to note that Freud, in his famous case history of the "Rat Man," draws an analogy between the indecision of the obsessional neurotic and the refusals of the German equivalents of Chancery to reach a judgment: [15]

> [Some obsessional neurotics] are incapable of coming to a decision, especially in matters of love; they endeavor to postpone every decision, and, in their doubt which person they shall decide for or what measure they shall take against a person, they are obliged to choose as their model the old German courts of justice, in which the suits were usually brought to an end, before the judgment was given, by the deaths of the parties to the dispute.

Almost as if he were conforming to Freud's description of the obsessional neurotic, Richard Carstone wears himself out by "premature anxiety, self-reproach, and disappointment" (li and xlv), and he dies not long before the verdict in the Jarndyce case becomes a moot point, the entire estate having been absorbed in legal costs.

The full psychological significance of the binding and narrowing of psychic energies manifested by Richard's failure to commit himself to a career warrants special attention, because it helps to define further Richard's relationship to Gridley and Esther. Dickens' explanation of the etiology of Richard's problem is interesting: "Having never had much chance of finding out himself what he was fitted for, and having never been guided to the discovery, he was taken by the newest idea, and was glad to get rid of the trouble of consideration" (xiii). A psychoanalyst might go on to suggest that Richard is in fact afraid to succeed and arranges his life in such a manner as to ensure instability, failure, and defeat. The medical literature notes that "occupational inhibitions" like Richard's indecision frequently stem from an inhibition of that aggressiveness which, under our cultural conditions, is necessary for success in life; and it suggests further that this inhibition of normal aggressiveness is actually a defense against rage and against longings for destructive revenge, which in turn are occasioned by the frustration of infantile sexual desires.[16] Rage, as already noted, is a conspicuous feature of the characters in *Bleak House,* either by its presence in the rabid hostility of Gridley toward Chancery or by its pronounced absence in Esther's character. Carstone occupies a middle ground here: Richard, like Gridley, surrenders his own identity to a compulsive preoccupation with Chancery, but, like Esther, he defends against his rage. Each of the characters is in his own way trying to discharge psychic energy whose direct avenues of expression have been blocked. Nor are these suppressions or diversions of psychic energy always completely successful. In Richard's case, for example, the anger and distrust he seems to be defending against seep through and are directed against his guardian and supposed rival in the lawsuit, John Jarndyce.

Although Richard starts out on good terms with his guardian, his growing involvement in Chancery litigation awakens his hostility. Hearing that John Jarndyce has "conflicting interests; claims clashing against his, and what not," Richard begins to "mistrust and suspect" him (xxxv). Viewing his ward's drift with some anxiety, Jarndyce moves to nullify Richard's engagement with Ada Clare, an act which later gives rise to Richard's feeling that Jarndyce "stepped in to estrange [Ada] from me" (xlv). Richard observes that his growing coolness toward Jarndyce derives from his involvement with Chancery, and he notes that "all this business puts us on unnatural terms with which natural relations are incompatible" (xxxvii). Such "division and animosity" within a previously harmonious family suggest an Oedipal configuration: participation in a Chancery suit, Richard might be saying, will show you what your "father" is really about and how fundamentally inimical his interests are to your own. Ada also observes that Chancery lawsuits seem principally to have this effect of setting members of a family against one another: "I am grieved that I should be the enemy— as I suppose I am—of a great number of relations and others; and that they should all be my enemies—as I suppose they are; and that we should all be ruining one another, without knowing how or why, and be in constant doubt and discord all our lives" (v).

Dickens' symbolism implies, then, that Chancery disputes are institutionalized versions of family conflicts, and this suggestion is reinforced by the parallel between his descriptions of the debilitating effects of active involvement in Chancery suits and his evocation of the consequences of the sin of Esther's parents on their child. Those "born into" a lawsuit suffer like Esther: "The legatees under the will are reduced to such a miserable condition that they will be sufficiently punished, if they had committed an enormous crime in having money left to them" (viii). In an unspecified way, the Jarndyce suit has "its share in making . . . both [Richard and Ada] orphans," and it is "the shadow in which . . . both were born" (xxxvii)—the language here strongly recalls Aunt Barbary's view of Esther's illegitimacy. The suit of Jarndyce and Jarndyce is termed the "family misfortune" (xxxvii), the "family curse" (xxxvii), the "fatal inheritance" (lx); and it is, so far as John Jarndyce is concerned, "forbidden ground" for conversation (xvii), again like the circumstances of Esther's birth.

Richard's obsession with Chancery and Esther's anxieties about her origin can be properly understood, then, only when they are both recognized as at bottom two aspects of the same instinct: for both Richard and Esther, the actions of the parents or ancestors are decisive in life, and each spends his life trying to come to terms with the family "legacy," whether literal or figurative. On a symbolic level, the family will proves to be the equivalent of the family sin; Chancery becomes the institutional symbol for the parents. The difference between Esther and Richard is that she will be afforded her modicum of happiness as a result of her acceptance and resignation, while Richard and the other obsessional neurotics will destroy themselves by their interminable and fruitless efforts. Among the psychological alternatives presented in the world of this novel, the inhibition of the desire to look or investigate proves to be preferable to the conversion of that impulse into an obsession.

— *3* —

The character in *Bleak House* who is able most fully to act out his hostility, curiosity, and desire is, interestingly enough, the novel's principal villain, the lawyer Tulkinghorn. At first glance, however, Tulkinghorn appears to have identified himself completely with the paternal and authoritarian elements in his society. The features of Tulkinghorn's appearance and personality that are emphasized as his leitmotiv through the novel are his rustiness, his belonging to the old school, his black clothes which never shine, his speechlessness and oyster-like closeness, and his quality as a "depository of family confidences." The message conveyed by such descriptions is that Tulkinghorn—"the steward of the legal mysteries, the butler of the legal cellar, of the Dedlocks" and other members of the aristocracy—is "eminently respectable" and "retainer-like" (ii) as a consequence of his being "severely and strictly self-repressed" (xli). He appears, in short, perfectly trustworthy, obedient, and controlled.

Before long, however, Dickens reveals that Tulkinghorn's respectability is, like Bradley Headstone's "decency" in *Our Mutal Friend,* a matter of surface appearance only. Dickens introduces doubts as to Tulkinghorn's reliability rather early in the novel: "Whether his soul is devoted to the great, or whether he yields them nothing beyond the services he sells, is his personal secret. He keeps it, as he keeps the secrets of his clients; he is his own client in that matter, and will never betray himself" (xii). Later Tulkinghorn is described as, "in face, watchful behind a blind; habitually not uncensorious and contemptuous perhaps. The peerage may have warmer worshippers and faithfuller believers than Mr. Tulkinghorn, after all, if everything were known" (xxvii). Lady Dedlock, then, correctly assesses Tulkinghorn as "mechanically faithful without attachment," but her evaluation of his motive in uncovering secrets—that he is "very jealous of the profit, privilege, and reputation of being master of the mysteries of great houses"—is less helpful, unless one stresses the unconscious determinants behind the choice of such words as "jealous," "master," "mysteries," and "great houses" (xxxvi). In fact, Tulkinghorn's motives for peeping at the indiscretions of his betters, for being so "watchful behind a blind," seem to be obscured by the novelist.

Tulkinghorn himself claims that his sole concern is "Sir Leicester's feelings and honor, and the family reputation" (xli and xlviii), yet this is obviously mere subterfuge. Thus Tulkinghorn considers Lady Dedlock's sending away of Rosa as a serious threat to his purpose, presumably because Rosa's absence diminishes his power to control her. Tulkinghorn suggests to Lady Dedlock during their final interview that he may reveal his knowledge of her affair with Hawdon to Sir Leicester on the very next morning, though he declines to state this definitively (xlvii). In a conversation with Sir Leicester (liv), Inspector Bucket of the detective police seems to accept the notion that Lady Dedlock's exposure was imminent at the time of Tulkinghorn's murder; however, Lady Dedlock's declared intention of going.to Tulkinghorn the evening of his death to petition him not to "protract the dreadful suspense" but "mercifully [to] strike next morning" again casts doubt on Tulkinghorn's intention and motive (lv). Was Tulkinghorn at the time of his death about to reveal Lady Dedlock's secret or not? And what were his real motives in unearthing the secret in the first place?

Taylor Stoehr is surely right in dismissing blackmail as a motive and in discounting Tulkinghorn's avowals that his investigation is all "for Sir Leicester's sake," but Stoehr does not shed much light on the situation by declaring that "it is in [Tulkinghorn's] character and calling to root out and gobble up such family secrets—not to divulge them." [17] A close attention to textual detail and to metaphor might, however, take us beyond the widely held view of Tulkinghorn as a mid-nineteenth-century version of "motiveless malignancy." For example, Lady Dedlock remarks that Tulkinghorn's "calling is the acquisition of secrets, and the holding possession of such power as they give him" (xxxvi), and it is significant that Tulkinghorn's "love of power" is directed so single-mindedly through the length of the entire novel at an effort to control this extremely forceful woman. At one point the novelist himself offers a deliberately evasive—though in some ways quite revealing—analysis of Tulkinghorn's possible motives:

> It may be that my Lady fears this Mr. Tulkinghorn, and that he knows it. It may be that he pursues her more doggedly and

steadily, with no touch of compunction, remorse, or pity. It may be that her beauty, and all the state and brilliancy surrounding her, only gives him the greater zest for what he is set upon, and makes him the more inflexible in it. Whether he be cold and cruel, whether immovable in what he has made his duty, whether absorbed in love of power, whether determined to have nothing hidden from him in ground where he has burrowed among secrets all his life, whether he in his heart despises the splendor of which he is a distant beam, whether he is always treasuring up slights and offences in the affability of his gorgeous clients—whether he be any of this, or all of this, it may be that my Lady had better have five thousand pairs of fashionable eyes upon her, in distrustful vigilance, than the two eyes of this rusty lawyer, with his wisp of neckcloth and his dull black breeches tied with ribbons at the knees. (xxix)

Tulkinghorn's voyeurist instincts appear to be stimulated especially by ideas about "gorgeous clients," "splendor," "state and brilliancy," and "beauty," that is, by superior station and physical attractiveness. He feels inferior to and slighted by his social betters, and he seeks to engage them in a struggle for power, a struggle which has sexual overtones, as the imagery of inflexibility and burrowing in the ground as well as the emphasis on the beauty of his quarry suggest. The "horn" in the laywer's name also reveals his phallic as well as his aggressive nature (is his name an amalgam of "stalking" and "horn"?), and through such clues as these, the reader comes intuitively to understand Tulkinghorn's sexual motivation as well as his ambition, even though the author does not spell all this out in the text.

It is interesting that Dickens is much more explicit in describing the motives involved in the case of the prototypes for Tulkinghorn and Lady Dedlock who appear in *Dombey and Son,* written five years before *Bleak House.* Tulkinghorn's harboring of grudges and his rebellion against his employer suggest his close resemblance to James Carker the Manager in the earlier novel, while the beautiful Edith Dombey, the wife of Carker's employer, prefigures Lady Dedlock's combination of icy hauteur and inner passionate intensity. Carker is, however, an avowed seducer, and he elopes with Edith in an attempt to shame and dishonor Mr. Dombey, whose business affairs he has already undermined. In that novel, humiliation of the male "parent" is accomplished by acquiring a hold over his wife, and the apparently faithful employee finally becomes an openly hostile, rebellious, and even seducing "son."

While the motives and intentions ascribed to Tulkinghorn are vague, scrambled, and contradictory, it does seem clear that he is driven by the same hostile envy that his predecessor Carker feels toward his superiors. It may be that after gaining power over Lady Dedlock, Tulkinghorn intends to try to seduce his employer's beautiful wife, because of his desire for her and because of his envious hatred of Sir Leicester. Or it may be that Tulkinghorn will be satisfied with the possession of certain knowledge of her passionate fling which resulted in the birth of an illegitimate child. Perhaps Tulkinghorn's knowledge of Lady Dedlock's love affair may be an adequate substitute for her seduction. Freud observes that fantasies or claims of the mother's infidelity to the father (it is a matter of indifference whether the affair took place before or after her marriage to him) are common expressions of the child's own desire for the mother and of his wishes for revenge against the father.[18] So by exposing the affair, or perhaps merely by learning all the details of it, Tulkinghorn may be gratifying his curiosity, hostility, and, vicariously, his desire. Though Dickens appears a bit reluctant to present and examine Tulkinghorn's motives, they do seem rather similar to Carker's, and they apparently include sexual desire as well as envy and ambition. Tulkinghorn is a "filial" rebel, attempting to gain control of the "mother" and to act out his hostility toward the "father" who possesses her.

Since Tulkinghorn's tracking down of Lady Dedlock is essentially an assault on the "parents" and an act of rebellion, it is interesting to note that the Dedlocks are closely identified with Chancery and with social institutions generally. The "world of fashion" centered on Sir Leicester Dedlock is as decayed and stultifying as Chancery itself, and the baronet implicitly connects the two by his approval of Chancery as "a slow, expensive, British, constitutional kind of thing" (ii). From Chesney Wold elections are manipulated, the government of Britain is discussed as if it were a rivalry between families, and good government is conceived of as nepotism and influence peddling. Sir Leicester may have a point in his oft-expressed belief that "the country was going to pieces" and that the floodgates were opening, cracking the entire framework of society (see especially xxviii and xl), but the causes of this dissolution are other and more immediate than he supposes: the rottenness is located within his family circle, and it is exemplified by Lady Dedlock's sexual mystery and by the feed attorney who will not keep his place. Nor is this domestic threat to stability and the social order without precedent: the legend of the Ghost's Walk, after all, tells of an earlier Lady Dedlock who betrayed her husband by aligning herself with "the rebels who leagued themselves against that excellent King," Charles I (vii). Rebels and unfaithful wives, rather than any political conspiracy, are the true sources of anarchy identified by this novel.

Tulkinghorn, then, must be seen in relation to the other "filial" characters. He shares with Esther, Richard, and the others an intense curiosity about "parents," a curiosity directed particularly at their sexual mysteries, a curiosity which seems to represent or be a displaced expression of his own sexual desire. But Tulkinghorn is more active than the others in following up his will to power, his rebellion, his hostility, and his desire. His curiosity breaks out into active pursuit and rebellion, for which he—as surely as Carker, though the causal nexus is less clear in *Bleak House*—is destroyed.

— *4* —

Inspector Bucket seems at first to be identified with the forces of rebellion and self-assertion as manifested in Tulkinghorn, for example, but he is in the later portions of the novel able to identify himself with the goals of parental authority. He is not destroyed by his aggressions or compulsions, nor does he survive by means of an inhibited passivity. Instead, like the Leonardo of Freud's essay, he comes to adapt his curiosity so as to conform with socially acceptable aims through the process of sublimation. Finally, he identifies himself with the "parents."

During Tulkinghorn's life, Bucket is merely an agent for the lawyer, and he is closely identified with him and the worst injustices of the legal system. His intimidation of Jo, tracking down of Gridley, and arrest of George Rouncewell are not likely to endear Bucket to the sympathies of the reader. Yet once his association with Tulkinghorn is dissolved by the latter's death, Bucket's moral status seems to undergo a drastic alteration. He is instrumental in discovering Tulkinghorn's real murderess, so that George and Lady Dedlock may be exculpated, and he even seeks to restore Lady Dedlock to Sir Leicester with a minimum of adverse publicity.

Bucket's dramatic change has provoked critical attack: "Bucket is a monster whitewashed, a character who begins as a fittingly grotesque representative of law and order but ends as a kind of hero." [19] The critic, Michael Steig, then goes on to compare Bucket with other ambiguous figures in the Dickens canon, but he fails to make anything of the reasons why Tulkinghorn and Bucket are linked with one another, nor does he mention the character who seems to be the immediate prototype for both of them, Nadgett in *Martin Chuzzlewit*. Nadgett's secrecy and closeness are very like Tulkinghorn's, but his role as a detective-spy markedly anticipates Bucket, down to the "musty old pocketbook" which Nadgett produces "from somewhere about the middle of his spine" (*Martin Chuzzlewit*, xxvii) and which Bucket draws forth "from somewhere about the middle of his coat" (*Bleak House*, xlix, liii, liv). Bucket and Tulkinghorn, then, share the same origin and spring from the "Nadgett" corner of Dickens' mind. Indeed, all three share a propensity for surreptitious activity and a desire to possess knowledge and power. Bucket's shrewdness, his thrusting forefinger, and his great power and skill tend to identify him with Tulkinghorn as a filial rebel, but he turns out to be in fact the bright, active, and assertive "child" who is on the side of the good parents, ready to protect them against all accusations. He is able at last to dissociate himself from the covert but active rebellion of Tulkinghorn in favor of a socially acceptable adaptation of curiosity and aggression. Political institutions and civil law may lend themselves to abuses in the world of Dickens' novels, but when fundamental criminal and moral laws are violated, then higher sanctions are brought to bear and authority is supported. Under these circumstances, identification with the law and the social establishment proves to be a much more viable solution than acting out the hostility and desire one feels for one's superiors, however glaring their failures may be known to be. The ambiguity of Bucket's moral status, his "whitewashing," stems from Dickens' very mixed feelings about any character who plays such an active role: he is as likely to be a villain as a hero. Still, Bucket is perhaps the only "son" in the novel able successfully to sublimate his impulses, and it is his role as a detective which provides him with the means to do so.

A psychoanalytic study by Geraldine Pederson-Krag describes how detective stories generally come to suggest one path to the mastery of conflicts about looking at and unearthing parental secrets.[20] Dr. Pederson-Krag claims that the reader, by coming at last to identify himself with the detective, is in effect able to gratify his curiosity about parental sexuality with impunity: "In an orgy of investigation, the ego, personified by the great detective, can look, remember and correlate without fear and without reproach, in utter contrast to the ego of the terrified infant witnessing the primal scene."[21] The detective, after all, can gratify his curiosity without guilt, since his function is to solve mysteries rather than to commit crimes. He is the one character who can be permitted to *know* and escape unscathed.

Identification with the detective also offers the reader a route to mastery over the dangerous content of mysteries, a goal the reader has sought from the very first puzzling pages of *Bleak House*. In the success achieved by the detective as an organizer of the wealth of circumstances which seem at first to lack any coherent pattern, a possible resolution to the conflict which lies at the heart of the novel is indicated: curiosity can be indulged if it is exercised on behalf of the parents and without any trace of hostility or desire. The old order may be criticized, but it must finally be maintained.

The novel is, then, not only the expression of a conflict about curiosity in Dickens, but it also represents an attempt to work through that conflict and toward a resolution, an attempt which is recapitulated in the mind of every reader of the book. The experience of reading follows a progression through curiosity and disorder to an understanding of the coherence of events. When the reader at last becomes aware of this coherence, he experiences the triumph of a Bucket at the solution of a mystery. He is assured that order and not fragmentation prevails, and he can gratify his curiosity with impunity, without guilt. *Bleak House* deserves to be considered one of Dickens' first achievements precisely because its formal design as a mystery so successfully expresses and attempts to work through its latent content, its concern with the investigation of the mysteries associated with parental sexuality.[22]

Yet the novel's ambivalence on the question of whether or not Oedipal mysteries are actively to be investigated is not fully resolved at the book's end: the psychological "message" of *Bleak House* remains an ambiguous one. Although Bucket represents the child as hero and detective, and despite his prominence in the later pages of the novel, the book's principal hero remains Esther Summerson, even though her passive and inhibited response to the challenges of mystery and curiosity is not as attractive to most readers as Bucket's assertion and command. While Dickens seems intellectually to perceive the sublimation of Bucket as the only possible successful adaptation of the investigative impulse in the real world, he still hopes against hope for the triumph of the passive child as well. Dickens' realism seems in conflict with his wish to believe in the possibility of a passive solution, so the novel concludes on a note of unresolved tension.

In any case, Dickens has spent much more energy in exploring the extremes on the spectrum—helpless rage and passive submission—than in delineating the potential mean solution that Bucket represents. Ambivalence and conflict energize Dickens, while resolution, though sought, characteristically escapes him. The principal affective resonances of *Bleak House* remain, on the one hand, the indignation and rage expressed against Chancery, which most readers—especially most modern readers, with their preference for activist confrontation with the unreasonable demands of parental authority—regard as the novel's success; and, on the other hand, Esther's passive disengagement from curiosity, which leaves many readers of the book less than satisfied. Nevertheless, the active but sublimated solution of "desexualized" mysteries is something which every reader of *Bleak House* must work through after the model of Detective Inspector Bucket, even though emotionally the book's author clearly remains more drawn to Esther's mode of repression and to the Chancery litigants' obsessions and anger as responses to the dangerous attractions of mystery, curiosity, and desire.

Edward Heatley

THE REDEEMED FEMININE OF
LITTLE DORRIT

You still preach the pact Jehovah
Made with man five thousand years ago.
Every generation must make its own pact with God.
Our generation is not to be scared by rods
Of fire, or by nurses' tales about damned souls.
Its first commandment, Brand, is: Be humane.
                                        Brand, Act 3

LITTLE DORRIT shares with Ibsen's *Brand* that tendency of the human imagination to give expression to the powerful feeling that every generation must make a new pact with its own God, by the tearing down of the house of the old God and his burial in the debris. The collapse of the house of Mrs. Clennam, the figure, like the Jehovah-pact of *Brand,* of "dark law," represents precisely this impulse. The interaction of Mrs. Clennam and Amy Dorrit always looks forward to the resolution of the question of what the "first commandment" is for the new generation; this is the basis on which the claim of their interaction to aesthetic coherence rests. Indeed, in the context of the bringing-down of the old temple (in *Brand* it is the burial of the "ice-priest" beneath the crashing "ice-church"), it is seen that the religious emotion of *Little Dorrit,* centered in Amy, has roots feeding far more deeply in the total creative life of the novel than is suggested by Trilling's brilliant but foreshortening description of Amy Dorrit as "the Beatrice of the *Comedy,* the paraclete in female form." The terms of reference for the religious experience of *Little Dorrit* are so much more substantial than this. She is in fact the bearer of the first commandment for the *new* generation, the spiritual center of the impulse of the "Master Builder" to construct the house for the *new* God. Trilling's alignment of *Little Dorrit* with *The Divine Comedy* has the further disadvantage of suggesting an affinity between Dickens' novel and the great metaphysical system of twelfth-century Catholic Europe, whereas the religious experience of Dickens' novel is substantiated by the radical religious ethos of the mid–nine-

[153

teenth century. Founded upon scientifc materialism, this radical religious ethos looks to a doctrine of Man and Earth; *Little Dorrit* has so thoroughly opened up the frontiers for the massive humanity of such nineteenth-century figures as Ibsen that the way has been blocked to Dante and his metaphysical system.

The unapproachable, ruthless, vindictive God of the dark law has a larger presence in *Little Dorrit* than in any other of Dickens' novels; *Bleak House* is its nearest rival, with the punishing God of Lady Dedlock's and her sister's puritan religion. The God of dark law of *Little Dorrit* exists not only in the theological sense, but also, as I shall discuss later, in the psychological dimension of the unapproachable Father, or the Super-Male. Theologically His temple is seen to be massive and menacing enough. Arthur Clennam stands by in the horror of childhood memory as his mother reads her Testament,

> sternly, fiercely, wrathfully—praying that her enemies . . . might be put to the edge of the sword, consumed by fire, smitten by plagues and leprosy, that their bones might be ground to dust, and that they might be utterly exterminated. As she read on, years seemed to fall away from her son like the imaginings of a dream, and all the old dark horrors of his usual preparation for the sleep of an innocent child to overshadow him. (Oxford Illustrated Dickens, 1953, pp. 35–36)

Figuratively, the private dwelling of Mrs. Clennam, in which she presides over the rule of gloom and darkness, is one and the same thing as the religious temple of revenge and destruction: "Do you consider [she retorts to a questioning Arthur] that a house serves no purpose, Arthur, in sheltering your infirm and afflicted—justly infirm and righteously afflicted—mother?" (46). The house is the "impious" construct just as her habitual communions with her God are: " 'Smite, Thou my debtors, Lord, wither them, crush them: do Thou as I would do, and thou shalt have my worship': this was the impious tower of stone she built up to scale Heaven" (47).

Amy Dorrit, like Agnes the teacher of gentleness in *Brand,* is the holder of the new Galilean covenant, "the blessed later covenant of peace and hope that changed the crown of thorns into a glory" (793):

> "O, Mrs. Clennam, Mrs. Clennam," said Little Dorrit, "angry feelings and unforgiving deeds are no comfort and no guide to you and me. . . . Be guided only by the healer of the sick, the raiser of the dead, the friend of all who were afflicted and forlorn, the patient Master who shed tears of compassion for our infirmities. . . . There is no vengence and no infliction of

suffering in His life, I am sure. There can be no confusion in
following Him, and seeking for no other footsteps, I am certain!" (792)

Characteristic of the great spirits who can no longer serve the supernatural God, but who passionately retain the religious impulse, is the in-
tensification of their veneration of the life of Jesus the great seer of
Galilee. Dickens, like Ibsen, devoted much of his creative energy to the
new mid-nineteenth-century humanistic rededication to the great Galilean. It is the energy of Dickens' commitment to the spirit of the Galilean covenant which, following directly upon Amy Dorrit's offering of
the new covenant to Mrs. Clennam, brings down the old "impious
tower": "In one swift instant the old house was before them; . . . another thundering sound, and it heaved, surged outward, opened
asunder in fifty places, collapsed and fell. . . . The great pile of chimneys, which was then alone left standing like a tower in a whirlwind,
rocked, broke, and hailed itself upon the heap of ruin" (793–94).

For Dickens, as for Ibsen, the supernatural God is no party to the
Galilean covenant of gentleness and compassion; it is a doctrine of
Earth centered upon the Man-Savior, assured by the reality of love
revealed in a multitude of lives and by the earth's own inherent beauty
and bounty. "Duty on Earth, restitution on earth, action on earth"
(319), the earth—although from the majority of existing perspectives it
is the universal prison—that is yet capable of assuring men like Clennam of "that sense of peace."

> Everything within his view was lovely and placid. The rich fo-
> liage of the trees, the luxuriant grass diversified with wild
> flowers, the little green islands in the river, the beds of rushes,
> the water-lilies floating on the surface of the stream, the distant
> voices in boats borne musically towards him on the ripple of
> the water and the evening air, were all expressive of rest, . . .
> the prevailing breath of rest, which seemed to encompass him
> in every scent that sweetened the fragrant air. The long lines of
> red and gold in the sky, and the glorious track of the descend-
> ing sun, were all divinely calm. . . . Between the real landscape
> and its shadow in the water, there was no division; both were so
> untroubled and clear, and, while so fraught with solemn mys-
> tery of life and death, so hopefully reassuring to the gazer's
> soothed heart, because so tenderly and mercifully beautiful.
> (332–33)

The new temple of the "master builder" of *Little Dorrit* is very like the
"Church of Life" in *Brand:*

> Our church is boundless. It has no walls.
> Its floor is the green earth,
> The moorland, the meadow, the sea, the fjord.
> Only heaven can span its roof. (Act 5)

In the world of *Little Dorrit* the impulse to establish the temple of earth and doctrine of man is intensified by the increasing redundancy and disarray of the institutional church. Thus, Clennam listens to the dismal importuning of the London church bells:

> At the quarter, it went off into a condition of deadly-lively importunity, urging the populace in a voluble manner to Come to church, Come to church, Come to church! At the ten minutes, it became aware that the congregation would be scanty, and slowly hammered out in low spirits, They *won't* come, they *won't* come, they *won't* come! At the five minutes, it abandoned hope, and shook every house in the neighbourhood for three hundred seconds, with one dismal swing per second, as a groan of despair. (29)

This is Dickens' farewell fantasia for a dying church, given in antiphonal form: "come," "they *won't* come." Indeed it is in this novel that Dickens coined the phrase "a congregationless Church" (31). Thus the echo here is manifestly that of the futile importuning of the redundant theological church of *Dombey and Son*.

So far I have considered the novel from the historical perspective of the radical religious ethos of the mid–nineteenth century, having its creative expression in the pervasive figure of the temple and the covenant. A change in the medium of analysis from history to psychology provides us with a structure which can more adequately accommodate the full dynamic of the religious life of *Little Dorrit*. Thus placing the interaction of the ruthless temple of Mrs. Clennam and the gentle covenant of Amy Dorrit in its psychological dimension, it becomes clear that they trace out a series of oscillations between the Super-Male, unapproachable Father-Religion, and the Feminine orientation of the Christ ideal: the lamb of gentleness and compassion. Perhaps none of Dickens' novels gives more overt expression to the conflict between the masculine and feminine in Dickens' own nature than *Little Dorrit*. The operation of the masculine-feminine split is the energy source which groups so much of the creative life of the novel within its two poles of worship. Thus the existential crisis of Arthur Clennam is always looking toward the feminine spirituality, centered in Amy, for its resolution. Conversely, the Father-Religion of Mrs. Clennam draws into itself the super-male energies of characters like Henry Gowan, Miss Wade, and Ferdinand Barnacle. In calling the latter configuration the masculine pole of worship, I of course have in mind the question of male-identification illuminated by the Freudian concept of the Father-Religion, but, more especially, in my use of the idea of poles of worship I am invoking Jung's description of religion as an integrated "psychotherapeutic system": "Religions are psychotherapeutic systems in the truest sense of the word. . . . They *express the whole range* of psychic problems in powerful images" (*Collected Works,* trans. R. F. C. Hull [Princeton: Princeton University Press, 1961] 8: par. 805). The most fundamental qualities of the religion which emerges from such a system depends on whether the masculine images or the feminine images gain ascendancy. In *Little Dorrit* the feminine images of worship are affirmed only after the male images have challenged them to their most resistance.

The masculine images of hate, brutality, and mental disruption are both powerful and authentic in *Little Dorrit.* Characteristic of the novel's masculine powers is the episode in which Henry Gowan, the sophisticated, cynical master-male, brutally reduces his dog to submission.

> "Lion! Lion!" He was up on his hind legs, and it was a wrestle between master and dog. "Get back! Down, Lion! Get out of his sight, Blandois. What the devil have you conjured into the dog?" . . .
> The master, little less angry than the dog, felled him with a blow on the head, and standing over him, struck him many times severely with the heel of his boot, so that his mouth was presently bloody.
> "Now get you into that corner and lie down," said Gowan, "or I'll take you out and shoot you." (494)

The master-male image of Gowan is more sharply focused when it is projected into the jungle world of Miss Wade. In her savage eyes everyone else is "tame in comparison with Mr. Gowan, who knew how to address me on equal terms, and how to anatomise the wretched people around us" (670). Here the worship of the boot has changed the object of its onslaught from dogs to "wretched" people. Together Wade and Gowan form a communion of torment of the type already familiar to the Dickens reader in the relationship of Carker and Edith:

> He [Gowan] was the first person I had ever seen in my life who had understood me. He was not in the house three times before I knew that he accompanied every movement of my mind. In his cold easy way with all of them, and with me, and with the whole subject, I saw it clearly. (669)

The question as to whether Miss Wade is lesbian is a subject of endless fascination, especially when viewed from the point of view of Dickens' intention. For the present purpose it will suffice to say that she is a female on a masculine rampage of neurotic intensity, and that the role of the neurotic tormentor must have been a seductive one for Dickens in his heightened masculine aspect. If Miss Wade herself seduces the young females with whom she comes in contact, it is less the seduction of one female by another than the exertion of the mesmeric will by a Dracula-type figure. Pet Meagles is intimidated by her in this way in the quarantine episode, but it is Tattycoram who is marked out by Dickens to bear the main stress of Miss Wade's hypnotic power. Thus in the scene in which Mr. Meagles attempts to win back Tattycoram from Miss Wade, from "that passion fiercer than yours, and temper more violent than yours," he refers to "that lady's eyes so intent upon you" and "that power which she exercises" (329). The episode closes with the Dracula in female clothing taking possession of her quarry: "Miss Wade, who had watched her under this final appeal [of Meagles] with that strange attentive smile, . . . then put her arm about her waist as if she took possession of her for evermore. . . . And there was a visible triumph in her face when she turned it to dismiss the visitors" (330).

The hypnotic power of the rogue male is well established in the Dickens world; one immediately thinks of Steerforth's mesmeric hold over David, Carker's over Rob the Grinder, and Jasper's over Rosa. It seems clear, then, that in *Little Dorrit* the imagination of the boot and demonic, hypnotic seduction, upon which the character of Miss Wade draws its lifeblood, has long since left behind the social psychology of the illegitimate child, and, equally it suggests boundaries rather more elemental then lesbian psychology. She is locked in the satanic embrace of the dance of hate, the super-masculine Dickens himself her principal partner; she, of all his things of darkness, his greatest seducer.

A *seemingly* objective handling of masculine power is found in Dickens' treatment of Ferdinand, "the best and brightest of the Barnacles." After the collapse of the Merdle empire he delivers the doctrine of power and corresponding powerlessness with charm, flair, and numbing finality.

> "The next man who has as large a capacity and as genuine a taste for swindling, will succeed as well. Pardon me, but I think you really have no idea how the human bees will swarm to the beating of any old tin kettle; in that fact lies the complete manual of governing them. . . . Good day! I hope that when I have the pleasure of seeing you next, this passing cloud will have given place to sunshine. Don't come a step beyond the door, I know the way out perfectly. Good day!" (738–39)

His is a limitless capacity for defining every situation by a reductive set of rules, with the detachment of a systems analyst brought in from another universe: "You have no idea how many people want to be left alone. You have no idea how the Genius of the country (overlook the Parliamentary nature of the phrase, and don't be bored by it) tends to being left alone. . . . We must have humbug, we all like humbug, we couldn't get on without humbug. A little humbug, and a groove, and everything goes on admirably, if you leave it alone" (737–38). The objectivity here is more illusory than real, for the goal of detachment is sought after at the level of fantasy. It's the fantasy of the hollow man who takes on life in the spirit of a game, reducing the complexities and unknowns to a series of rules which allow of prediction; it's really a sign which the gamesman wears, announcing that he does not wish to be involved in the complexities of life outside the rules of his game or in the multitudinous variability of the inner life. A declaration of intent it remains, of course, for the inner life cannot be switched off. But the whole exercise which Dickens puts Ferdinand through does generate a powerful fantasy of control. This is the same fantasy control which Pirandello reproduced in his *The Rules of the Game.* For Dickens the "game of life" is more properly characterized as an insistent imaginative possibility, an aspect of his psychic life finding expression in the fictive medium; for the twentieth century, in the face of the accelerated collapsing of value systems, it has increasingly become a way of life.

One can see why Shaw was so impressed by *Little Dorrit,* for in his own works there are many systems analysts who operate with the same superhuman detachment as Ferdinand. But the brightest of the Barnacles is not really a Barnacle at all. Placed within a higher social cast and with a much more concrete politico-social framework, Ferdinand is the reincarnation of Carker of the power game, Carker shuffling the firm's business letters, deciding his next move against his rivals. The difference between the two creations is that Dickens has shifted the axis of the fantasy from rampant engagement within the power game to an ideal of manipulation effected in a mood of absolute detachment. Together with the intrinsic nightmare attributes of the Circumlocution Office, Ferdinand, the power gamesman, turns the laughter of the broad satire directed against the public service into awe.

The existential crisis of Arthur Clennam represents the swing of the creative pendulum away from the centers of either effective or active masculine power, Mrs. Clennam, Miss Wade, Gowan, and Ferdinand: "I am such a waif and stray everywhere, that I am liable to be drifted where any current may set" (20). Essentially the major problem confronting Clennam is his inability to cope wholesomely with the feminine aspect of his own being. Surrounded from childhood onwards by menacing images of masculine power, he periodically retreats into a degenerate feminine submissiveness, characterized by his self-proclaimed absence of will, and, to a lesser extent, by his fear of asserting himself with Pet Meagles. Arthur Clennam is a personality in crisis, and it is the integration of this personality through the psychotherapeutic functioning of the masculine-feminine complex of images that constitutes the primary creative activity of *Little Dorrit*.

Clennam's personal crisis is indeed one of integration, or rather its absence. He is a man "who had deep rooted in his nature a belief in all the gentle and good things" of life, and this "had rescued him to judge not, and in humility to be merciful, and have hope and charity" (165). But more than this he is a man whose feminine gentleness of heart has lead him to a degenerate submissiveness in the face of the great questions of his life; in his lonely lodgings he poses the question, "From the unhappy suppression of my youngest days, through the rigid and unloving home that followed them, through my departure, my long exile, my return, my mother's welcome, my intercourse with her since, down to the afternoon of this day with poor Flora," said Arthur Clennam, "what have I found!" (165). It is a submissive retreat from the masculine powers of his life experience, as earlier revealed at the quarantine station: "I have no will. That is to say," he coloured a little, "next to none that I can put in action now. Trained by main force; broken, not bent; heavily ironed with an object on which I was never consulted and which was never mine; . . . what is to be expected from *me* in middle life?" (20). What have I found, what is to be expected from me? Indeed the questioning is endless, but always in this nervous, essentially passive way.

The questioning widens the base of its submissive tendencies when it acknowledges itself as part of the absurd phantasmagoria of Mistress Affery's dream world. Here one could expect to find the two "clever ones," Mrs. Clennam and Jeremiah Flintwinch, "kissing Little Dorrit next, and then the two clever ones embracing each other and dissolving into tears of tenderness for all mankind" (343). A novel in which an intending suicide reaches the highest point of self-expression in rejecting a mother-of-pearl penknife in preference for "one with a darker handle," clearly has running through it a devastating feeling for the reality of the absurd. But it is to the dream world of Mistress Affery's "two clever ones" in particular that Clennam addresses his nervous questioning, the world whose "close air was secret. The gloom, and must, and dust of the whole tenement, were secret. At the heart of it his mother presided, inflexible of face, indomitable of will, firmly holding all the secrets of her own and his father's life, and austerely opposing herself, front to front, to the great final secret of all life" (543). The oppressive secrets have extensively to do with the guilt inherent in bourgeois monetary practices. But Mrs. Clennam's oppressiveness—

"his mother presided, inflexible of face, indomitable of will"—is finally much larger, more fundamental than the abuses of economic power. The quest for insight into these hidden things, "the great secret of all life," is always foremost in response to Clennam's loss of the masculine energies of will and self-assertion. Thus he will "make a desperate appeal to Affery. If she could be brought to be communicative and to do what lay in her to break the spell of secrecy that enshrouded the house, he might shake off the paralysis of which every hour that passed over his head made him more acutely sensible" (680). But the hope of Clennam's satisfying his great hunger for insight is reduced to absurdity by the ludicrous venue and accompanying circumstances of the moment of possible revelation. Dickens can offer only a parody of an oracle-giving. Affery is at once the veiled matron of the darkened grotto, bearer of life's mystery, and the half-witted domestic who, during the bizarre interview in an unlighted basement closet, has her apron over her head. The oracle-giving is brought to an abrupt and unceremonious close when one of the clever ones, Jeremiah, descends upon her with "such umbrage at seeing his wife with her apron over her head, that he charged at her, and taking her veiled nose between this thumb and finger, appeared to throw the whole screw-power of his person into the wring he gave it" (691).

Literature has many doors and closets of enigma and riddle, and the most frequent sound that emerges when the door-opening is taking place is the sound of mocking absurdity. It's the great cosmic joke that resounds from the charades of Lear and Gargantua and echoes through the dream works of Lewis Carroll, Strindberg, and Beckett. Clennam's meeting with Affery of the closet is clearly within this imaginative configuration. But it is still the insistent imaginative possibility for Dickens rather than the confirmed vision of life of someone like Beckett. For even here, Dickens occupies a position midway between the masculine-feminine poles; on the heightened masculine side there is Dickens taking part in the satanic comedy of the cosmic joke, and on the other, there is the feminine pathos with which Dickens has manifestly endowed this account of the failure to solve the riddle of his life: " 'I make an imploring appeal to you, Affery, to you, one of the few agreeable early remembrances I have, for my mother's sake, for your husband's sake, for my own, for all our sakes' " (689).

The type of submissiveness I have been considering has been the paralysis of the existential will. The second type of submissiveness in Clennam, which shows itself in his relationship with Pet Meagles, is less easy to put a name to; to call it sexual resignation or sexual defeatism is perhaps to be too reductive. It's not precisely clear what it is Arthur Clennam expects from Pet Meagles. Indeed neither Dickens nor Henry James' Strether of *The Ambassadors* has fully unveiled this type of expe-

rience for literature. But that it feeds on some deep-seated sense of
masculine deprivation or inadequacy there is little doubt. In Clennam's
inability to assert himself with Pet Meagles, it's the disproportionate
sense of age, the loss of control on the descent of the hill, the sense of
the drying up of the springs of the masculine demands upon life. The
complexity of the experience resides in the fact that Clennam at once
submits wholly to the sense of age, and yet is aware that he is yielding
too much too soon: "At that time, it seemed to him, he first finally
resigned the dying hope that had flickered in nobody's heart so much
to its pain and trouble; and from that time he became in his own eyes,
as to any similar hope or prospect, a very much older man who had
done with that part of his life" (334).

Thus Clennam's "paralysis" is both of the mind and of the body in
the truest sense of the duality. He can neither lash out with tooth and
claw like Miss Wade at the universal powers that preside over human
experience, nor affront them like Gowan, nor manipulate them like
Ferdinand. It is Amy Dorrit who redeems the feminine from the
degenerate course on which it is in full career. It is she whom Clennam,
to his own acknowledged shame, sees

> toiling on, for a good object's sake, without encouragement,
> without notice, against ignoble obstacles that would have
> turned an army of received heroes and heroines; . . . [she] in
> whom [I had] watched patience, self-denial, self-subdual, chari-
> table construction, the noblest generosity of the affections.
> (720)

Within the great psychic life of this novel she functions as an image of
the courageous, effective feminine, completing the image-complex
which releases the healing emergies in the Jungian manner. To describe Amy Dorrit in this way is to depart from the actual texture of the
narrative only moderately. Thus when Clennam is reduced to an ailing
body and spirit in the Marshalsea, "in the despondency of low, slow
fever," Amy comes to him as the active, administrant feminine, like the
Galilean "healer of the sick": "all the devotion of this great nature was
turned to him in his adversity, to *pour out its inexhaustible wealth of
goodness upon him*, . . . inspir[ing] him with an *inward fortitude,* that rose
with his love" [emphasis mine] (758).

Throughout this episode we see in evidence Dickens' unfailing
feeling for the archetypal rebirth through the feminine healer. It is an
archetypal ritual, superbly celebrated in the language of myth, and
having the life-giving potency of the sacred act. At its inception, there
enters into Clennam's fevered sleep the fragrance of Amy's symbolic
offering of flowers, "some abiding impression of a garden stole over

him—a garden of flowers, with a damp warm wind gently stirring their scents. . . . Nothing had ever appeared so beautiful in his sight. He took [the flowers], up and inhaled their fragrance, and he lifted them to his hot head, and he put them down and opened his parched hands to them" (755–56). And now the great creating feminine enters into the ritual. "One of the night-tunes was playing in the wind, when the door of his room seemed to open to a light touch, and, after a moment's pause, a quiet figure seemed to stand there, with a black mantle on it," revealing Amy Dorrit "with her tears dropping on him as the rain from Heaven had dropped upon the flowers" (756). The operation of this feminine archetype is recurrent in Dickens: together with Clennam, Dombey, Copperfield, Carstone (plus Esther Summerson), Pip, and Wrayburn, each figure in one or other kind of ritual healing *de profundis*. The ubiquity of this archetype clearly indicates that it embodied profound and enduring emotional significance for Dickens, to the extent that it must be very close to being the most fundamental myth presiding over his fiction.

Thus following upon the psychotherapeutic confrontation of the masculine and feminine in both its sacred and profane modes, the resolution of *Little Dorrit* represents a reaffirmation of the feminine in Arthur Clennam's and, finally, Dickens' own nature. The resolution is neither a courtship of death, nor a renouncement of society, although it does of course make total withdrawal from the capital "S" society. It is an existential reengagement based upon a commitment to the divinity of man, to his capacity to rise high above his egotism in gentleness and sympathy of heart. To cherish these attributes is for Dickens, in accordance with the new consciousness of humanist religion, to be among the "blessed," just as Clennam and Amy are said to be "inseparable and blessed" (826). The more habitual state of man is "the noisy and the eager, and the arrogant and the forward and the vain." In placing himself in relation to these two states of man, or rather in being thus placed by Dickens, and in affirming the feminine and the religious outlook, Clennam has attained personality. It is an imaginative experience very much akin to Jung's religious "individuation" or integration of the psychic life. Jung has this to say in *Modern Man in Search of a Soul* of those who have been overwhelmed by the modern void, and with whom he has had dealings:

> There has not been one whose problem in the last resort was not that of finding a religious outlook of life. . . . [They] had lost that which living religions of every age had given to their followers, and none of them had been really healed who did not regain his *religious outlook. This of course has nothing whatever to do with a particular creed or membership of a church* [emphasis mine]. (*Collected Works*, 11:334)

Little Dorrit, then, may be described as a richly diversified soul-complex in search of personality. In this search for personality the part played by Dickens' adherence to the mid-nineteenth-century radical religious ethos is a paramount one artistically. For it is through this ethos that the personality, dynamically evolved from the immense spectrum of images of the psychic life, finds so much of the language of its being, and which joins with the feminine archetypes to form the structure of its being. Far from being an elementary John Bull, Dickens is a great European, the spiritual friend of Feuerbach, George Eliot, Mathew Arnold, and Ibsen. I hope to have suggested the gross inadequacy of a position such as that of Robert Garis, who asserts in his *The Dickens Theatre* that Dickens in *Little Dorrit* "has taken conventional images of conventional moral and social excellence and imparted to them a radiance which is strictly the work of his own will and his own theatrical method" (184). If Garis had understood the great moral seriousness and the psychological implications of the radical religious ethos of nineteenth-century Europe, and how intensely Dickens responded to this consciousness, and appreciated how it commands such continuous expression throughout the creative life of *Little Dorrit,* and with what depth of archetypal endowment, he could never have attempted to beat Dickens with such a "conventional" and "theatrical" stick.

NOTES
INDEX

NOTES

STEPHEN L. FRANKLIN: *Dickens and Time*

[1] "It was in the nineteenth century, especially in Victorian England, that many modern attitudes toward the whole temporal process first emerged. The Victorians, at least as their verse and prose reveal them, were preoccupied almost obsessively with time and all the devices that measure time's flight." Jerome H. Buckley, *The Triumph of Time* (Cambridge: Harvard University Press, 1966), pp. 1–2.

[2] George H. Ford in "Dickens and the Voice of Time," *NCF* 24 (1970), 428–48.

[3] John Henry Raleigh, *Time, Place and Idea: Essays on the Novel* (Carbondale and Edwardsville: Southern Illinois University Press, 1968), p. 128.

[4] Ford, "Dickens and the Voice of Time," p. 437.

[5] See Graham Greene's "The Young Dickens," collected in *The Dickens Critics*, ed. George H. Ford and Lauriat Lane, Jr. (Ithaca, N.Y.: Cornell University Press, 1961), pp. 244–52; and J. Hillis Miller's analysis of *David Copperfield* in *Charles Dickens: The World of His Novels* (1958; rpt. Bloomington: Indiana University Press, 1969), pp. 152–59.

[6] Besides Raleigh's work, see Humphry House's *The Dickens World,* 2d ed. (1942; rpt. London: Oxford University Press, 1965), p. 34.

[7] Alexander Welsh's last chapter in *The City of Dickens* (Oxford: Clarendon Press, 1971), entitled "The Novel and the End of Life," treats apocalyptic views of time. Robert L. Patten's study of *A Christmas Carol,* "Dickens Time and Again," *DSA*, vol. 2 (Carbondale and Edwardsville: Southern Illinois University Press, 1972), pp. 167–96, treats Christian temporal views extensively.

[8] To cite only one pertinent example of this pattern, see Patten's discussion of Dickens as Dostoevsky's "great Christian" in contrast to what such critics as House and A. O. J. Cockshut have said about Dickens' religious feeling: Patten, "Dickens Time and Again," pp. 194–96 and notes.

[9] See Henri Bergson, *Time and Free Will,* trans. F. L. Pogson (London: George Allen and Unwin, 1910), pp. 90 ff.

[10] Spatialization of temporal concepts, as Bergson notes (pp. 183, 236, et passim), is verbally necessary, owing to the limitation of language, as well as being convenient.

[11] Bergson explains that duration cannot be measured and that, in truth, the significance of the workings of a clock is that they "count simultaneities": "there is never more than a single position of the hand and the pendulum, for nothing is left of past positions" (p. 108). Dickens' clocks almost invariably imply the same idea.

[167

12 See Bergson, p. 227, et passim, and also Hans Meyerhoff's *Time in Literature* (Berkeley and Los Angeles: University of California Press, 1955), pp. 5–6, 26–29. Of the many studies of time in literature (A. A. Mendilow's *Time and the Novel*, Georges Poulet's *Studies in Human Time*, etc.), Meyerhoff's is the best at explaining the philosophical and historical ramifications of the subject, and I have drawn on it extensively.

13 In spite of the mystical and transcendental tendencies of certain branches of Christian thought, the idea of the external temporal world as the arena for man's development is inherent in Christianity: "[Christian] time is the *ever-present possibility of renewing* our existence and giving it fresh meaning." Jean Mouroux, *The Mystery of Time*, trans. John Drury (New York: Desclee Co., Inc., 1964), p. 76. Quoted in Patten, "Dickens Time and Again," p. 191.

14 Kathleen Tillotson's assertion, in "The Middle Years from the *Carol* to *Copperfield*," supplement to the September *Dickensian* (1970), p. 14, that Dickens' interest in new methods of treating time begins with the Christmas Books, needs this addition, that his "old" method of treating time was begun in earnest in *Master Humphrey's Clock* and never abandoned. I would argue, in fact, that what happens, for example, in *A Christmas Carol*, *The Chimes*, and *David Copperfield* with reference to time is an outgrowth of what happens earlier.

15 From the preface to *The Old Curiosity Shop*, The Oxford Illustrated Dickens (London: Oxford University Press, 1948), p. xi.

16 What little commentary exists on *Master Humphrey's Clock* invariably puts emphasis on the club's dwelling in the past. See, for example, Malcolm Andrews' "Introducing Master Humphrey," *Dickensian* (1971), pp. 70–86.

17 Quoted in John Forster, *The Life of Charles Dickens* (1872–74; rpt.

London: Chapman Hall, n.d.), p. 122. My text for the novels is the Oxford Illustrated Dickens, but I have documented quoted passages with chapter rather than page numbers for easier reference to other editions. All references to *Master Humphrey's Clock* are to Chapter i, unless marked otherwise.

18 "Mr. Weller's Watch," which appears later, is instituted for the same purpose.

19 A famous London watch and clock shop, the Sir John Bennett Jewelry Store (now reconstructed in Greenfield Village, Dearborn, Mich.) may also have been in Dickens' mind, for it also has huge statues of Gog and Magog on its front which move to strike the chimes of a large clock every quarter hour.

20 The first story tells of a young girl—daughter of a bowyer and money-lender—who runs off with a worthless nobleman, and the bowyer's apprentice who is murdered by a mob years later after he has fought with and killed the nobleman; the second story tells how a man murders his dead brother's son in order to gain an inheritance; the third tells how a young man is hired to confront ghosts near a gibbet and finds instead the weeping relatives of a man recently executed for political reasons.

21 See, for example, Welsh, *City of Dickens*, pp. 119–21.

22 Miller, *Charles Dickens*, pp. 94–95; Malcolm Andrews, "Introducing Master Humphrey," p. 72.

23 House, *The Dickens World*, p. 34. Several critics, including House, have used the evidence of the false bookbacks ("The Wisdom of Our Ancestors—I. Ignorance. II. Superstition," etc.) at Gad's Hill to infer Dickens' rejection of the past. What they fail to add is that Dickens' own book-backs show a similar rejection of the present: The Wisdom of Our Contemporaries: I. Treatment of Children (*Oliver Twist*). II. The Law, Parliament, and the Aristocracy (*Bleak House*). III. Industrialism (*Hard*

Times). IV. Bureaucracy (*Little Dorrit*), etc. The point, of course, which George Orwell made long ago, is that Dickens was the enemy of wrong and the champion of good and decency: "He has no constructive suggestions, not even a clear grasp of the nature of the society he is attacking, only an emotional perception that something is wrong. All he can finally say is, 'Behave decently,' which . . . is not necessarily so shallow as it sounds. Most revolutionaries are potential Tories, because they imagine that everything can be put right by altering the *shape* of society; once that change is effected, as it sometimes is, they see no need for any other. Dickens has not this kind of mental coarseness. . . . What he is out against is not this or that institution, but, as Chesterton put it, 'an expression on the human face.' " *The Collected Essays, Journalism, and Letters of George Orwell*, ed. Sonia Orwell and Ian Angus (1968; rpt. London: Penguin, 1970), pp. 501–2.

24   Nell's death, however bathetic readers like Aldous Huxley think it ("The Vulgarity of Little Nell" in Ford and Lane, *The Dickens Critics*, pp. 153–57), thus has tremendous relevance. Whatever its failings, it is not a mere exercise in sentimentality.

25   The temporal problem in *Martin Chuzzlewit*, as Steven Marcus suggests in *Dickens: From Pickwick to Dombey* (New York: Basic Books, 1964), p. 254, relates to the primeval past and involves considerations deserving a separate treatment. The other Christmas Books carry on temporally from *A Christmas Carol* but in simpler fashion. The very title of *The Chimes* indicates their significance in the story's form, if, as I interpret the term, "form" means the relationship of a story's ideas to the way the author works them out in his fiction. J. Hillis Miller's idea of form overlaps this one, but it involves other considerations. See *The Form of Victorian Fiction* (Notre Dame: Notre Dame University Press, 1968), p. xi.

26   See Forster, *Life of Charles Dickens*, pp. 81 ff.

27   Learned men, naturally, were aware of this situation long before. John Stuart Mill notes this manifestation among the more educated classes in *The Spirit of the Age* (1831): "Before men begin to think much and long on the peculiarities of their own times, they must have begun to think that those times are . . . distinguished in a very remarkable manner from the times that preceded them" (rpt; Chicago: University of Chicago Press, 1942), p. 1.

28   "Framed within the twenty-four hours in Scrooge's fictional life the *Carol* re-creates at least five past times, a fictive present from Christmas morning through Twelfth Night, and a potential future encompassing the deaths of Tiny Tim and Scrooge himself. The multiplicity of the story's temporal dimension points up its central concern . . . for the *Carol* is about Time: Scrooge's conversion is effected, in multiple ways, by the agency of Time itself." Patten, "Dickens Time and Again," p. 166.

29   See, for example, Bergson's conclusion, pp. 222–40.

30   In *Tradition and Tolerance in Nineteenth-Century Fiction*, ed. John Lucas, David Howard, and John Goode (New York: Barnes and Noble, 1967), pp. 99–140.

31   Forster, p. 506.

32   Miller, *Charles Dickens*, pp. 154–55.

33   Stanley Tick, "The Memorializing of Mr. Dick," *NCF* 24 (1969), 142–53.

34   See Forster, p. 25, for Dickens' well-known evaluation of this experience.

35   Miller's ideas about the self-commentary built into each novel may apply here. See, for instance, his introduction to *Bleak House* in the Penguin English Library Edition.

36   Meyerhoff's section on "Order and Association" in *Time in Literature* (pp. 18–26) offers a peculiarly lucid

discussion of the literary ramifications of this problem.

[37] A. E. Dyson, *The Inimitable Dickens* (London: Macmillan, 1970), p. 182.

[38] See Philip Rogers, "Mr. Pickwick's Innocence," *NCF* 27 (1972), 21–37.

[39] Miller, *Charles Dickens,* pp. 212–19.

[40] Loren Eiseley, in *The Immense Journey* (New York: Random House, 1957), pp. 148–54, gives an excellent general discussion of this doctrine of "geological prophecy" which held sway for the fifty years prior to the publication of *The Origin of the Species* (1859) and which "saw the world as a complex symbolic system pointing in the direction of man, who was foreknown and prefigured from the beginning."

[41] Edgar Johnson's description of the plot of the novel is the best: "The movement of *Bleak House* becomes a centripetal one like a whirlpool, at first slow and almost imperceptible, but fatefully drawing in successive groups of characters, circling faster and faster." *Charles Dickens: His Tragedy and Triumph,* (New York: Simon and Schuster, 1952), II, 765.

[42] In *The Maturity of Dickens,* Monroe Engel states: "In *Bleak House,* as in *Dombey and Son,* death functions as a touchstone of reality. It is a measure of the wretchedness of man's earthly sojourn, awful and profound" (Cambridge: Harvard University Press, 1959), p. 117.

[43] The temporal issues of *Hard Times* are basically those of *A Christmas Carol.* In *Little Dorrit,* as K. J. Fielding suggests ("Dickens and the Past: The Novelist of Memory," in *Experience in the Novel,* ed. Roy Harvey Pearce [New York: Columbia University Press, 1968], pp. 107–31), the pervasive theme of imprisonment is in many cases expressed as imprisonment in the personal past, and thus *Little Dorrit* runs parallel to *David Copperfield. A Tale of Two Cities,* like *Barnaby Rudge,* juxtaposes temporal lack of awareness and Christian accep-

tance of time.

[44] K. J. Fielding makes a similar connection: "But this concern with the moral is shown not only in phrases struck off here and there, it is a part of the whole meaning of the book. It is the story of several minds which have shut themselves off from ordinary life and everyday affection, turned in upon themselves, and began to corrupt. Satis House stands for them all." *Charles Dickens: A Critical Introduction,* 2d ed., rev. (1964; rpt. Boston: Houghton Mifflin, 1965), p. 212.

[45] G. R. Stange in "Expectations Well Lost," Ford and Lane, p. 301, argues that "Miss Havisham *is* death. . . . Money, which is also death, is appropriately connected with the old lady rotting away in her darkened room."

[46] *The English Novel: Form and Function* (1953; rpt. New York: Perennial, 1967), pp. 154–55.

[47] Time in *Our Mutual Friend* focuses on the river as a Christian regenerative force. As in *Martin Chuzzlewit,* its temporal concerns stand rather apart from—although in agreement with—the ideas I am tracing here.

[48] Dickens told Forster that the novel was to be highlighted by a "review of the murderer's career by himself at the close, when its temptations were to be dwelt upon as if, not he the culprit, but some other man, were the tempted." Forster, p. 891.

[49] Vol. 1 (Carbondale and Edwardsville: Southern Illinois Univ. Press, 1970), pp. 265–72.

[50] Miller writes, "If *The Mystery of Edwin Drood* had been completed it might have marked a new departure for Dickens, a radical rejection of any possibility of the reconciliation of surface and depth, of 'celestial' and devilish." In *Charles Dickens,* p. 321.

[51] Fielding argues that "there is some reason to think that the design on the right-hand side of the cover . . . showing figures hurrying up a spiral staircase and led on by Jasper,

is not merely emblematic of the pursuer pursued, but that the story might have culminated in a chase up the great Tower of the Cathedral and along the narrow galleries between

the vaulting and the leaded roof." *A Critical Introduction*, p. 246.

[52] *The Consolation of Philosophy*, bk. V.

MARGARET GANZ: *Pickwick Papers*

[1] George Gissing, *Charles Dickens: A Critical Study* (London: Blackie, 1903), p. 165.

[2] Ada Nisbet, "Charles Dickens," in Lionel Stevenson, ed., *Victorian Fiction: A Guide to Research* (Cambridge: Harvard University Press, 1966), p. 147.

[3] See Edmund Wilson, "Dickens: The Two Scrooges," *Eight Essays* (New York: Doubleday, 1954), pp. 18–21; Sylvère Monod, *Dickens the Novelist* (Norman: University of Oklahoma Press, 1958), pp. 83–115; J. Hillis Miller, *Charles Dickens: The World of his Novels* (Cambridge: Harvard University Press, 1958), pp. 1–35; Steven Marcus, *Dickens: From Pickwick to Dombey* (New York: Basic Books, 1965), pp. [13]–53.

[4] G. K. Chesterton, *Charles Dickens: The Last of the Great Men* (New York: Readers Club, 1942), p. 59.

[5] Miller, *Charles Dickens*, p. 16.

[6] Steven Marcus, "Language into Structure: Pickwick Revisited," *Daedalus* (Winter 1972), p. 191.

[7] Miller, *Charles Dickens*, p. 24.

[8] George Orwell, "Charles Dickens," *Dickens, Dali & Others* (New York: Reynal & Hitchcock, 1946), p. 65.

[9] Barbara Hardy, *The Moral Art of Dickens* (London: Athlone Press of University of London, 1970), pp. 81–82.

[10] Despite his very different approach to the material, Miller makes a similar point in stating that "the true dramatic center of *Pickwick Papers* is not the unraveling of any plot, nor is it the chance of Pickwick or of any other character. It is Pickwick's grad-

ual discovery of the real nature of the world." *Charles Dickens*, p. 27.

[11] Seymour's idea itself was based on certain series which appeared in annuals and monthlies like Cruikshank's *Comick Almanack* and the *New Sporting Magazine* (*Jorrocks's Jaunt and Jollities* was published in the latter) and on Pierce Egan's *Life in London*. See John Butt and Kathleen Tillotson, *Dickens at Work* (London: Methuen, 1957), p. 64.

[12] *Pickwick Papers*, The Oxford Illustrated Dickens (London: Oxford University Press, 1948), p. 92. Other references to the novel will be placed in the text.

[13] These appropriate terms are used by Edgar Johnson in discussing Dickens' ability to transfigure "stock characters and stock situations." *Charles Dickens: His Tragedy and Triumph* (New York: Simon and Schuster, 1952), I, 159, 162.

[14] For some sharp observations on the limited appeal of "the farcical exposure" of the Pickwick Club members, see Hardy, pp. 87–90. The satirical approach is perhaps given more power by Hardy (*Moral Art of Dickens*) than is its due: to say that "where [Dickens'] comedy is neither satiric nor dark it is always least successful" (p. 85) is to minimize the impact of *humour* as distinguished from *comedy of humours*.

[15] The creation of the humorist can be in his own right a humorist, or can be humorous *malgré lui*. Sterne's Uncle Toby refighting military engagements in his backyard is unaware that he arouses the sense of humor; Sam Weller coining his "Wellerisms"

is a willful humorist. The creator of humorous characters must of course be in complete control of his vision. As Louis Cazamian says in "Le mécanisme de l'humour": "L'humour peut être l'expression spontanée d'un tempérament particulier, la simple expansion de son activité; encore faut il que cette originalité ait conscience d'elle-même." *Études de psychologie littéraire* (Paris: Payot, 1913), p. 103.

[16] From Wilson onward, the interpolated stories in *Pickwick Papers* have on the whole been given very serious consideration as evidence of the more somber aspects of Dickens' nature and concerns. It is refreshing to contrast such comments as those of Marcus (*Dickens,* p. 42: "The vindictive impulse of [some of] these stories is clearly antithetical to the emotional and moral climate of the novel as a whole, which is not only so preeminently benign but altogether Christian and affirmative of the greater Christian virtues") and of Miller (*Charles Dickens,* p. 28: "[The] submission to evil forces is expressed in several of the stories by hallucinatory, nightmarish visions in which the phenomenal world is a dark enclosure, swarming with ghosts or monsters") with the recent verdict of John Lucas in *The Melancholy Man: A Study of Dickens's Novels* (London: Methuen, 1970): "Of course, it is customary to say that the tales are a way of drawing off the darker side that Dickens couldn't allow into his idyll and I myself have spoken of their containing the evil that is automatically banished from the main narrative. But I want to add that this evil is a decidedly literary and inauthentic concoction. . . . Indeed, the . . . tales . . . cannot seriously be felt as constituting a potential threat to the idyllic world from which they have therefore to be kept apart, because they are so contrived and otiose an expression of Dickens's imagination" (pp. 9, 10).

[17] See A. O. J. Cockshut, *The Imagination of Charles Dickens* (New York: New York University Press, 1962), p. 24. The increased satiric bent is well resuméd by Sylvia Manning's statement: "The first novel celebrates life; the later books tend increasingly to attack whatever defiles, tramples on it, or seeks to confine it." *Dickens as Satirist* (New Haven: Yale University Press, 1971), p. [35]. For a detailed discussion of the progressive muting of Dickens' humor see my article "The Vulnerable Ego: Dickens' Humor in Decline," *DSA,* vol. 1, ed. R. Partlow (Carbondale, Ill.: Southern Illinois University Press, 1970), pp. 23–40, 276–80.

[18] As John Killham notes, an element directly meaningful to Dickens comes into play here: Jingle, he says, "collapses . . . because we can no longer sustain the image we have built up of him in face of an event which Dickens thinks too important (because too painful for him personally) for Jingle to convert into his own nature." "Pickwick: Dickens and the Art of Fiction," in John Gross and Gabriel Pearson, eds., *Dickens and the Twentieth Century* (London: Routledge, 1962), pp. 43–44.

[19] W. H. Auden, "Dingley Dell and the Fleet," *The Dyer's Hand* (New York: Random House, 1962), p. 428. Sam Weller likewise does not escape the blight of seriousness as he is made to philosophize on the injustice of imprisonment for debt which penalizes honest debtors far more than it does irresponsible ones, *Pickwick Papers,* pp. 573–74.

[20] There is most probably a connection between the change in mood and the death of Mary Hogarth, which took place before the appearance of chap. xi (see Monod, pp. 94–95). But *Sketches by Boz* already gives ample evidence of Dickens' preoccupation with injustice, misery, death. For contemporary criticism of Dickens' technique see "Charles Dickens and his Works," *Fraser's Magazine* 21 (1840), 383–94 and "Charles Dickens and David Copperfield," *Fra-*

ser's Magazine 42 (1850), 700–701. See also "The Pickwick Papers," *Westminster Review* 27 (1837), 198–200: this article does not challenge the consistency of characters but deplores their lack of individuality.

21 Susanne K. Langer, *Feeling and Form* (New York: Charles Scribner's Sons, 1953), pp. 335, 333.

22 Killham, p. 43. Falstaff's *language* is of course the basic element of transfiguration. Miller's comment in "The Sources of Dickens's Comic Art," *Twentieth-Century Fiction* (1970), p. 474, is essentially applicable here. "Within the novel," Miller says, "the meaning of a given motif is constituted by relations among linguistic elements rather than from reference to the external world." While an inevitable dependence on linguistic structuring, conspiring to promote what Miller calls (in relation to *Bleak House*) "a complex linguistic fabric," makes realistic portrayal impossible, that a novel is such a "self-generating web of meaning" (p. 474) guarantees the processes of humor in it.

23 "The Pickwick Papers," *Westminster Review* 27 (1837), 199, 200, 199.

24 His own forebears Cervantes, Fielding, Smollett, and Sterne, along with many other comic writers were after all perpetuating that connection established in Roman comedy between the lower class and the attributes of cleverness and sophistication (on the initial assumption, no doubt, that the perpetual exposure of such a class to the unpleasant aspects of reality must inculcate a protective familiarity with the arbitrary lashings of life and—better still—a mode of dealing with its threats). See the section "*Servus:* Clever Trickster and Faithful Servant" in George E. Duckworth, *The Nature of Roman Comedy* (Princeton: Princeton University Press, 1952), pp. 249–53.

25 It was probably inevitable that academic resourcefulness would go Serjeant Buzfuz one better in the as-

sessment of Pickwick's nature. Not only does Christopher Herbert inform us that "the very notion of the innocent Pickwick as lustful ravisher has a resonance not wholly comical" in its possible connections with the world of the actual rapists in Gothic romances like *The Castle of Otranto* and Lewis' *The Monk,* but (after mentioning the lady with the yellow curlpapers incident and the boarding house and Mrs. Bardell imbroglios) he promulgates with seemingly perfect seriousness the central Buzfuzian principle of handling evidence: "one cannot easily make sense of this series of incidents perhaps, but one can construe them to contain a sinister implication." "Converging worlds in *Pickwick Papers,*" *NCF* 27 (June 1972), 10. Marcus not only exhibits Buzfuzian ingenuity in discoursing on the meanings of the first advertisement for the First Number of *Pickwick Papers* but also betters Pickwick on the subject of "BILL STUMPS, HIS MARK" (see "Language into Structure," pp. 183–84, 194).

26 Sigmund Freud, "Humour," *The Complete Psychological Works of Sigmund Freud,* trans. and ed. James Strachey (London: Hogarth Press and the Institute of Psycho-Analysis, 1927–31), XXI, 162, 166.

27 Northrop Frye's terms in "The Mythos of Spring: Comedy." The connection between this negative role and the larger view of comedy manifesting what Ludwig Jekels calls "a mechanism of inversion," as *"the feeling of guilt which, in tragedy, rests upon the son, appears in comedy displaced on the father; it is the father who is guilty,"* has endlessly fascinating reverberations where Dickens' treatment of authority figures is concerned—even setting aside the reversed Oedipal situation posited here by Jekels. Whatever later ambiguities mark the comic handling of father-son relationships in Dickens (e.g., David and Micawber *in loco parentis*), the role reversal in *Pickwick* is wholly benign, both Sam and Pick-

wick fulfilling at times the parental and filial responsibilities with positive results. For the whole significant question of the reversed Oedipal element in comedy see Frye's essay mentioned above, pp. 143, 141–62; Ludwig Jekels' "On the Psychology of Comedy," pp. 264, 263–69; Eric Bentley, "Farce," pp. 284–85, rpt. in Robert W. Corrigan, ed., *Comedy: Meaning and Form* (San Francisco: Chandler, 1965). See also Martin Grotjahn, *Beyond Laughter* (New York, McGraw-Hill, 1966), pp. 86–91, 260–61.

28   Freud, "Humour," p. 163.

29   Carried out in metaphysical terms, that impulse finds its most subtle manifestation in the humor of Samuel Beckett.

30   Miller, *Charles Dickens*, p. 29.

31   James R. Kincaid, *Dickens and the Rhetoric of Laughter* (Oxford: Clarendon Press), p. 35. For a general assessment of his viewpoint see my review of this work in *Dickens Studies Newsletter* 4 (1973), 89–93.

32   For a possible origin of the technique of the Wellerisms, see J. B. Van Amerongen, *The Actor in Dickens* (London: Cecil Palmer, 1926), p. 241; Sir William H. Bailey, "Wellerisms and Wit," *Dickensian* 1 (1905), 32; Earle Davis, *The Flint and the Flame: The Artistry of Charles Dickens* (London: Gollancz, 1965), pp. 43–46.

33   Sam's "gen'l'm'n" on the way to Tyburn is reminiscent of Freud's "rogue" who "being led out to execution of a Monday remarked: 'Well, this week's beginning nicely.' " Freud goes on to comment that "humour is concerned in the *making* of such a joke—that is, in disregarding what it is that distinguishes the beginning of this week from others, in denying the distinction which might give rise to motives for quite special emotions." *Jokes and their Relation to the Unconscious, The Complete Psychological Works of Sigmund Freud* (1905), VIII, 229. The conclusion of this significant essay on comedy anticipates the brilliant contribution of Freud to the understanding of humor itself in the later essay "Humour."

34   J. Cuming Walters, "The Place of Pickwick in Literature," *Dickensian* 23 (1927), 98.

35   Marcus sees in the treatment of Tony Weller "the sole occasion when Dickens achieves enough impersonality to regard such vagrant parenthood with humor and understanding" (*Dickens,* p. 32). One might say rather that Dickens' capacity to show parental irresponsibility in a work of art as an incongruous, comic shortcoming rather than a destructive failing is not *made possible* by "impersonality" but *allows* a momentary transmutation and thus a negation of the personal hostility aroused in him by parental betrayal.

36   Barbara Hardy speaks of "the terrors of marriage, the law, the doctors, and death" as "all held at bay in the violent jokes, the tall stories which manage to convert the threat into humour and yet, asserting the incongruity of laughing at this, recognize the threat as real" (*Moral Art of Dickens*), pp. 97–98. But the process in Sam's jokes and stories (as in Tony's pronouncements) seems a somewhat different one: the threat is converted into humor by emphasizing the incongruity in those sources of fear rather than the incongruity of laughing at them. In the process the threat is divested of its reality rather than ultimately asserted as real.

37   See Butt and Tillotson for the possible influence of the Norton-Melbourne trial, which Dickens reported for the *Morning Chronicle* on 23 June 1836. Like Serjeant Buzfuz, the lawyer for the prosecution invested simple words with reprehensible meanings, in this case the terse "I will call about half past 4. Yours, Melbourne" (p. 71, n. 1). It is Auden who finely realizes that moral judgments of Dodson and Fogg are wide of the mark: "they have no malevolent intent," he comments; rather "their clients are the pieces with which they play the

legal game, which they find as enjoy-
able as it is lucrative" (p. 424).
[38] Wilson, "Dickens: The Two
Scrooges," p. 21.
[39] Writing to John Macrone (July
1836) about an undelivered parcel of
letters, Dickens concludes with a jubi-
lant and cryptic reference to the popular success of his first novel—two
words hugely capitalized: "PICK-
WICK TRIUMPHANT." *The Letters
of Charles Dickens,* ed. Walter Dexter
(Bloomsbury: Nonesuch, 1938), I, 76.

STEVEN V. DANIELS: *Pickwick and Dickens*

All citations to *Pickwick Papers* (and the one citation to *Hard Times* late
in my discussion) will be to The Oxford Illustrated Dickens (London:
Oxford University Press, 1948); page references are placed in parentheses after the quotation.

[1] Steven Marcus, "Language into
Structure: Pickwick Revisited," *Daedalus* (Winter 1972), p. 201.
[2] *Pickwick Papers,* "Preface to the
First Cheap Edition."
[3] Ibid.
[4] Sylvère Monod, *Dickens the Novelist* (Norman: University of Oklahoma
Press, 1968), p. 110.
[5] George H. Ford, *Dickens and His
Readers* (1955; rpt., New York: Norton, 1965), pp. 5–6; John Butt and
Kathleen Tillotson, *Dickens at Work*
(1957; rpt. London: Methuen, 1968),
pp. 66, 69–70.
[6] Edgar Johnson, *Charles Dickens:
His Tragedy and Triumph* (New York:
Simon and Schuster, 1952), I, 174.
[7] Steven Marcus, *Dickens: From
Pickwick to Dombey* (New York: Basic
Books, 1965), p. 17.
[8] Johnson, I, 285.
[9] *Oliver Twist,* "The Author's Preface to the Third Edition."

ANNE HUMPHERYS: *Dickens and Mayhew on the London Poor*

[1] One commentator has dug into
London Labour for possible sources of
Our Mutual Friend. See Harland S.
Nelson, "Dickens's *Our Mutual Friend*
and Henry Mayhew's *London Labour
and the London Poor,*" NCF 20 (December 1965), 207–22. Nelson points
out several parallels between *LL&LP,*
II, and the novel; an additional connection is the similarity between a
long-song seller (*LL&LP,* I, 272) and
Silas Wegg. Other links between Mayhew's work and the novels of Dickens
include the rag and bottle man (in
LL&LP, II, 109–10), who bears similarities to Krook in *Bleak House;* and
the man in *LL&LP* (I, 360), who calls
himself, rather like Mrs. Gummidge
in *David Copperfield,* a "poor forlorn
creatur'." Recently Harvey Peter
Sucksmith has extended the discussion by finding "echoes" of Mayhew's
The Great World of London in *Little Dorrit.* See NCF 24 (December 1969),
345–49.
[2] In his introduction to *The Children of Sànchez* (1961; rpt. London:
Penguin, 1964), Lewis says "If one
agrees with Henry James that life is
all inclusion and confusion while art is
all discrimination and selection, then
these life histories have something of
both art and life. I believe this in no
way reduces the authenticity of the
data or their usefulness for science"
(p. xxi).
[3] See "The Topicality of *Bleak
House*" in Kathleen Tillotson and
John Butt, *Dickens at Work* (London:
Methuen, 1957), pp. 177–99, and Mi-

chael Slater, "Dickens's Tract for the Times" (on *The Chimes*) in *Dickens 1970*, ed. Michael Slater (New York: Stein and Day, 1970), pp. 99–133.

4   *Oliver Twist* (London: Oxford University Press, 1949), p. xvii. All references to Dickens' novels are to The Oxford Illustrated Dickens.

5   From October 1849 to the end of 1850, Mayhew published eighty-odd "letters" or articles on "Labour and the Poor" for the *Morning Chronicle*. (Selections from these articles have been reprinted in E. P. Thompson and Eileen Yeo, *The Unknown Mayhew* [New York: Pantheon, 1971] and my edition of *Voices of the Poor* [London: Frank Cass, 1971].) In December 1850 Mayhew began to publish a weekly serial *London Labour and the London Poor* which ran through February 1852. Sometime in 1851 a two-volume edition was published made up of bound-up parts. The 1851–52 parts include all of Volume I, Volume II to page 432, and Volume IV to page 192. (Copy of the 1851 text is in the British Museum.) Material for the final parts of Volume II and for Volume III of *London Labour* was collected but not published in 1856. (See internal dates plus the advertisement on the back of the March 1856 number of *The Great World of London*.) When the four-volume edition of *London Labour* was prepared in 1861–62, Volume IV was completed by other contributors and the 1856 material for Volume III was filled out with selected reprints from the original 1849–50 *Morning Chronicle* letters. See the appendices in both Thompson and Yeo, and Humpherys for full particulars. The edition of *London Labour* used in this essay is the 1967 reprint by Frank Cass, London. References are abbreviated *LL&LP*, volume, page.

6   *Morning Chronicle*, 24 September 1849, p. 4; rev. rpt. in *Meliora*, ed. Viscount Ingestre (London: John Parker, 1851).

7   Humphry House in *The Dickens World* (1942; rpt. London: Oxford University Press, 1961), p. 180, notes the "metrical excitement" in a similar passage in *The Old Curiosity Shop*. A number of critics have pointed out the use of symbolism in Dickens' descriptions: see, for example, Arnold Kettle, "Oliver Twist" in *Introduction to the English Novel* (1951; rpt. New York: Harper, 1960), I, 137; Grahame Smith, *Dickens, Money and Society* (Berkeley: University of California Press, 1968), p. 77; Steven Marcus, *Dickens: From Pickwick to Dombey* (New York: Basic Books, 1965), p. 72. See also Alexander Welsh, "Satire and History: The City of Dickens" *VS* 11 (March 1968), 393.

8   "The Dickens World: A View from Todgers," in *The Dickens Critics*, ed. George H. Ford and Lauriat Lane (Ithaca, N.Y.: Cornell University Press, 1961), pp. 213–32.

9   Dickens had a "trick . . . of dealing with low life in a detached and whimsical style." Butt and Tillotson, *Dickens at Work*, p. 44.

10   In *London Characters* (London: Chatto and Windus, 1874), pp. 348–49, Mayhew lists a number of personal experiences he had had in his investigations of the poor. His stint on the treadwheel is one of these; in *The Criminal Prisons of London* (1862; rpt. London: Frank Cass, 1968), p. 136, he recounts being shut up in a dark punishment cell.

11   Accounts of how he found his informants are contained in *Chronicle* articles II and X and throughout *London Labour*.

12   See Michael Steig, "The Whitewashing of Inspector Bucket: Origins and Parallels," *Papers of the Michigan Academy of Science, Arts and Letters* 50 (1965), 575–84, for a discussion of this aspect of *Bleak House*.

13   *Household Words* 3 (14 June 1851), 266. In *Reprinted Pieces* (Oxford Illustrated Dickens edition), p. 516.

14   "On an Amateur Beat," *All the Year Round* 21 (27 February 1869),

300. In *The Uncommercial Traveller* (Oxford Illustrated Dickens edition), p. 345.

15 "A Small Star in the East," *All the Year Round* 21 (19 December 1868), 62. *The Uncommercial Traveller,* p. 322.

16 *Morning Chronicle,* 9 November 1849, p. 5. This passage represents about one-third of the interview.

17 For Mayhew biography see John L. Bradley, "Introduction" to *Selections from London Labour and the London Poor* (London: Oxford University Press, 1965), pp. vii–xl, and Thompson, "Mayhew and the *Morning Chronicle*" in Thompson and Yeo, pp. 11–50. Dickens and Mayhew knew each other well enough for Mayhew to take part in Dickens' amateur theatrical *Every Man in his Humour* in 1845. An account of the theatrical appears in the *Illustrated London News,* 29 November 1845, with a picture of Mayhew in costume. Nelson ("Dickens's *Our Mutual Friend*"), gives other indications of the connection. Dickens never refers to Mayhew in his work or in his letters, nor does he ever mention *London Labour.*

18 For Dickens' views see Philip Collins, *Dickens and Education* (1963; rpt. London: Macmillan, 1965), pp. 143, 188. Mayhew's views are scattered, but his pamphlet *What to Teach and How to Teach It* (London: William Smith, 1842) gives a fair summary.

19 Mayhew attacked the Ragged Schools in his series in the *Chronicle* (Letters XLIII through XLV). See Thompson in Thompson and Yeo, pp. 32–35, for an account of the debate.

20 *Dickens and Crime* (1962; rpt. Bloomington, Ind.: Indiana University Press, 1968), pp. 180–81.

21 See *Figaro in London,* 13 January 1838. According to Bradley, Gilbert à Beckett was editor of *Figaro* in 1831–34, and Mayhew in 1835–38. There is a Mayhew family tradition that Henry was in Wales in 1835–38 avoiding creditors, but so far no real corroboration of these dates exists. In his only book, *A Jorum of Punch* (London: Downey and Co., 1895), Athol Mayhew, Henry's son, claimed his father had left the editorship of *Figaro* by 1838.

22 "The Ruffian," *All the Year Round* 20 (10 October 1868), 423. In *The Uncommercial Traveller,* p. 307.

23 Henry Mayhew, "On Capital Punishments" in *Three Papers on Capital Punishment* (London: Cox and Wyman, 1856), pp. 32–61.

24 *The Criminal Prisons of London,* p. 414.

25 When *London Labour* was being published in numbers in 1851–52, Mayhew used the inside covers of each part for an "Answers to Correspondents" column in which he discussed among other questions his intentions for the project, his attitudes toward poverty, and his conclusions about low wages. On the cover for 10 January 1852, discussing the effects of machinery on employment, Mayhew asks what is to be done with those thrown out of work "since you could not exactly do with them as Mr. Carlyle humanely recommends, 'shoot them and sweep them into the dustbin.'" This quotation is probably a paraphrase of Carlyle's remark in "Model Prisons": "If I had a commonwealth to reform or to govern, certainly it should not be the Devil's regiments of the line that I would first of all concentrate my attention on! . . . To them one would apply the besom, try to sweep *them* with some rapidity into the dustbin." *Works* ed. H. D. Traill (New York: Charles Scribner's Sons, n.d.) XX, 58.

26 The research for this book was done in 1856 when 498 pages appeared in numbers as *The Great World of London* (copy in British Museum). According to the publisher's preface dated April 1862, the last 130 pages were written by John Binny, and the whole volume was first published in book form in 1862.

27 Mayhew's work in the 1850s

compared to that of Dickens qualifies somewhat Bradley's insight about Mayhew, namely that in his choice of subjects he was acutely attuned to his readers' interests from one decade to the next. (John L. Bradley, "Henry Mayhew and Father William," *English Language Notes* 1 [September 1963], 40–42.) Although prison conditions were of perennial interest and thus always a good subject, Mayhew's attitudes on the treatment of prisoners and the abolition of capital punishment were not popularly supported positions in the mid-fifties and hence not likely to win him enthusiastic readers.

28   See Thomas Willert Beale, *The Light of Other Days* (London: Richard Bentley, 1890), I, 271–75 for an account of this incident between Henry and his father.

29   John D. Rosenberg makes a similar point in his introduction to the Dover Press edition of *London Labour* (1968), p. v.

30   In a letter to the editors of the *Morning Chronicle* in February 1850, Mayhew described the aims of his survey, then five months old: "The labour question was to be investigated without reference to any particular prejudice, theory, party, or policy, and it was with this spirit that I set out upon my mission. I made up my mind to deal with human nature as a natural philosopher or a chemist deals with any material object; and, as a man who had devoted some little of his time to physical and metaphysical science, I must say I did most heartily rejoice that it should have been left to me to apply the laws of the inductive philosophy for the first time, I believe, in the world to the abstract questions of political economy" (quoted in "Report of the Speech of Henry Mayhew" [London: Committee for the Tailors of London, 1850], p. 6). Both E. P. Thompson ("The Political Education of Henry Mayhew," *VS* 11 [September 1967], 58) and Gertrude Himmelfarb ("Mayhew's Poor:

A Problem of Identity," *VS* 14 [March 1971], 316) think that H. Sutherland Edwards' remark that Mayhew "redictated" the tales of his informants "with an added colour of his own" (*Personal Recollections* [London: Cassel, 1900], p. 60) discredits Mayhew's claims of objectivity. Edwards' remark is ambiguous, however; it could simply mean that Mayhew "added" descriptions of the rooms, surroundings, and physical characteristics of his subjects, as he did. There is no reason to assume Edwards' vague remark means Mayhew changed any details in the actual interviews themselves, especially since he always insisted that he did not and the internal structure of the interviews strongly supports his self-defense.

31   See Yeo, "Mayhew as a Social Investigator" in Thompson and Yeo, pp. 51–95, for a discussion of some of the conclusions Mayhew drew about the causes of low wages. Many of these appear in *Low Wages, Their Causes, Consequences and Remedies*, a weekly serial begun in November 1851 (reprinted in Thompson and Yeo). The serial apparently folded after the fourth number at the same time that *London Labour* ceased publication due to a suit in Chancery.

32   In "Answers to Correspondents," 2 August 1851, Mayhew stated that "viewed as a working man's question, the weight of the argument appears to lean towards the side of Protection; and that, viewed as a capitalist's or trader's question, the facts are in favour of Free Trade."

33   On the cover for Part 5 of *London Labour* (undated), Mayhew outlined what his weekly serial was going to contain. The first six months were to be "devoted to an exposition of the condition and earnings of the several varieties of the London Street-folk. . . . This done, Mr. Mayhew proposes directing his attention to the Producers; beginning with the Workers in Silk, Cotton, Wool, Worsted, Hair, Flax, Hemp, and Coir as well as

the Workers in Skin, Gut, and Feathers, comprising both the Manufacturers and Makers-up of these materials."
[34] In the prospectus for *London Labour* printed on the cover of Part 9 (undated), Mayhew says he begins with the street folk to "afford to the Author the time necessary to obtain all and every information bearing upon the condition of the Metropolitan Artizans through the several Trade Societies of London."
[35] "Mayhew's Poor: A Problem of Identity," p. 308. Although her general charge in this essay that Mayhew enthusiasts have claimed a scope for *London Labour* that is unjustified has merit, the extension of this confusion to Mayhew himself is unwarranted. Mayhew's plans for *London Labour* (see note 33) show how small a part he considered the street folk as such played in the overall labour pattern of London. Nor does Himmelfarb mention that *London Labour* as a project was interrupted toward the end of Volume II by a law suit. If he had completed his work as he sketched it out, it would have fulfilled the promise of the title.
[36] John Forster remarked that Dickens felt a "profound attraction of repulsion" for the slums. *Life of Charles Dickens*, ed. A. J. Hoppé (London: J. M. Dent, 1962), I, 14.
[37] *Charles Dickens. A Critical Study* (New York: Dodd, Mead, 1898), p.

96. Consider also Orwell's remark: "Dickens's early experiences have given him a horror of proletarian roughness. He shows this unmistakably whenever he writes of the very poorest of the poor, the slum dwellers. His description of the London slums are always full of undisguised repulsion," in "Charles Dickens" in *The Collected Essays, Journalism, and Letters,* ed. Sonia Orwell and Ian Angus (New York: Harcourt, Brace & World, 1968), I, 434.
[38] As the Brothers Mayhew, Henry and Augustus published six novels. They include: *The Good Genius that Turned everything into Gold,* 1847; *The Greatest Plague of Life,* 1847; *Whom to Marry and How to Get Married,* 1848; *The Image of his Father,* 1848; *The Magic of Kindness,* 1849; *Fear of the World,* 1850.
[39] Henry and Augustus began *Paved with Gold* in 1857. According to the covers for the monthly numbers, Henry dropped out of the project after the fourth number. When the novel was published in book form (1858; rpt. London: Frank Cass, 1971), it appeared under Augustus' name alone. *Kitty Lamere* (1855) is another novel by Augustus based on the *Morning Chronicle* survey.
[40] *Young Benjamin Franklin* (London: James Blackwood, 1861), p. 250, n.
[41] Collins, *Dickens and Crime,* pp. 184–85.

LAWRENCE FRANK: *"Through a Glass Darkly"*

[1] Frank Kermode, "Survival of the Classic," in *Shakespeare, Spenser, Donne: Renaissance Essays* (New York: Viking Press, 1971), p. 170.
[2] Charles Dickens, *Bleak House* (London: Oxford University Press, 1962), vii. References to Dickens' novels are all to the Oxford Illustrated Dickens; subsequent quotations are identified by chapter number in parentheses.

[3] See William Axton, "Esther's Nicknames: A Study in Relevance," *Dickensian* 62 (1966), 158–63, for a discussion of the implications of Esther's nicknames.
[4] See Alex Zwerdling, "Esther Summerson Rehabilitated," *PMLA* 88 (1973), 429–39. Mr. Zwerdling's essay appeared when my essay was in the final stages of revision. There are obvious parallels between our views of

Esther. However, I believe my own concern with certain patterns of language in *Bleak House* and my effort to make Esther a part of the novel as a whole, in a manner different from Mr. Zwerdling's, will become clear.
5 See J. Hillis Miller, *"Bleak House,"* in *Charles Dickens: The World of His Novels* (Cambridge: Harvard University Press, 1958), pp. 160–224.
6 See J. Hillis Miller, "Introduction," in *Bleak House,* ed. Norman Page (Baltimore: Penguin Books,

1971), pp. 11–34.
7 See Rollo May, "Contributions of Existential Psychotherapy," in *Existence,* ed. Rollo May, Ernest Angel and Henri F. Ellenberger (New York: Simon and Schuster, 1958), p. 68.
8 Ibid., p. 43.
9 José Ortega y Gasset, "History as a System," in *History As A System and other Essays Toward a Philosophy of History,* trans. Helene Weyl (New York: W. W. Norton, 1961), p. 203.

HARVEY PETER SUCKSMITH: *Sir Leicester Dedlock, Wat Tyler, and the Chartists*

1 *Bleak House,* The Oxford Illustrated Dickens (London: Oxford University Press, 1948), p. 13; this edition of the novel is hereafter cited in the text.
2 See, for example, Sir James Fitzjames Stephen's reviews of *Little Dorrit, Saturday Review* 4 (4 July 1857), 15, and *A Tale of Two Cities, Saturday Review,* 17 December 1859, pp. 741–43, the latter reprinted in *The Dickens Critics,* ed. George H. Ford and Lauriat Lane, Jr. (Ithaca, N.Y.: Cornell University Press, 1961), esp. pp. 44–46.
3 See, for example, Humphry House, *The Dickens World* (London: Oxford University Press, 1942), pp. 176–77; A. O. J. Cockshut, *The Imagination of Charles Dickens* (London: Collins, 1961) pp. 50–65.
4 See, for example, James Fitzjames Stephen in *The Dickens Critics,* pp. 41–43; G. H. Lewes, "Dickens in Relation to Criticism," *Fortnightly Review* (February 1872), pp. 141–54, reprinted in *The Dickens Critics,* esp. pp. 61–62; Robert Garis, *The Dickens Theatre: A Reassessment of the Novels* (Oxford: Clarendon Press, 1965), esp. pp. 103–43.
5 Dickens to John Overs, 30 December 1840, *The Letters of Charles Dickens,* ed. Madeline House and Graham Storey (Oxford: Clarendon

Press, 1969), II, 176.
6 Certainly, in view of this, it does not seem surprising that Dickens expressed the opinion in 1846 that bigamists should be punished with more than one flogging and transportation for life; see Philip Collins, *Dickens and Crime* (London: Macmillan, 1965), p. 348 n. 98, citing John Forster, *The Life of Charles Dickens,* bk. V, chap. iv. Dickens may well have regarded the second bigamous marriage as a devious kind of indecent assault.
7 See Collins, *Dickens and Crime,* pp. 16–17, 21–22, 90, 193–95, 244–48, 319, 324.
8 *Household Words* 5 (12 June 1852), 304–6.
9 See, for example, Walter E. Houghton, *The Victorian Frame of Mind, 1830–1870* (New Haven: Yale University Press, 1963), pp. 353–61; Stephen Marcus, *The Other Victorians* (New York: Basic Books, 1970), pp. 13–18.
10 See, for example, *Encyclopaedia Britannica,* 22d ed., s.v. "Wat Tyler." Though modern historians are sceptical about attributing the incident to Wat Tyler and his daughter, which derives from the story of the killing of a tax collector by John Tyler of Dartford in John Stow's *Annales,* ed. E. Howes (London, 1631), such indecent assaults did occur as one cause of the

Peasants' Revolt of 1381; see R. B. Dobson, *The Peasants' Revolt of 1381* (London: Macmillan, 1970), pp. 395 n., and 135–36 citing Henry Knighton, *Chronicon*, ed. J. R. Lumby, 2 vols., Rolls Series, 1889–95.

[11] Marcus, *Other Victorians,* p. 111; David Daiches, *George Eliot: Middlemarch* (London: E. Arnold, 1963), p. 21; cf. Lydgate's "general sense" in boyhood "of secrecy and obscenity in connection with his internal structure," *Middlemarch*, bk. I, xv.

[12] Houghton, *Victorian Frame of Mind,* pp. 365–66; Marcus, *Other Victorians,* pp. 130–41.

[13] Houghton, pp. 353–59; Marcus, pp. 29–32.

[14] His grandmother had been a maid at the Marquis of Blandford's house, later on housekeeper to the Marquis of Crewe, to whom Dickens' grandfather had been butler.

[15] John Overs' view, which we can deduce from Dickens' letter to him, is rather untypical; he was very much the workingmen trying to climb out of his class.

[16] This popular work was first published in 1837 but Dickens used the 2 vol. edition of 1845, a copy of which in his library at the sale of his books was found to be well marked with pencil in the margins; see *Catalogue of the Library of Charles Dickens,* ed. J. H. Stonehouse (London: Piccadilly Fountain Press, 1935), p. 67. The 5th edition was stereotyped and I quote from the 2 vol. edition (London, 1859) I, 222–26, which contained no alterations.

[17] *Letters of Charles Dickens,* ed. M. House and G. Storey, II, 177.

[18] *Household Words* 5 (11 September 1852), 614.

[19] *Times* (London) (31 May 1848), p. 5.

[20] Ibid., (2 June 1848), p. 5.

[21] Ibid., (16 September 1848), p. 4.

[22] Ibid., (21 December 1848), pp. 6–7.

[23] Needless to say, children were being transported for long sentences for felonies almost daily and, more strikingly here perhaps, men were being sentenced throughout 1848 to savage sentences for seditious statements and rebellious conduct in Ireland which were treated as treason-felonies. Admittedly, the prisoners at York were convicted only of misdemeanor, but even as late as this century a convicted person could receive a maximum of seven years for illegally drilling others and two years for being so drilled and, since the Second World War, at least one person has received a longer sentence than any of the prisoners at York for a somewhat similar offense.

[24] John Butt and Kathleen Tillotson, *Dickens at Work* (London: Methuen, 1957), pp. 183–87, 188.

[25] See Dickens' letter to Miss Coutts (24 May 1848), *Letters from Charles Dickens to Angela Burdett-Coutts, 1841–1865,* ed. Edgar Johnson (London: Jonathan Cape, 1953), pp. 119–20.

[26] I can find no evidence to suggest Dickens knew of the *more general* tendency among the Chartists to resurrect Wat Tyler as a popular hero after centuries of infamy and neglect. A Chartist song contains the lines: "For Tyler of old, a heart-chorus bold / Let Labour's children sing!" *Poetical Works of Thomas Cooper* (London, 1877), p. 285. On their homemade banners, the Sheffield Chartists of the 1840s painted the portraits of their heroes, "ranging from Wat Tyler to Byron and Shelley" (see Brian Simon, *Studies in the History of Education, 1780–1870* [London: Lawrence & Wishart, 1960], p. 249). Both pieces of information are cited by Dobson, *Peasants' Revolt,* pp. 30, 31. Though it should be added that Dickens' illustrator, Phiz, was accurately informed as to one design, the skull and crossbones that did feature on Chartist banners, as Gammage points out (see "A Procession of the Unemployed," *The Old Curiosity Shop,* Oxford Illus-

trated Dickens [1951], p. 337). It seems unlikely, though not impossible, that Dickens knew of the reference to Isaac Jefferson, the Chartist blacksmith, in Fergus O'Connor's *Northern Star* (3 June 1848).

27 R. G. Gammage, *History of the Chartist Movement, 1837–1854,* (1854; 2d ed. 1894, rpt. New York: Kelley, 1969), p. 333. G. D. H. Cole and Raymond Postgate, *The Common People, 1746–1946* (London: Methuen, 1961), p. 324.

28 See *Dombey and Son,* Oxford Illustrated Dickens (1950), pp. 384, 387.

29 Paul Mantoux, *The Industrial Revolution in the Eighteenth Century: An outline of the beginnings of the modern factory system in England,* trans. Marjorie Vernon (London: Jonathan Cape, 1968), pp. 370, 372–73.

30 Samuel Smiles, of course, stresses the point in *Self-help* (1859), especially chap. 2. Dickens' interest is confirmed by the copy in his library of Smiles' *Life of George Stephenson* (London, 1867); see *Catalogue of the Library of Charles Dickens,* p. 102. Watt was the son of a merchant in a small way but was thrown into the proletariat as an artisan on his father's ruin. The important role played in the Industrial Revolution by a few aristocrats, like the Duke of Bridgewater, does not invalidate this general statement.

31 The arrogance of unproductive members of the upper classes would inevitably excite a bumptious inferiority-superiority complex in the less well-balanced, less sophisticated industrialists who had risen up the ladder, but James Watt, for example, was a cultivated, modest man.

32 Cf. Asa Briggs, *The Age of Improvement, 1783–1867* (London: Longmans, 1963), p. 312.

33 Ibid., pp. 261, 323–25.

34 W. L. Burn, *The Age of Equipoise: A Study of the Mid-Victorian Generation* (London: Allen & Unwin, 1964), pp. 304–20.

35 Cf. Briggs, *Age of Improvement,*

pp. 245–46, 264, 266–67; Cole and Postgate, *The Common People,* p. 257.

36 Trevor Blount, "The Ironmaster and the New Acquisitiveness: Dickens's Views on the Rising Industrial Classes as Exemplified in *Bleak House*," *EIC* 15 (1965), 414–27; Blount, "Dickens's Ironmaster *Again*," *EIC* 21 (1971), 429–36; David Craig, "Fiction and the Rising Industrial Classes," *EIC* 17 (1967), 64–74; Anne G. M. Smith, "The Ironmaster in *Bleak House*," *EIC* 20 (1971), 159–69; F. R. and Q. D. Leavis, *Dickens the Novelist* (London: Chatto & Windus, 1970), pp. 142–47 (review by K. J. Fielding, *Dickens Studies Newsletter* 2 [1971], 37–39, esp. p. 38).

37 Northrop Frye, *The Anatomy of Criticism* (Princeton, N.J.: Princeton University Press, 1957), pp. 21–24.

38 *Letters from Charles Dickens to Angela Burdett-Coutts,* ed. E. Johnson, 18 April 1852, p. 199.

39 No. IX of *Bleak House,* containing Chapter xxviii, was published at the beginning of November 1852 but Dickens usually kept several numbers ahead of publication. No. XIII, containing Chapter xl, appeared in March 1853 and the Final Double No., containing Chapter lxiii, in September 1853, and was therefore written not much more than twelve months later than the letter to Miss Coutts.

40 Butt and Tillotson, *Dickens at Work,* p. 199.

41 Smith, "Ironmaster in *Bleak House*," p. 169 n. 5.

42 Dickens in 1851–52, of course, looks back to a great extent on the decade of the "Hungry Forties"; the "Golden Fifties" were only beginning and do not, in any case, seem to have impressed Dickens as much as they have modern historians.

43 Scholars, drawing largely on *The Old Curiosity Shop, Barnaby Rudge,* and *A Tale of Two Cities,* have argued that Dickens expressed disapproval of mob violence in general and that of the Chartists in particular (see Butt

and Tillotson, *Dickens at Work,* p. 82; Collins, *Dickens and Crime,* p. 217). Yet Dickens also expressed a limited approval of genuine working-class Chartism and its aims (see *Letters from Charles Dickens to Angela Burdett-Coutts,* ed. E. Johnson, 30 August 1849, p. 150 and n. 2), and what on earth are we to make of Dickens' wholehearted approval of Wat Tyler's violence at the time he was writing *The Old Curiosity Shop* and *Barnaby Rudge* and, later, *Bleak House?* I do not believe we are here in the presence of Edmund Wilson's pathological Dickens but of the contradictory attitudes of many decent men (surely the events of 1939–45 have taught us something) at the spectacle of cruelty, injustice, and oppression. The psychological mechanisms we are familiar with in ambivalence may go some way toward explaining how it is possible for contradictory attitudes to exist side by side, but hypocrisy or psychopathology are hardly adequate as terms to explain what is happening here. Dickens constantly warns his readers that rebellion and violence are the natural and inevitable consequences of certain social and psychological conditions and, indeed, a retribution on those who create or help to perpetuate such conditions; *Hard Times* and *A Tale of Two Cities* are both intended as object lessons in this respect. Nevertheless, as a civilized, peace-loving man, on the whole, Dickens prefers a constructive rather than a destructive solution to social and personal problems and the urgent and wholly sane warning, "before it is too late," is constantly on his lips.

44   In his interesting article, N. C. Peyrouton, "Dickens and the Chartists," *Dickensian* 40 (1964), 78–88, 152–61, does not cover the material presented here.

GORDON D. HIRSCH: *The Mysteries in* Bleak House

1   J. Hillis Miller makes this point brilliantly in *Charles Dickens: The World of his Novels* (Cambridge: Harvard University Press, 1968), pp. 160–224. Miller points out that the world of *Bleak House* seems at first to be "a collection of unrelated fragments plunged into a ubiquitous fog" and that the reader and the characters must try to make sense of this seemingly chaotic world. Miller fails, however, to see the relationship between the various mysteries in the book, nor does he fully comprehend the significance of the varied emotional responses to mystery which the characters have. Miller's optimistic and moralistic biases are exemplified by his participation in Dickens' wishful faith that Esther Summerson's "creation of a small area of order and significance around her" represents a satisfactory solution to the problems depicted in the novel.

2   All quotations of Dickens' works are taken from The Oxford Illustrated Dickens (London: Oxford University Press, 1948).

3   Sigmund Freud, *Leonardo da Vinci and a Memory of his Childhood,* in *The Standard Edition of the Complete Psychological Works of Sigmund Freud,* ed. James Strachey (hereafter abbreviated *S.E.*), 24 vols. (London: Hogarth, 1953–66), XI, 78–80.

4   Sylvère Monod, "Esther Summerson, Charles Dickens and the Reader of *Bleak House,*" *Dickens Studies* 5 (1969), 17.

5   Ibid., p. 17.

6   Taylor Stoehr, *Dickens: The Dreamer's Stance* (Ithaca, N.Y.: Cornell University Press, 1965), pp. 140–44.

7   This sort of "splitting" and "displacement" is a common attribute of literature and of fantasy in general: guilty wishes are frequently denied in the hero and projected onto another

character. The hero may, however, still suffer the consequences of having such wishes, even though they do not find expression in his own character. The classic instance of such displacement is the guilt and anxiety Hamlet experiences as a result of his unconscious identification with the murderer of his father and successor to his mother's bed. See Ernest Jones, *Hamlet and Oedipus* (Garden City, N.Y.: Doubleday, 1954), esp. pp. 81–103.

8   After this essay was written, an interesting article by Alex Zwerdling appeared, which argues, along the same lines as I do here, that Esther Summerson is to be regarded as an almost clinical study by Dickens of the long-range psychological effects of the denial of love to a young child. Zwerdling engages, however, in an unpersuasive attempt to trace what he sees as Esther's effort "to become a more assured and self-possessed woman," whereas I believe that the unremitting effects of her conviction of her guilt and unworthiness are much more pervasive and important for explaining her behavior. The evidence Zwerdling finds for Esther's growing self-assertion seems extremely doubtful to me. Her dismissal of Guppy's marriage proposal, for instance, hardly requires "an extremely healthy sense of her own innocence and worth," as Zwerdling claims, because she has no positive emotional involvement whatever with this young man; self-confidence is not a necessary condition for the pronounced aversion which motivates her brusque rejection of his suit. Zwerdling also makes little effort to relate Esther's psychology to that of the other major characters in *Bleak House,* though he does have some provocative things to say about Ada's role as a double for Esther. The subject of my essay, on the other hand, is the range of possible responses to curiosity about "parental" behavior, which Esther defines in part, but which I believe informs the structure of the entire novel. From my point of view, Esther is merely one aspect of the composite hero of *Bleak House;* she is the Dickensian hero as a "female." See Alex Zwerdling, "Esther Summerson Rehabilitated," *PMLA* 88 (1973), 429–39.

9   Edgar Johnson, *Charles Dickens: His Tragedy and Triumph* (New York: Simon and Schuster, 1952), p. 779; and Morton Dauwen Zabel, ed., *Bleak House* (Boston: Houghton Mifflin, 1956), "Introduction" p. xxv.

10   Freud's suggestion about the relatedness of the latent content of the sections of dreams which appear divided and dissimilar is applicable as well to literary works containing more than one plot or narrative: "In interpreting dreams consisting of several main sections or, in general, dreams occurring during the same night, the possibility should not be overlooked that separate and successive dreams of this kind may have the same meaning, and may be giving expression to the same impulses in different material. If so, the first of these homologous dreams to occur is often the more distorted and timid, while the succeeding one will be more confident and distinct." *The Interpretation of Dreams,* in *S.E.,* IV, 334.

11   See Robert A. Donovan, "Structure and Idea in *Bleak House,*" *ELH* 19 (1962), 180–81; and Leonard F. Manheim, "The Law as 'Father,' " *American Imago* 12 (1955), 17–23.

12   Primal scene memories or fantasies are the real or imagined traumatic recollections, common to many children, of having viewed the parents in the sexual act. Though the effects of such experiences (or fantasies) are variable, frequently the child interprets the parental sexuality in them sadistically, and he associates these "memories" with his own fears about sexuality, and specifically with his castration anxiety. Memories or fantasies of the primal scene, then, express the child's early perceptions of, and responses to adult sexuality;

they are connected with an individual's early ambivalences and conflicts about sexual desire and about "looking." For the significance of primal scenes see, for example, Freud's case history of the "Wolf-man": "From the History of an Infantile Neurosis," *S.E.,* XVII, 7–122. Steven Marcus discusses the importance of primal scene memories or fantasies for Dickens—with particular reference to the role of Fagin in *Oliver Twist* and to Dickens' autobiographical account of the intense feelings occasioned by his father's watching him while he was at his "degrading" work in the blacking factory—in the appendix of *Dickens: From Pickwick to Dombey* (New York: Basic Books, 1965), pp. 358–78. See also the treatment of primal scene content in some of Dickens' recollections from his early childhood in my essay, "Charles Dickens' 'Nurse's Stories,' " in *The Psychoanalytic Review,* in press.

13 A. O. J. Cockshut, *The Imagination of Charles Dickens* (New York: New York University Press, 1962), p. 131.

14 The last words in Miss Flite's list, "Gammon and Spinach," suggest the roguery and trickery manifested in Chancery practice, like the other words in the third group. The word "gammon" originates in thieves' cant, means humbug or deception and appears frequently in Dickens' novels. The phrase, "Gammon and Spinach," is probably modeled after the colloquial expression, "gammon and patter," and is part of a nonsense refrain to the nursery song, "The Love-Sick Frog." Thus "Gammon and Spinach" is probably intended to suggest trickery or deceit through the use of cant, nonsense, or some other verbal device. Another curious little lady, Miss Mowcher, also uses the phrase in this sense in Chapter xxii of *David Copperfield*. See Eric Partridge, *A Dictionary of Slang and Unconventional English* (London: Macmillan, 1967); and Partridge, *A Dictionary of the Underworld* (London: Macmillan, 1968).

15 Freud, "Notes Upon a Case of Obsessional Neurosis," *S.E.,* X, 236. It is conceivable that Freud may even have been thinking here of *Bleak House,* which he read but did not think highly of, considering it "deliberately hard" and having "too much mannerism in it," according to Ernest Jones, *The Life and Work of Sigmund Freud* (New York: Basic Books, 1957), I, 174.

16 See Otto Fenichel, *The Psychoanalytic Theory of Neurosis* (New York: W. W. Norton, 1945), pp. 178–83.

17 Stoehr, p. 163.

18 Freud, "A Special Type of Object Choice Made by Men," *S.E.,* XI, 171.

19 Michael Steig, "The Whitewashing of Inspector Bucket: Origins and Parallels," *Papers of the Michigan Academy of Science, Arts, and Letters,* 50 (1965), 575.

20 Geraldine Pederson-Krag, "Detective Stories and the Primal Scene," *Psychoanalytic Quarterly* 10 (1941), 373–81.

21 Ibid., p. 213.

22 For a full discussion of the complex manner in which the reader participates in the unconscious content of a work of literature, despite the fact that the work's form serves to disguise partially and defend against the core fantasy, see Norman N. Holland, *The Dynamics of Literary Response* (New York: Oxford University Press, 1968); also Frederick C. Crews, *Psychoanalysis and Literary Process* (Cambridge, Mass.: Winthrop Publishers, 1970), pp. 1–24.

INDEX

Auden, W. H.: considers Pickwick, 42

Barnaby Rudge: time in, 3, 6, 14–19; John Willett and belief in stasis, 14–15; Gabriel Varden as moral center, 15
Bergson, Henri, and Dickens: time and free will, 2–3, 7; non-spatialization of time, 2–3, 7, 35; duration, 3, 13–14, 16, 167
Bleak House: time and Christian belief in, 19–27; cosmic clock in, 19–20, 25–27; as religious novel, 19–21, 22–27; opening paragraphs, 20–21; Sir Leicester Dedlock and evil of oldness, 21–24; the Small-weeds, 22–23; flawed characters in, 22–26; deaths in, 24–26; double narrative in, 91, 92, 93, 110–11, 134; ending of, 105–12
—Freudian analysis of: past in, 132–34; repression in Esther Summerson, 133–40; guilt in Esther, 135–40; guilt in Lady Dedlock, 136–37; obsessional thinking, in Gridley, 140–41; law in, 140–46, 146–50, 150–52; in Miss Flite, 141–43; in Richard Carstone, 143–46; analysis of Tulkinghorn, 146–50; Tulkinghorn and James Carker, 148–49; sublimation in Inspector Bucket, 150–52
—political background of: Middle Ages and Dickens, 113, 114, 115–19, 122–23, 124; Sir Leicester Dedlock, 113, 122–23, 123–27, 130–31; Wat Tyler, 113–24, 126–27; Chartism, 114–15, 119–23; Mr. Rouncewell, 114, 123–31; Keightley as source, 117–19; police in, 119–22; Times (London) as a source, 119–23, 128; industrialism and commercialism in, 123–31; Trevor Blount on, reply to, 127–31
—psychological analysis of Esther Summerson: guilt feelings of, 92–93, 94–96, 99, 101; the past in, 92–93, 96, 105–6, 107–9; willed failure to understand, 92–95, 99–106; triad of Esther, Lady Dedlock, and Hortense, 92, 95–99, 102–3, 106–10; symbols in, 92, 99–103, 107; Christian beliefs in, 93, 94–95, 96; as Dame Durden, 93–94, 99–104, 106, 111; relationship with Ada, 93, 95, 103–4, 105; mirrors and veils in, 96–97, 99, 101–3, 105, 106, 111; rebirth of, 99–112
Blount, Trevor: views on Rouncewell criticized, 127–31
Buckley, Jerome: on time, 167

Chartism: in Bleak House, 114–15, 119–23, 125–26
Child's History of England, A: on Peasants' Revolt of 1381 and Wat Tyler, 115–17
Chimes, The: Mayhew's criticism of, 89–90
Christian beliefs, and time: in Master Humphrey's Clock, 3–6; in The Old Curiosity Shop, 6–13; in Barnaby Rudge, 14–15; in A Christmas Carol, 15–16; in Dombey and Son, 16–17; in David Copperfield, 17–19; in Bleak House, 17–27; in Great Expectations, 27–31; in The Mystery of Edwin Drood, 31–34
—and evil: Quilp, 8–9, 11–12; moral centers, 11–13, 15, 18–19, 22–27, 31–33; Smallweeds, 22–23; Sir Leicester Dedlock, 23–24; John Jasper, 31–34; Mrs. Clennam, 153–62
Christmas Carol, A: temporal flow in, 3, 14, 15–16
City, the: as present reality, 7–11; Cloisterham in Drood, 32–34; in Bleak House, 98–99. See also Mayhew, Henry
Clocks. See Time, in Dickens

[187